RADIO PROGRAMMING

A Basic Training Manual

RADIO PROGRAMMING

A Basic Training Manual

by

RALPH MILTON

PUBLISHED BY

GEOFFREY BLES · LONDON

© RALPH MILTON, 1968
SBN: 7138 0216 2

Printed in Great Britain
by Cox & Wyman Ltd, Fakenham

Published by
GEOFFREY BLES LTD
52 Doughty Street, London, W.C.1
33 York Street, Sydney
353 Elizabeth Street, Melbourne
246 Queen Street, Brisbane
CML Building, King William Street, Adelaide
Lake Road, Northcote, Auckland
100 Lesmill Road, Don Mills, Ontario
P.O. Box 420, Barbados, B.W.I.
P.O. Box 2800, Salisbury, Rhodesia
P.O. Box 8879, Johannesburg
P.O. Box 834, Cape Town

First published in 1968

Foreword

The World Association of Christian Broadcasting, which is responsible for this book, is an association of agencies and churches throughout the world, concerned with raising the standards of religious broadcasting and encouraging responsible broadcasting of all kinds. One of its major activities is training. This can be done in many different ways and the varying conditions in developing countries demand different methods.

When a man seems destined to become a leader in the broadcasting field in his own country the WACB has found it a good investment to bring him to Britain or some other European or North American country, to expose him to the high professional standards of such organisations as the BBC. In this way some twenty people pass through the hands of the WACB in any year.

It is of course expensive to bring men to Europe or North America yet many more need training each year. For this reason use is made of regional training centres at Nairobi in Kenya, at Jabalpur in India, at Tokyo and other well equipped centres. Again, the majority cannot leave their country to spend several months training in one of these centres or even in training courses provided by public corporations nearer home.

It is for this majority that we encouraged Ralph Milton to write this manual so that they can learn at home or in their own studio. While an experienced friend is needed to supervise the course, anyone who is ready to work can learn how to improve what he is doing in religious or other broadcasts.

Ralph Milton brings to this work years of experience in the studios of Dumaguete in the Philippines and observations on a world tour of Christian stations. He provides all that a broadcaster needs who wants to raise the standards of programmes in his studio. I would urge that every studio concerned with the production of purposive broadcasting should have copies of this manual around for its young helpers who aspire to become radio producers.

E. H. ROBERTSON
Executive Director of the World
Association for Christian Broadcasting

Introduction

When I first began to work in broadcasting, the station which employed me had a slogan, "Wherever you go, there's radio." This is becoming more true every day. The "transistor revolution" is bringing small inexpensive radios to more people in ever more remote parts of the world.

This "transistor revolution" offers a great opportunity for all those persons and organisations who are looking for ways in which to help people in their individual and national development. These radios, spreading throughout the world, can be an efficient tool in nation building, or an effective weapon for national destruction.

We hope this manual will help those who are beginning in the field of broadcasting, to learn the basic principles of responsible radio programming. The manual is designed for the nations of Asia, Africa, the Middle East, and Latin America, and as such is quite different from many of the books on radio which have come out of the Western world. However, many who have read the first drafts have felt there was no reason why it could not also be useful in Europe and North America.

This manual began its life in 1963 with the South East Asia Radio Workshop held in the Philippines, when men from five countries came together to study the art of sound broadcasting. It was not until several years and several workshops later that work on the manual was begun in earnest. At that time it became possible to visit stations and studios in Asia, Africa and the Middle East, to study the problems and the possibilities, and to find the exact form such a manual should take. The one-year sabbatical, granted by the United Church of Canada, made it possible for me to concentrate entirely on this work. Otherwise it could not have been done.

Such a manual could never be a one-man project. There are many people to whom we owe a great debt.

Most important among these are the fine people at stations DYSR and DZCH in the Philippines. If I lean too heavily upon them, it is because they taught me so much. Much of what is found in the manual grew out of the five happy years spent with these fine broadcasters.

I am also grateful to the team of consulting editors who carefully studied each and every portion of this manual. Their comments and criticisms were extremely useful. In fact, this manual could not have been written without them. They were: Mathew Ogawa, Japan; William Haney, Brazil; Melchizedeck Solis and Juan Pia, the Philippines; John Poulton and Edwin Robertson, Great Britain; Otto DeCamp, Korea; Jan van Dis, Netherlands; William Haddad, Lebanon; Ulrich Fick and Ann Voltz, Ethiopia; Kenneth Carmichael, Kenya; Beverley Chain and Barnerd Luben, U.S.A., and Clemence David, India. Many others offered comments and helpful suggestions, among them Eugene Nida of the American Bible Society.

Thanks should also be extended to Kathleen Smith, who patiently typed and retyped each part of this work; to Norma Robson, who did the basic proofreading; to Marvin Hunt who gave us the line drawings; and to my mother, Mrs. Marie Friesen who gave not only practical assistance, but also her love and encouragement.

The largest thanks must go to Beverley, who was much more than a patient wife. She offered constant encouragement and real help by reading each project at every stage of its development. Her grasp of the basic problems involved, and her ability to suggest needed improvements have been invaluable. In fact, it was she who suggested the project in the first place. It is with love and gratitude that I dedicate this book to her.

G.R.M.
June, 1967
Winnipeg, Canada.

Contents

FOREWORD BY THE REVEREND E. H. ROBERTSON   5

INTRODUCTION   7

A Word to the Student

ABOUT THIS MANUAL (A1)   21

The Glossary (A2)   21
Learning (A3)   22
Honest Broadcasting (A4)   22
Danger (A5)   23

Project A. Making a One-minute Talk

THE BEGINNING (A6)   25
Preparing to Write a Short Talk (A7)   25
Audience Research (A8)   26
Programme Research (A9)   27

WRITING (A10)   27
The Outline, Step One (A11)   28
Writing the First Draft, Step Two (A12)   29
A Sample Talk (A13)   30
Rewriting the Talk, Step Three (A14)   32
Recording the Talk, Step Four (A15)   34
Evaluation, Step Five (A16)   35
Check-list for a Short Talk (A17)   36

GLOSSARY (A18)   36
Glossary Assignment (A19)   37

Project B. Writing a Five-minute Talk

ABOUT THIS PROJECT (B1)   39

BUILDING RESOURCES (B2)   39
The Notebook (B3)   40
Some Day it May be Useful (B4)   41
Writers Must Read (B5)   42

The Studio Magazine Shelf (B6)   43
The Idea File (B7)   44

BUILDING A RADIO TALK (B9)   45
Unity, Clearness and Emphasis (B10)   46
Building a Bridge (B11)   47
An Example (B12)   48

A FIVE-MINUTE TALK (B14)   48
The Outline (B15)   49
The First Draft (B16)   49
The First Edit (B17)   51
Using Other People's Ideas (B18)   51
The Second Draft (B19)   51
Timing (B20)   52
Recording the Talk (B 21)   52
Evaluation (B22)   52
Check-list for a Five-minute Talk (B23)   53
One Last Word (B25)   54

ASSIGNMENTS (B8, B13, B24)

Project C. Translation

OUR WONDERFUL LANGUAGE (C1)   55
A Language to Love (C2)   55
Your Language (C3)   56
Studying Your Language (C4)   57
Listening to Your Language (C6)   58
Looking for a Linguist (C7)   58
Consult a Foreigner (C8)   59
"The Rabbit and the Turtle" (C11)   60

FROM ONE LANGUAGE TO ANOTHER (C12)   61
Adaptation (C13)   62
"Young Eyes" (C15)   63
Check-list for an Adaptation (C16)   63
Translation (C17)   64
Check-list for a Translation (C19)   65

ASSIGNMENTS (C5, C9, C10, C14, C18)

Project D. Research, Spot Announcements and Your Voice

THINGS A BROADCASTER MUST KNOW (D1)   67
Audience Research Continued (D2)   67

Where is My Listener? (D3)   68
Research in Libraries (D4)   68
Research Through People (D5)   69
Finding out from the Listener (D6)   69
Asking Questions (D7)   69
Attention Span (D9)   71

SPOT ANNOUNCEMENTS (D10)   72
What Spot Announcements Can Do (D11)   72
What Spot Announcements Cannot Do (D12)   73
Writing a Spot Announcement (D13)   73
The Outline (D14)   74
Spot Examples (D15)   75
Learn by Listening (D16)   76
Timing the Spot (D17)   76
Check-list for Spot Announcements (D19)   77
One Last Word (D20)   77

THE SPOKEN LANGUAGE (D21)   79
The Sound of Language (D22)   79
Marking Copy (D23)   80
Sample of Marked Script (D24)   80
Check-list for Radio Speaking (D25)   81
Improve Your Speaking (D26)   82
Clear Speech (D27)   82
Speech Texture (D28)   83
Speech Colour (D29)   83

ASSIGNMENTS (D8, D18, D30)

Project E. Interviews: Section One

WHY STUDY INTERVIEWS (E1)   85
The Art of Description (E2)   85
Check-list for Description (E4)   87
Practise Description Any Time (E5)   88

PEOPLE LIKE PEOPLE (E6)   88
Preparing an Interview (E7)   88
What Would the Listener Ask? (E8)   89
Preparing the Guest (E9)   89
The Interview Rehearsal (E10)   90
A Flexible Plan (E11)   90
Introducing the Guest (E12)   91
Be Polite (E13)   91

Move Along Quickly (E14)   92
Asking for Criticism (E16)   92
Check-list for a Short Interview (E17)   93

ASSIGNMENTS (E3, E15, E18)

Project F. Interviews: Section Two

PRACTICE MAKES PERFECT (F1)   95
Three Kinds of Interviews (F2)   95
Interview Formats (F3)   96
One-time Interviews (F4)   96
Serial Interviews (F5)   97
Spot Interviews (F6)   98
News Interviews (F7)   98
Special Event Interviews (F8)   99
Always be Ready (F9)   99

THE COMMON PEOPLE (F11)   100
Alertness and Other Qualities (F12)   101
The Art of Asking (F13)   102
Three Ways of Asking (F14)   103
Keep Control (F15)   104
It Depends on You (F16)   105
The Studio Interview (F17)   105
Using a Microphone Outside (F18)   106

EDITING AN INTERVIEW (F19)   109
Dangers of Editing (F20)   109
Dubbing (F21)   110
Splicing (F22)   110
Check-list for Tape Editing (F25)   112
Check-list for an Interview (F28)   113

ASSIGNMENTS (F10, F23, F24, F26, F27)

Project G. The Panel Discussion

WHY A PANEL DISCUSSION (G1)   115
What is the Topic? (G2)   115
The Moderator (G3)   117
Choosing the Panel (G4)   117
Preparing the Discussion (G5)   118
Rehearsal (G6)   119
Planning with the Panel (G7)   120

Preparing the Panel Members (G8)   120
The Moderator's Summary (G9)   121
Suggestions to the Panel (G10)   121

A PANEL THAT DISAGREES (G12)   124
A Panel that Searches (G13)   124
Panel Discussion Formats (G14)   124
A Panel Discussion Series (G15)   125
Scripted Panel Discussions (G16)   125
Check-list for a Panel Discussion (G18)   126

ASSIGNMENTS (G11, G17, G19)

Project H. Audience Studies

THE IMPORTANCE OF RESEARCH (H1)   129
Culture (H2)   130
What Has Already Been Done (H3)   132
UNESCO (H4)   132
Background Information (H5)   133
Population (H6)   133
Language (H7)   133
Economics (H8)   134
Culture (H9)   134
Religion (H10)   135
Radio Placement (H11)   135
Education (H12)   136
New Information (H13)   136
Analysing Cultural Groups (H15)   137
Cultures and Sub-cultures (H16)   137
Not Knowing is Expensive (H19)   140

HOW TO FIND OUT (H20)   140
What Do You Think? (H21)   141
Your Friends Might Not Help (H22)   141
What Does a Comment Mean? (H23)   142
Letters (H24)   143
Analysing Letters (H25)   144
What Does the Chart Say? (H26)   145
What Does the Chart Not Say? (H27)   146
Audience Survey (H28)   146
Bicycle Survey (H29)   147

ASSIGNMENTS (H14, H17, H18, H30)

Project I. Communication

MEDIA AND COMMUNICATION (I1)   149
  Five Parts of Communication (I2)   149
  Encoding and Decoding (I3)   150
  Distortion (I4)   151
  Feedback (I5)   152
  Field of Experience (I6)   153
  Interference (I7)   154

BRINGING CHANGE THROUGH RADIO (I12)   155
  Dr. Schramm's Book (I13)   156
  A Culture is Tied Together (I14)   156
  People Live in Groups (I15)   157
  The Radio Forum (I16)   157
  The Use of Mass Media (I17)   158

WHAT THE MASS MEDIA CAN DO (I18)   160
  Telling Us What is Important (I19)   160
  Making People Want Things (I20)   161
  Helping People Decide (I21)   161
  Person-to-person Communication (I22)   162
  Changing Ideas a Little (I23)   163
  Making a Leader Important (I24)   163
  Helping People Learn to Enjoy Things (I25)   163
  Radio in the Schools (I26)   164
  What Radio Cannot Do (I27)   164
  Programme Targets (I28)   165

ASSIGNMENTS (I8, I9, I10, I11, I29, I30)

Project J. Music Programme

MUSIC PROGRAMMES (J1)   169
  What is Music? (J2)   169
  Music and Emotions (J3)   170
  Many Kinds of Music (J4)   171
  The Record Library (J5)   171
  Kinds of Music Programmes (J6)   172

PLANNING A MUSIC PROGRAMME (J7)   172
  Arranging the Order of the Music (J8)   173
  Making Selections Shorter (J9)   174

Writing a Music Programme Script (J10)   175
Resources (J11)   175
Music Cues (J12)   176

PROGRAMME SERIES (J15)   179
Choosing a Name (J16)   179
Opening and Closing Announcements (J17)   179
Signature Music (J18)   181
Fitting the Words to the Music (J19)   182
Fading (J20)   182

PUTTING A SCRIPT ON PAPER (J22)   183
Suggestions for Script Typing (J23)   184
Check-list for a Music Script (J26)   187
Check-list for a Music Programme (J27)   188
A Sample Script (J28)   189

ASSIGNMENTS (J13, J14, J21, J24, J25)

Project K. Live Talent Programmes

FOR LARGE AND SMALL (K1)   191
Outside Talent (K2)   191
Searching for Talent (K3)   192
Training Talent (K4)   193
Keeping People Interested (K5)   193
Going to the Talent (K6)   193
Is It Worth It? (K7)   194

MICROPHONES, STUDIOS AND RECORDING TECHNIQUES (K8) 194
The Microphone (K9)   195
Microphone Presence (K10)   195
The Studio (K11)   196
Microphone Balance (K12)   198
Drawings of Microphone Positions (K13)   199
Short-wave Broadcasts (K14)   200
A Word of Warning (K17)   202

LISTENER PARTICIPATION PROGRAMMES (K19)   203
Taped Participation (K20)   203
Letter Participation (K21)   204
An Edited Letter (K22)   204
The Question and Answer Programme (K23)   206
Comments from Listeners (K24)   206

Music Request Programme (K25)   206
Greetings Programme (K26)   208
Message Programme (K27)   208
Other Letter Programmes (K28)   208
Letter Programme Check-list (K31)   210

ASSIGNMENTS (K15, K16, K18, K29, K30)

Project L. News

THE WATCHMAN (L1)   212
Freedom of Information (L2)   213
What is News? (L3)   213
News or Opinion? (L4)   213
Propaganda (L5)   214
We All Do It (L6)   214
Dangers in Selecting News (L7)   215
Accuracy (L8)   215
Newsworthiness (L9)   215

WHERE TO FIND NEWS (L10)   217
Asking Questions (L11)   217
The Telephone (L12)   218
Newspapers (L13)   218
News Releases (L14)   218
News Services (L15)   219
Wire Services (L16)   219
Other Radio Stations (L17)   220

MAKING A NEWS BROADCAST (L20)   221
Writing (L21)   221
The Important First Sentence (L22)   221
Five "W's" and an "H" (L23)   223
Other Suggestions (L24)   224
Editing a News Story (L25)   226
Compiling a Newcast (L26)   227
Voicing the News (L27)   228
Check-list for News Items (L31)   230
Check-list for News Broadcasts (L33)   231

ASSIGNMENTS (L18, L19, L28, L29, L30, L32)

Project M. Documentary and News-reel

OTHER KINDS OF NEWS PROGRAMMES (M1) 232
Pictures in Radio News (M2) 232
Taping Speeches (M3) 233
Interviews (M4) 234
On-the-spot Reports (M5) 234
Sound and Music (M6) 235
The Radio News-reel (M7) 235
Check-list for Recorded News Report (M9) 236

MAGAZINE PROGRAMME (M10) 236
Credits (M11) 237
Finding Materials (M12) 237
Planning a Magazine Programme (M13) 238
Magazine Outline (M14) 239
Editing Materials (M15) 239
Music Bridges (M16) 239
Timing (M17) 240

DOCUMENTARY PROGRAMMES (M18) 240
Kinds of Documentaries (M19) 241
Be Fair with the Listener (M20) 241
Documentary Formats (M21) 242
The Morgue (M22) 242
Check-list for a Magazine Programme (M26) 243

ASSIGNMENTS (M8, M23, M24, M25)

Project N. Drama: Section One

HOW DRAMA BEGAN (N1) 246
Drama Around the World (N2) 246
What is Radio Drama? (N3) 247

HOW TO TELL A STORY (N4) 248
"Threshold to Colour Bar" (a sample story) (N5) 249
What is a Story? (N6) 250
Something Happens (N7) 250
Developing Conflict (N8) 251
Secondary Conflicts (N9) 252
Plot Example (N10) 252
Movement (N11) 253
The Character Outline (N12) 253

The Plot Outline (N13)   254
The Beginning and the End (N14)   254
The Middle (N15)   255
Check-list for a Short Story (N18)   257

WRITING FOR RADIO (N19)   257
Narration (N20)   257
Dialogue (N21)   258
How do People Talk? (N22)   258
Characters Speak in Their Own Style (N23)   259
Putting Personality into Dialogue (N24)   260
Accents and Dialects (N25)   260
How Many People? N26)   261
Who is in the Scene? (N27)   261
Dialogue Tells Where (N28)   262
Give Eyes to the Listener (N29)   263
Much More to Learn (N30)   264
Check-list for Drama Script (N34)   266

"THE CONTRARY WIFE"(a sample drama script) (N35)   266

ASSIGNMENTS (N16, N17, N31, N32, N33)

Project O. Drama: Section Two

DRAMA PRODUCTIONS (O1)   270
The Three Tools (O2)   270
Volume (O3)   270
Sound Effects (O4)   271
Using Sound Effects (O5)   272
Let the Listener Know (O6)   272
Choosing Sounds (O7)   274
Background Effects (O8)   274
Making Sound Effects (O9)   275

MUSIC IN RADIO DRAMA (O10)   275
Background Music (O11)   276
Choosing the Right Music (O12)   276
What Kind of Music? (O13)   277
Use Only One Kind of Music (O14)   277

OPENING THE DRAMA (O15)   277
Opening with Speech, Music and Sound (O16)   278
Opening with Music and Speech (O17)   279
Opening with Sound and Speech (O18)   279

SCENE CHANGES (O19)   279
   The Pause (O20)   280
   The Narrator (O21)   280
   Scene Changes with Sound Effects (O22)   281
   Music (O23)   282
   Combinations (O24)   282
   Closing the Radio Drama (O25)   283
   Radio Tricks (O26)   283

THE DRAMA DIRECTOR (O32)   284
   Using Amateur Actors (O33)   285
   Developing an Acting Group (O34)   285
   Choosing the Right Actor (O35)   286
   Talent Card File (O36)   287
   Rehearsals (O37)   288
   Recording a Drama (O38)   290

COMMUNICATION THROUGH DRAMA (O39)   290
   Information (O40)   290
   Empathy (O41)   291
   How to Gain Empathy (O42)   291
   Drama in all Programmes (O43)   292
   What to Communicate (O44)   292
   Why Communicate (O45)   292
   Check-list for Drama Production (O49)   294

ONE FINAL WORD (O52)   295

Appendix W. A Glossary of Radio Words   296

Appendix X. Sound Effects
   (Some simple studio effects and how they can be produced.)

SOUND EFFECTS SOURCES   320
   Recording Local Sound Effects   321
   Live Sound Effects   322

LIVE EFFECTS AND HOW TO MAKE THEM   323
   (Effects listed alphabetically)

Appendix Y. Suggestions for Further Reading   333

(A selected bibliography for student and supervisor, plus a list of periodicals.)

Appendix Z. Supervisor's Notes

INTRODUCTION (S1)   336
   The Task of the Supervisor (S2)   336
   Supervisor's Preparation (S3)   337
   Working with the Student (S4)   338
   Adapting the Manual (S5)   339
   Working with Two or More Students (S6)   340
   Training Outsiders (S7)   341
   Encouraging the Student (S8)   342
   The Glossary Assignments (S9)   342
   Research and Idea Files (S10)   343
   Where to Go for More Help (S11)   343
   Translation of the Manual (S12)   344
   Future Revisions (S13)   344

Notes on all the projects are found in the Supervisor's Notes. These are designed to assist the person administering the work. We strongly suggest that no student attempt the work in the manual without such guidance.

A Word to the Student

About this Manual (A1):

This is a manual which we hope will help you begin to learn the art of radio programming. We say "help" because no book can ever teach this to anyone. You can *learn* radio, and the book may offer you some help. However, you will succeed only by your own efforts. A person who works hard will learn by himself, although he may learn faster if he uses this manual. The person who does not work will not learn, and no manual or book can help him.

As you work in this manual, it may sometimes seem that we ask too much. Often we say you "must" do this, or you "must" do that. This simply means that we think these things are very important, so important that they cannot be left out. It does not mean that we are giving orders. We would not want to do this, even if we could.

In each of the projects we talk about some part of radio programming. Please remember, however, that each time you learn about one kind of programme, you are also learning some things about other kinds of programmes. For that reason, we would like you to keep going back and reading the projects over again. We cannot repeat everything that has been learned in each project, for each new programme that you are asked to make. Therefore, what you learn in *Project A* must be remembered for *Project B*. What you learn in the first projects can also be used for the last ones, and all the projects in between.

The Glossary (A2):

A glossary of radio words has been put at the end of the manual. This glossary gives the meaning of some of the words used by radio people. Look at this glossary often and study the explanations. When you see a word in the manual written in capitals, like THIS, it means you can find that word in the glossary. We will write it in capitals only the first time it appears in the manual. After that it will be written just like any other word, because you should already know what it means.

Learning (A3):

You will be asked to study your own work and the work of others very often in this manual. You will be asked to criticise: to say what is good about it and what is bad.

This is very hard for some people to do, especially if they must criticise someone older or more experienced. We ask you to do this in order to help you learn how to separate the bad from the good. Even the most experienced broadcasters make mistakes.

Until you learn to criticise the work of others, you will never know which ideas can be used on your own programmes, and which cannot. Even worse, you will not know how to criticise yourself. Unless you can look at your own work and decide what is good and what is bad, you will not be able to improve.

As you work through this manual, you will be asked to take your work to your supervisor. He will try to help you improve your work. For this reason, your supervisor will need to tell you the things you did wrong. Do not feel badly if he tells you what was wrong with your work. It is a sign of strength, a sign of wisdom, to be able to hear someone tell you of your mistakes, and then say "thank you" to him for it. A person who gets very angry when he is told of his mistakes is usually a weak man. Such a man can never really learn anything well, because he will never know what mistakes he must correct.

Honest Broadcasting (A4):

As a broadcaster, you are a very powerful person. You also bear a great burden. You are able to talk to thousands of people at one time. You can help make your country greater, but you might also slow down its growth. You can help your people, or you may harm them. You may make many programmes and have no influence at all. What you will do depends on the kind of person you are, and how much honesty, hard work, and intelligence you give to your work.

This manual is intended for people in the growing nations of Asia, Africa, the Middle East, and Latin America. These nations need broadcasters who are much more interested in helping their own people than helping themselves.

Radio can be a powerful tool in the building of new nations. Such a tool needs honest workmen, who know how to use the tool well.

Danger (A5):

A warning before we start. This manual is only a beginning. When you have finished all the projects, then you have *begun* to learn the art of radio. There will still be much, much more to learn.

The United Church of Canada.

PROJECT A

Making a One-minute Talk

The Beginning (A6):   PART ONE*

We would like you to begin your work in this manual by writing a simple one-minute talk. That may seem very easy, but it is really quite difficult. Anyone can talk for one minute. However, it is difficult to make your listener feel that you have said something important for him.

Radio listeners are very hard to please. A friend will listen to you for one minute even if you are not saying anything interesting. He will be polite. A radio listener does not need to be polite. If you do not sound interesting to him as soon as you begin, he will turn off the radio or tune to another station.

The only way to please a listener is to know many things about him. You should know the ways in which you can talk to him about important things. That will not happen until you spend a great deal of time studying your listener. This is what we call *research*. You may feel that since you have been living in your country all your life, you know a great deal about the kind of people who listen to radio.

That is true, However, if you begin to study your listener, you will learn many new things that will be surprising and helpful. You will never finish learning about your audience, because our world and our listeners are changing.

In this project, we speak of only *some* of the things that must be learned about writing and research. There will be more to be learned later – much more!

You will be asked to report to the supervisor four times during this project. Please do not proceed to the next stage until you have reported.

Preparing to Write a Short Talk (A7):

The kind of talk we would like you to make in this project is very useful in radio programming. It can be used several ways:

* See page 347 for the significance of these numbered parts.

in between records in a music programme,
between two radio programmes, and
as part of a magazine programme.

There are four things which should be done for every programme if it is to be successful. They are as follows:

research,
writing,
production, and
evaluation.

Audience Research (A8):

Audience research is finding out the things we must know about our listeners before we can begin to write a programme.

Some people begin working on a radio programme by wondering, "What will I say?" That is wrong! The first question is to ask, "To whom am I speaking?"

> If someone said to you, "Please come and teach in my school," you would ask, "What kind of school? Is it a university, or a school for small children?" Until you know the answers to these questions, you will not be able to consider *what* you will be able to teach.

Here are five questions about your radio audience. Try to find answers to all of them. Perhaps a library near by, or a government office might have some of the answers. You should also visit people in your city and your towns to see for yourself. Ask others to tell you where you might find this information. Try always to get *facts*.

> What class of people in your area own radio receivers? Are they farmers? Office workers? Labourers? Students? Fishermen?
> How much education do most of them have?
> What language or dialect do they speak?
> What kind of work do most of them do?
> What kind of help or information do they need?

As you gather this information, write it down. You will need to look at it many times before you have finished making this talk. This information will also be needed for other projects. We would suggest that you place this information in a "Research File". There will be other information from other projects which you will also want to place in this file.

Now ask this question: "Do I have any friends or acquaintances who are just like the people I have described?" If not, then perhaps you need to make some new friends. You will need to know such people if you are going to make intelligent radio programmes. No one can talk well, if he does not know to whom he is talking.

Write down all you can find about these friends. Ask them how they feel about life, what kind of problems they have, what makes them happy and what makes them sad, what their religion is, and anything else you may wish to know about them.

That is the first part of your research. It is known as *Audience Research*, and few programmes are successful without it.

Programme Research (A9):

The next kind of research you should do is called *Programme Research*. The first two questions to ask are these:

> "What do I wish to say to these people?"
> "What are the things *they* wish to know?"

Among the things you wish to say, find one that fits the things your listener wishes to know. Do not try to answer questions that your listener would not ask!

There are probably many things that you would like to tell your listeners. Remember, they must be things *you* believe are true and honest. They must be things you feel will help the people in some way. Radio is a powerful tool. When you use it, you have a very great responsibility to speak the truth.

Have you decided *what* it is that you must say? Use only a single idea since we are making only a one-minute talk. You cannot say more than one simple thing in one minute. If you say more your listener may be confused.

Now go to your supervisor to talk about the things you have so far. Bring all the things you have written with you.

Writing (A10):   PART TWO

There are five steps to help you write a good radio talk.

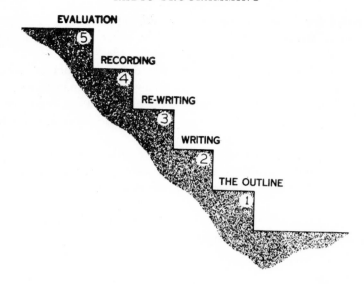

The Outline, Step One (A11):

Make a plan, or an outline for your talk. A plan before beginning will ensure a much better talk. This plan or outline should have the following four stages:

Object: Write down in *one* short sentence, what you would like to say in this talk. Be sure it is only one short sentence. If you cannot put your idea into one sentence, perhaps it is too complicated for a one-minute talk, or perhaps you do not understand it well enough. Think about your idea until you can say it in fifteen words or less.

Attention-catcher: This is the first sentence. It should always be a very short sentence, something that will make the listener want to hear what else you are going to say. Your first sentence might be an exciting question, or a challenging statement.

Direction-pointer: Here you should have one or two sentences that would help the listener to begin thinking about the subject you have in mind.

The Story-message: This will be the biggest part of the talk. It should really be a *parable*; that is, a story that helps to explain what you are talking about. It might be a folk tale, or an amusing joke, or it might be a story you made up in your own imagination. It might be something that you have read in the newspaper or in a magazine. However, it must always have two important virtues. It must help to explain your message, and it must be of interest to the listener. This section should be from thirty-five to forty-five seconds long.

The Quick Closing: This part should be very short, perhaps two or three short sentences. Here you must state again your message in a very few words. Sometimes it is best to think of your closing before you plan the rest of your talk. Choose your words well, so that your listener cannot forget them. This section should be from ten to fifteen seconds long.

The whole talk should be planned to last one minute. However, don't worry about the length as yet. Just be sure your idea is a good one.

A young African broadcaster named Esthon Hamadu wrote a good talk at a radio workshop in Nairobi. Here is the outline for his one-minute talk.

Object: We are only useful when we let God use us.
Attention-catcher: A tricky question about a hoe.
Story-message: About the proper use of the hoe. Somebody has to use the hoe well, otherwise nothing will grow on the farm.
Quick Closing: We are as useless as a hoe without the farmer, unless we let God use us.

Writing the First Draft, Step Two (A12):

Before beginning to write, turn to the *Glossary of Radio Words* at the back of the manual. Read the short section under SCRIPT, then follow those instructions as you write.

If the right words don't seem to come into your mind, then write down the ones that do come. Leave plenty of space between your lines so that you can write in new ideas later. Follow your outline, but write quickly, without worrying too much whether you are saying things the right way.

Now you are ready for your first edition. Read over the script you have just written. This is not the script you will use on the programme. It is only the beginning, your *first draft*.

As you read, think about the following things and change (or edit) your script where necessary.

Am I using words that the listener would not understand? If so, change them to easier words.

Are my sentences too long and difficult? Sentences should be very short and simple in a radio talk.

Is my writing interesting? Are there colourful words and phrases I could have used? Put them in, but only if they really fit.

Am I too serious? Would my script not be better if it made the listener smile sometimes? A smile, or a laugh, will turn a listener into a friend. A friend will listen to what you say.

Is it exactly one minute long? To find this out, you will need to read your script out loud with a stop-watch in your hand. Shorten or lengthen your talk as necessary.

Your script should now look rather messy. It should have many corrections and new words on every line. If not, then perhaps you should do your editing again.

Now you are ready for your second editing. This is more difficult. Take the information you have gathered in your research. Place it beside your script. Read over your research information again; then read your script. Ask yourself these questions:

Will the talk be interesting to these people?
Does it give them information they need or want?
Will they fail to understand any part of it?

If you answer these questions very honestly, you may be tempted to throw away your script and start again. If you do this you are beginning to be a good writer. The best writers do their work many times before they feel it is good enough.

When you have answered all these questions, and you are satisfied that you have a good script, move on to Step Three.

Before you do, however, study this sample script. What changes have been made in the editing? Why were the changes made? Do the changes in this script give you some ideas for changes you might make in your own script?

A Sample Talk (A13):

Here is Mr. Hamadu's talk the way it looked after he had edited his first draft.

~~Have you ever stopped to wonder whether~~
Do
you know how to use a hoe? Perhaps you ~~have~~
Think you do. Perhaps you don't.
~~never given the matter any thought. Here is~~
~~a story about a hoe.~~

My Grand~~father~~ (pa) had a hoe. He knew ~~the~~ that
a hoe had a blade and a handle.
~~was well aware of the way in which a hoe was~~
~~constructed.~~ ~~My~~ Grand~~father~~ (pa) also knew that
a handle ~~all by itself~~ alone coul'd not ~~properly~~ be
called a hoe. ~~My Grandfather was also aware~~
He knew that
~~of the fact that you could not call~~ a blade
is not
by itself, a hoe either. ~~And so he reached~~
~~the conclusion that a blade and a handle were~~
~~what you would call a hoe.~~

My Grand~~father~~ (pa) learned long ago, that ~~the~~
when a hoe is held with
~~proper use of the hoe is not to have~~ the blade
facing the sky, ~~because then~~ it cannot cut
He
the grass. ~~My Grandfather~~ also discovered
many years ago that the hoe, ~~will never really~~
~~work for him and~~ has no value, if he simply
puts it
~~allows it to remain~~ on the farm ~~and then~~
To
watches it work. ~~because~~ Grand~~father~~ (pa) is a man
of intelligence. ~~Although he is a man of~~
~~great age,~~ He knows that the hoe can never
farm all by itself. ~~Furthermore,~~ A hoe is
useless unless he holds it and moves it in the
right
direction. ~~it should go.~~
It seems to me
~~Therefore, do you not agree~~ that you and
like
I should be, ~~as~~ hoes in the hands of God?
We
Should ~~we not~~ learn our proper use? ~~Our mis-~~
~~take is frequently that we beleive we can hoe~~
We often think we can hoe alone
~~the grass alone, independant of the direction~~
without
~~of~~ the Master's hand. That certainly is ~~a~~
worth considering,
~~point to which we should give our attention,~~
isn't it?

Rewriting the Talk, Step Three (A14):

A famous writer once said, "Great authors do not write. They rewrite."

If you felt that your first writing was good enough for a radio programme, then you probably have not learned to judge yourself.

All of us find it hard to judge our own work, because we like to feel that what we have done is good. However, we must learn to judge ourselves more harshly than our worst enemy, if we are to become good writers.

You have finished your first writing, or your *first draft*. It should be covered with corrections and new ideas. You may have taken out some large pieces and put in new ones, and almost every sentence has been changed. However, as you worked through those corrections, the new script was forming in your mind.

Now you must rewrite. This time, write more carefully. Think about the words as you put them down. Choose them carefully, being guided by your first draft. If a better idea comes to your mind, use it.

You may decide to rewrite your talk a third time because you are not yet satisfied. This is good. Many excellent writers will rewrite their talk four or five times.

When you have typed your script, read it out loud again. Check the time. Is it exactly one minute long? If not, shorten or lengthen it.

Now you are ready for the final edit. You must go back to all the questions we asked about your first draft. Ask them again about your *second draft*. Make the corrections on your paper very neatly. If there are not too many corrections (not more than one per line) you may be able to use this script on the programme. Probably, however, you will find there are too many corrections and changes, and this will mean that you must type your script again. Check your time once more, to be sure your talk is exactly one minute long.

Now you have your air copy, neatly typed, with only a few corrections on it, and you are satisfied that it is the best script you can do.

Take your finished script, all of the other drafts, and your research material to your supervisor for his comments.

Do not feel badly if your supervisor asks you to write the talk again and to make some changes. Be grateful to him if he points out your mistakes. We can only improve our work if we can find our mistakes.

This Filipina radio writer often rewrote her script as many as four or five times. This was one of the reasons why the stories she wrote for radio were later published in a book.

C

Recording the Talk, Step Four (A15):

A short talk such as this, once it is written, needs little to get it ready for the programme. However, this little bit of work must be done very carefully, or your talk will fail. You have worked very hard while you were writing your talk. All of your hard work will be of little use if the listener does not like the way you speak.

Good radio speaking is not easy to learn. It takes a great deal of practice and hard work. You will help yourself very much if you spend a lot of time by yourself reading *out loud*. Read out loud from magazines and newspapers. Poetry is very good for this purpose.

For the moment, however, read over your talk very carefully, *out loud*.

> Read it a second time out loud, and try to sound as friendly as you can.
> Read it a third time, and try to sound as sincere as you can.
> Read your talk a fourth time, and try to sound as conversational as you can; that is, try to sound as if you were talking very *quietly* to somebody sitting right beside you.
> Read your talk a fifth time, very, very slowly, making sure that every sound in every word comes out clearly. It is best to make the sounds so clear and so sharp in this exercise, that they sound a little bit silly.
> Now, read over your talk silently. *Underline* all the important words. These are the words that you want to emphasise.
> Read your talk over once again, trying to remember all of the things we have just told you about.

Still, there is one more thing that is as important as anything we have said. SMILE! A smile on your face will make your voice more friendly, more relaxed, more pleasant, and it will keep you from making many mistakes.

Of course, there will be times when you are speaking on the radio that you will not want to smile. Sometimes you should sound angry. However, most of the time you will want a friendly sound in your voice, and you can have this by keeping a smile on your face.

> One friend I knew wrote the word "SMILE" in large letters on the top of every page of his script. Another friend, when he was learning to speak into a microphone, asked me to stand behind him and to pull his ear each time he stopped smiling.

Now you are ready. Go into your studio. Ask your technician to watch your time with a stop-watch. Sit down about 25 to 35 centimetres (10 to 14 inches) from the microphone. Relax! Smile! Yawn! Stretch! Enjoy yourself! You are speaking to friends! Now, go ahead and record your talk.

This African broadcaster is sitting just the right distance from the microphone, so that his voice will sound clear but not hollow. He is holding the script up off the table, and sliding the sheets of paper one by one off to his right. He does not turn his pages over.

Evaluation, Step Five (A16):

Step Five is the most important step of all! If you learn to evaluate your programme, you will learn new things. If you learn to judge yourself carefully each time, then you will become an expert programme writer and producer. If you do not learn to criticise yourself, then you will learn very slowly and your work will always be of low value.

Here are some questions about your talk. Answer them carefully and honestly as you listen to your tape. Remember that when we speak of "the listener", we mean the *one* kind of person you studied in your research.

Check-list for a Short Talk (A17):

1. Was my talk interesting to the kind of listener I had discovered in my research?   Yes ____ No ____
2. Was the talk simple enough for this listener to understand?   Yes ____ No ____
3. Did I say something that was important to my listener?   Yes ____ No ____
4. Did my talk have a beginning so interesting that the listener would really want to hear the rest of it?   Yes ____ No ____
5. Did the "story-message" in the middle explain my idea?   Yes ____ No ____
6. Was the "story-message" told in such a way that the listener would find it interesting?   Yes ____ No ____
7. Was my "quick closing" short and interesting?   Yes ____ No ____
8. Did it repeat the idea of the "story-message" but in different words?   Yes ____ No ____
9. Did I make my writing interesting, with colourful words and phrases?   Yes ____ No ____
10. Was the writing happy enough to make the listener smile a little?   Yes ____ No ____
11. Did my voice sound natural, as if I were talking to a friend sitting beside me?   Yes ____ No ____
12. Did I smile as I spoke?   Yes ____ No ____
13. Was the talk exactly one minute long?   Yes ____ No ____

Listen to the tape-recording of your talk several times, to be sure that you have answered these questions well. If you are able to answer "yes" to more than ten of them, then take your tape, all of your scripts, and your research to your supervisor.

If not, go back and correct your errors. If you are not certain whether some parts of your talk were successful or not, discuss them with your supervisor.

Glossary (A18):   PART THREE

At the end of this training manual you will find the *Glossary of Radio Words*. It is important that you learn to understand these words for two reasons:

They will help you understand other things you might read about radio work.

They will help you understand what broadcasters mean when they use these words.

In almost all of the projects, one of the assignments will ask you to look up some of these words. By the time you have finished the manual, you will have studied most of the words in the glossary.

We would like you to translate the meanings of these words into your own language. We know this may sometimes be very difficult. You may not be able to find the right words in your language. Even so, you should do the best you can, and use words taken from another language only when there is no other way. Sometimes you may even be able to find one word or phrase in your own language that means exactly the same thing as the word in the glossary.

These exercises will not only help you to understand the meanings of the words, but they will also make it easier to describe the meanings to others.

Use one notebook just for these *Glossary Assignments*. Keep your translations. When you have finished the manual, you will have your glossary in your own language, and this will be very useful in your studio.

Glossary Assignment (A19):

Look up these words in the glossary and translate the meanings of the words into your own language.

EDITING	OFF–MICROPHONE
ON–AIR	SCRIPT
ON–MICROPHONE	

When you have finished this assignment, take it to your supervisor and ask him to help you make some improvements.

The United Church of Canada.

PROJECT B

Writing a Five-minute Talk

About this Project (B1):

We hope that you have enjoyed the first project in this manual, and that you will enjoy working on *Project B* even more.

There is a great deal of work to do in *Project B*, but we are sure that it will help you learn the art of radio programming.

Please do not go on in your work or your readings if you do not understand some part of the manual. If something is not clear, read it again several times. If it still is not clear, go and talk about it with your supervisor.

If you go on to the next part without understanding everything in the first part, you will soon find many other things you cannot understand.

In *Project B* we hope you will learn some more things about making a talk programme. Everything you were told in *Project A* is also for *Project B*. It might help you read quickly through *Project A* before you continued.

Building Resources (B2):

A radio station is like an elephant.

  It eats a great deal of food.

  It must have food all the time.

  It can eat only certain kinds of food.

A radio station "eats" many programmes. You will soon discover that it takes many programmes and a great deal of work just to fill up the time on a radio station. It takes even more time and work to put things on the radio that are helpful to the listener.

A radio station must have its "food" always. Even if you feel tired, or if you have no more ideas in your mind, or you do not have enough time, the radio station must go on the air every day. Otherwise, the listeners will think the station has stopped, and they will find another station to listen to. Then you have an even harder task to get them back.

A radio station can use only certain kinds of programmes. There are some ideas that can be given easily on the air. There are some kinds of programmes and ideas that are *not* successful on the radio.

When you begin to write radio programmes, you may think you have many ideas in your mind for good programmes. No doubt they are good ideas. But they will soon be gone!

> Just like an elephant. When you buy an elephant, you may already have much food prepared for him. But an elephant is a very hungry animal. The food will soon be gone. While you still have some food left, you must begin to look for some more. If you do not begin to look now for more ideas for programmes, you will find very soon that there are no more ideas left!

Here are *three* ways to help you find "food" for your programmes:

> the notebook,
> reading, and
> the Idea File.

The Notebook (B3):

A good writer, whether he is writing for radio programmes, for a newspaper, or whether he writes books, always has four tools:

> his eyes,
> his ears,
> his notebook, and
> his pencil.

Wherever he goes, a good writer sees things, and hears things that can be used in his writing. These ideas are written down in his notebook.

What does he write down? He writes:

> interesting colourful words,
> new ways of saying old things,
> little stories he hears from other people,
> things that happen to him, to his friends, and to his neighbours, and
> good ideas that come into his mind.

He writes things down as soon as he sees or hears or thinks them. He may hear a good joke or a wise saying in the market when he buys his food. He writes it down immediately. He may have a good idea as he lies in his bed waiting for sleep to come. He picks up his notebook and writes it down because he knows that if he waits for the morning, the idea will be gone.

Why does he write these things down?

> Because when he writes them down, he also makes them stay in his mind. Because he knows that in the future, he may need those memories. As he sits at his typewriter wondering how to convince a listener, he will glance through his notebook, and new, fresh thoughts will come into his mind.

Frank Palomares, DYSR, Philippines.

This broadcaster has seen something interesting in this fishing boat, and is writing it in his notebook.

Some Day it May be Useful (B4):

It is true that many things in a writer's notebook will never be used. A good writer knows, however, that even if only a few of the things he writes become part of a programme, the notebook has proved very helpful.

There is an even more important reason why a good writer always carries a notebook with him, and always writes things in it. The notebook helps him to see. It helps him to hear.

Because he knows he should find things for his notebook, he looks for things. The more he looks, the more he sees. Because the good writer wants new words and thoughts for his notebook, he listens to people. The more he listens, the more he really hears what is going on around him.

A good writer works hard to learn all he can about people and listens to them, simply because he loves them. He also knows that he cannot remember all the interesting things he sees and hears. So he writes them in his notebook.

We suggest that you start a notebook now. It need only be a small one, just the right size for your pocket. Carry it and a pencil or pen with you always.

A good way to begin a notebook is by walking for two or three hours through your city or town. Do not ride. You see much more when you walk. Look for interesting things about people. Do not look for big, important things. Look for the little things that people say and do.

We said in *Project A*, that there were four things that should be done for every programme. The first thing was *research*. Later on in *Project B* we will ask you to write a five-minute talk. The walk will be your research. We hope you will find some good ideas for your talk as you are walking.

If you were writing the talk in English, it might have a title like: "Walking Through My Town" or "People are Interesting". Since you are writing in your own language your title will, of course, be quite different and I hope, much better.

Now take your walk. Walk through places where there are many people, perhaps the market. Walk slowly. Look at everything and everybody. Listen! Write it down! When you come back from your walk, do *not* begin writing your programme. There are other things you should do first.

Writers Must Read (B5):

A great statesman was once asked "What kind of a person do you admire most?" He answered, "The man who reads."

Your country is changing quickly. Our world is changing quickly. Even if you finished your school study only one year ago, then you should know that many of the things you learned are no longer true. Things in government, science, medicine, and art are changing very fast. There is only one way you can keep from becoming a man from the past. That is to read.

There are also other reasons why you should read. These are almost the same as the reasons why you should learn to observe the way people act and speak. A good writer reads, and watches and listens, because he needs this material for the things he writes.

> A bucket of water will soon be dry if you keep taking water out, and you don't put any back in. You must keep filling your mind with new ideas, new thoughts, new words, new information.

The Studio Magazine Shelf (B6):

Your station or studio should try to receive certain newspapers and magazines regularly. What kind? Here are some suggestions:

> The most important newspapers in your country. (If possible, get two or three that have different political views.)
> One or two popular magazines published in your country or a neighbouring country.
> A popular magazine from a far-away country.
> One or two magazines that have articles about your kind of programming. (If you are doing school programmes, then you should have the best magazines about education. If you are doing religious programmes, you should have magazines about your own faith and others.)

You should try to spend at least an hour every day reading.

"But I have no time!" you may say. It *saves time* to read, because your mind and your notebook are full of ideas from your reading.

> It is easier to get water when the bucket is full, than to get the last little bit from the bottom when it is almost empty.

Of course, you should not read only magazines and newspapers. You will want to read many books as well. Perhaps there is a library in your studio. Perhaps there is a public library or a school library near by. Find out if it is possible to borrow books, or to sit in the library and read. Many of your friends may also have books that are interesting and useful.

As you read, you should have three things beside you. Your notebook. Your pencil. A pair of scissors. The scissors are for your idea file.

The Idea File (B7):

Every good writer has an idea file. It is a place where he keeps ideas and information until he needs them. If you are going to write programmes successfully, you will also need an idea file.

There are many ways to make an idea file. You can use:

some old brown envelopes,
some filing folders and a filing cabinet, or
a large scrap-book.

Mark different parts of your idea file for different kinds of ideas. If you are doing programmes on farming, you may have parts or sections like this:

rice planting,
rice harvesting,
diseases of rice, and so on.

It depends on the kinds of programmes you are preparing.

This Ethiopian broadcaster is looking for programme information in her idea file.

When reading, you might see a short newspaper story that could be used as a parable (story-message) about the best way to plant rice, or how to feed children, or how to love your neighbour. Cut it out and put it in your idea file.

If you are not permitted to cut from the pages, then write the information in your notebook, tear out the page, and put it in your idea file. It doesn't matter if the information is not used right away. Perhaps you may use it two years from now in a very surprising way.

> My father had an idea file. He wrote stories for magazines, not for radio.
> My father has been dead for many years, but I often use the things he put in
> his file so many years ago.

Assignment One (B8):

The first assignment in *Project B* is to talk to your supervisor about making an idea file. Then spend an hour or more cutting items from newspapers and magazines that may be useful some day in your programmes. Put them in your idea file. If your studio already has a file, then spend an hour studying it carefully. Become familiar with the way in which things are put into it, and how to find things. If there is someone in charge of the idea file, ask him to explain it to you. Write a short *report* on your idea file for your supervisor, describing the way the idea file works, what is in it, and its value.

Now, bring your *notebook* and the work you have done on your *idea file* to your supervisor. Please do not proceed to the next part of *Project B* until you have done this.

You have just begun a very important part of your training as a radio writer and producer. If you keep writing interesting things in your notebook, and if you constantly put exciting materials in your idea file, then you will certainly improve your work as a writer.

Building a Radio Talk (B9):   PART TWO

If you have made some public speeches then you have already learned something about a radio talk. You will already know that in a speech where you can see the people before you, the talk must be interesting and exciting. It must be clear and well planned. Most important, the speaker must have something worthwhile to say.

However, a radio talk is different in almost every other way:

> The listener cannot see your face.
> He cannot see the way you wave your arms.
> He cannot see your nice clothes.

Most important, your radio listener does not have many other people beside him. When many people are standing together, they help each other get excited about what is being said. Each person helps the other one get more angry, or more excited, or more interested, or makes him laugh louder. A radio listener usually has only a few friends or his family near by.

A political leader knows that a speech in the market-place is a good way to persuade people. He also knows that it is even better if he can go from house to house, from person to person, and talk to each one by himself.

When a political leader speaks to one person in his home, he talks in a different way than he does when making a speech in the market-place. He talks quietly as a friend. He uses the same way of speaking as you should on the radio.

Whenever you write a programme for the radio, or whenever you talk on the radio, think of your listener as one person, a friend sitting beside you.

Unity, Clearness and Emphasis (B10):

A good talk is like a stool with three legs. If you remove one of the legs, it will fall. The three legs of a good talk are:

> *Unity:* Your talk must stick together. You must always stay with the main idea. There should be no words or sentences that do not help tell about the main idea.
> *Clearness:* Your talk must be easy to understand. Your sentences should be easy to say. It means that each part of your talk flows easily out of the one before it, and easily into the one that follows.
> *Emphasis:* Your talk makes the listener remember what you have said. It means that you caught his interest at the beginning, made him even more interested by the things you said in the middle, and finally left him at the end with something that *he* feels is important.

Unless your talk has unity, clearness and emphasis, it will be like a stool with some legs missing. The one who writes, and the one who speaks a talk both help in giving a talk these three legs. In this project, you are both the writer and the speaker. Therefore, your work is even more difficult.

Building a Bridge (B11):

Do you remember the research you did in *Project A*? Spend a few minutes looking at it again. Try to think of the single person you found in that research. One person only. It may not be a real person. It might be a person you imagine. If so, think of a name for that person, and try to form a picture in your mind of what he or she looks like.

You should try to make your talk as if it was intended only for this one person.

Of course, there are many different people in a radio audience. However, if you keep just one listener in your mind, your talk will seem more *personal*. Every listener will have the feeling that you are talking *to him alone*.

> Think of one person, and you will reach many.
> Think of many people, and you may reach none.
> One very successful broadcaster draws a little picture of the listener he has in his mind. He is not an artist, and so his picture is not very beautiful. But he puts the picture on the table beside him, and keeps saying to himself, "I am talking to *that* person!" Many listeners write to him and say, "I had the feeling that you were talking only to me!"

What are you going to say to this *one* person? Did you find something interesting in your walk? Did you see anyone suffering? Did you see anyone happy? Did you see anyone angry? Every human being knows about such things.

When you speak of something your listener knows, you are building a bridge. Your listener says to himself, "Yes, I understand that! That has happened to my family and to me," or he may say, "I know a man like that!" You now have a bridge you may use. On that bridge you may talk of many things. Remember, people are interested in people.

Perhaps you are making programmes about farming. Did you see people in the market arguing about the cost of rice or corn? Did you see children suffering because they don't have enough food?

These things are bridges you can use to cross over to your listener. Those same bridges could be used for broadcasts about education, social problems, or religion.

An Example (B12):

Here is one way in which a bridge like this was used:

> "Abu Wazir was angry. He was so angry, his eyes were growing large in
> the front of his head. "Why?" he shouted, "Why should I pay so much
> money for a cupful of rice? This is worse than robbery!"
> I saw Abu Wazir in the market this morning. There were others there, too,
> trying to buy rice. They were not all as angry as Abu Wazir, but none of
> them were happy.
> Why the high cost of rice? Because the farmers do not grow enough for
> our country.
> Let me tell you about another man. He was a farmer. His name was . . ."

. . . the story continues about a farmer who learned to irrigate, and tells people
where to write for more facts about good farming practices.

Did you find some bridges you can use? You may need more than one bridge
for each talk. Look over your notes, and think about it for a while.

Assignment Two (B13):

Write a five-minute talk. Choose a subject that you know well, and one that
your listener would find useful. Before you begin, study the following suggestions. They will tell you how to go about writing such a talk.

First, however, look over the outline you used for your talk in *Project A*. The
outline you should make for this talk is very much like it, but a little longer.

A Five-minute Talk (B14):

What do you wish to say to your listener? What would your listener like to
know? What problems is he worried about? How can you help him solve the
problems he worries about? Do you have a solution to one of his problems? Can
you tell him about that solution in a way that he would accept your advice?
Will he be interested?

If you can answer these questions, you will begin to see some of the places
where you, as a broadcaster, can help your listener. You may also find a worthwhile subject for the talk.

The Outline (B15):

After you have chosen your subject here is one way of making an outline:

Object: Write down in *one* short sentence, the idea that you will use on your programme. Write it down in not more than twenty-five words. Unless you can do this, your idea is too big and difficult, or else you do not really understand it very well yourself.

Attention-catcher: This is the same as in *Project A*, except that you could spend more time on this. You may use perhaps forty-five seconds just to make the listener interested in what you say. Something from your note-book, perhaps?

Direction-pointer: A few sentences to tell the listener *what* you want to say. Do not tell everything, but do tell enough so that the listener will know what you are doing, and will not be afraid he will be tricked.

The First Story-message: This is the same as in *Project A*. It should be a short story about a minute long that will help the listener understand your message. Once again, you may find something in your notebook or idea file.

Second Direction-pointer: Because you have explained your subject a little with your first story-message, you can now add a little more information to your first direction-pointer. You should also repeat the information you have in your first direction-pointer, but with different words.

The Second Story-message: This second story-message should tell even more about your idea, so that when you have finished the listener has in mind all of the idea you wanted him to understand.

The Quick Closing: Do not add any new information in your closing. Repeat the information you gave in your first and second direction-pointers, but use a new and interesting way of saying it. Make this part as short as possible, but choose your words very well. If it is done well, this is the part the listener will remember most.

Now outline your talk. Write down each of the six parts and a few words to remind you of what you want to do with each part. Read over the instructions for outlining a talk in *Project A*, to refresh your memory on how this is done.

The First Draft (B16):

After you have done your outline, gather together the notes and magazine clippings you may need to look at as you write, and begin your first draft.

Remember to write quickly when you are doing your first draft, and do not worry too much about the way you say things.

Here are some suggestions that may help:

Use action-words. Use words and phrases that tell about things happening or moving. Use stories and ideas that tell of a lively life.

Help the listener see and hear. Use words and phrases that will help the listener imagine easily the things you describe.

Make the listener understand. Do not say, "The flood covered seventeen million hectares of land." Rather say, "The flood covered a piece of land about the size of our smallest province." Do not say, "There will be a 12 per cent increase in taxes," say, "Every time you earn one dollar, you will give twelve cents to the government."

Use a little suspense. The listener will want to understand what you are talking about. But if you can make him wonder about a few things, and then give him the answer before the end of the programme, it will help him to keep listening.

Use conversation. People like to hear other people speak. Whenever possible, use the actual words that people said, but only when they are very interesting words. Do not use long quotations from a book or magazine.

Use simple words. Unless you use words people understand, they will not listen. If you use big words, the listener will say to himself. "That man is very clever. He uses big words. I will listen to somebody else who is not so clever." Your friends may listen to you if you can show them your great knowledge. A radio listener does not need to be polite. He can turn off your programme, just as you would close a book if it is not interesting.

Do not "talk-down". Never talk to your listener as if you are more clever than he is. Even if you are educated and he is not, that still does not give you the right to "talk-down". In any case, it will simply make the listener turn off his radio.

Do not harangue or scold. Few people will accept advice from someone they do not like. They do not like a radio speaker who sounds as if he is always angry. Although there will be times when you should be angry, usually you should talk as one friend to another friend. It is the only way people will listen to you.

The First Edit (B17):

Use each of those suggestions for judging your talk as you write. Of course, you will want to make many changes as you do the first edit. When you have finished your page it should look very messy. It should be covered with marks and corrections. You may wish to write your first draft again.

Before you move on to your second draft, read your first draft over quickly out loud. Try to determine if it is close to five minutes. Of course, you can only make a guess at this time, but it is easier to make a big change now, if it is necessary.

Using Other People's Ideas (B18):

If you are using someone else's ideas or words, be sure you tell your listeners where they come from. It is simply dishonest to use somebody else's work and then make the listener think it is yours.

Also try to get the permission of the author whenever possible, even if your law does not say you must.

Now bring your outline and first draft to the supervisor. Please do not go on to the second draft until you have done this.

The Second Draft (B19):   PART THREE

Now you are ready to write your second draft. Re-read the part of *Project A* which tells how this is done. No doubt, you will feel sometimes that it is not necessary to write and edit, then rewrite and edit everything. You can be sure, however, that the quality will be lower if you try to leave out one stage.

What did I say? That is an important question. After you have written your second draft, read your script over, and ask yourself, "What did I say?" Is it the same thing as you intended to say? Check the "Object" in your outline to be sure. Did you say something worth while? Was it useful to the listener? Was it important? If you can answer some of these questions carefully, the answers may not be pleasing. You may wish to do a third draft in order to rewrite parts of your talk.

Timing (B20):

Read over your talk, to see how long it is. It should be five minutes long.

If your programme is very much too short or too long, you will have to rewrite some parts.

If it is only about ten to thirty seconds too *long*, then find out if there are four or five sentences near the end of your talk that could be removed. Do not cross them out. Put a line under them. When you actually get behind your microphone, you probably will be a little nervous, and you will speak faster. You may need the extra few sentences to fill in the extra time.

If your programme is ten or twenty seconds too short, then you will need to write some extra material for the end of your programme. Write enough so that your programme is about fifteen to twenty seconds too long. Put a line under these extra sentences, so that if you do not need them, you can easily leave them out. If you write extra sentences be sure they fit into your script, and are just as interesting as the rest of your talk.

Now take your script (including your outline and first drafts) to your supervisor. Do not go on to the next step until you have done this.

Recording the Talk (B21):   PART FOUR

If you and your supervisor have agreed that your script is satisfactory, you may prepare to record your programme. Turn back to *Project A*. Review the steps necessary for the *Production* of your talk. We asked you to read your talk out loud seven times. There was something to watch out for each time. Later when you have gained more experience, you may be able to record your programme after practising your script only a few times. But that is later on. Unless you have several years of microphone experience, you cannot do your talk successfully, if you do not read and study your script carefully *at least seven times*. When you have done this, make arrangements to record your talk.

Evaluation (B22):

When you are satisfied it is the best recording you can make, ask yourself the following questions. Answer them very carefully. Listen to your tape as many times as necessary to be sure your answers are true.

Here are the questions. Remember, when we talk about "the listener" we mean only *one* person. This is the one person you were thinking about in your research earlier in this project.

Check-list for a Five-minute Talk (B23):

1. Was the talk interesting to the listener?   Yes ____ No ____
2. Was the talk simple enough for this listener to understand?   Yes ____ No ____
3. Did I say something that was important in the mind of the listener?   Yes ____ No ____
4. Did my talk have a beginning so interesting that the listener would really want to hear the rest of it?   Yes ____ No ____
5. Did the "story-messages" in the middle help explain my "idea"?   Yes ____ No ____
6. Was my "quick closing" done in such a way that the listener was able to remember the message easily?   Yes ____ No ____
7. Was my "quick closing" short and interesting?   Yes ____ No ____
8. Did I use "action-words" in my talk? The kind that tell of things happening and moving?   Yes ____ No ____
9. Did I repeat the main idea of my talk at least twice, using different words each time?   Yes ____ No ____
10. Did I use my language correctly, at the same time talking as if I was having a quiet conversation?   Yes ____ No ____
11. Was the writing happy enough to make the listener smile a little?   Yes ____ No ____
12. Did my voice sound natural, as if I were talking to someone sitting beside me?   Yes ____ No ____
13. Did I smile as I spoke?   Yes ____ No ____
14. Was my talk exactly five minutes long?   Yes ____ No ____

After you have been over this list several times, find out how many of your questions were answered "yes". If more than eleven were answered "yes", then you may go on to the next assignment. If less than eleven were answered "yes", then go back and correct all the mistakes.

Glossary Assignment (B24):

Translate the meaning of these words into your own language.

    IDEA FILE   RECORD

   Now take your recorded talk, your script (including the first and second drafts) and your check-list to your supervisor.

One Last Word (B25):

We have told you how to prepare a one-minute and a five-minute talk. Of course, there are other good ways of doing a good radio talk. As you continue through this manual you will learn other ways to make a talk successful.

   For instance, almost all the things you will learn about dramas can be used in writing a talk. Because you will not be asked to write any more talks, it does not mean that you have learned all you should know about this kind of programme.

   There is still much more to learn.

PROJECT C

Translation

Project C is a little different from the first two. You will not make any programmes, although the poem we will ask you to translate might be used as part
of a programme.

We think you will enjoy *Project C* because it has to do with something that is
very close to all of us. If you come to this project with your mind open to new
ideas, you will gain a better understanding not only of your language, but of
your people and yourself as well.

There are many things that make men higher than animals. One of the most
wonderful is man's ability to speak.

It is most amazing that you and I learned to talk when we were very small
children. By the time we were a few years old, we could make many sounds
with our little mouths, and thousands of words with those sounds.

With these words and these sounds we could tell of the things we felt. We
could tell of our joy, our hate, our sorrow, our love, our loneliness, our needs.

Through these words and these sounds, we could learn from our family and
our friends. We could learn of their joys and sorrows. They could tell us of
things we had not seen, and about people we had not known.

Later we learned to read, and the world opened up to us.

We found there were people like us in other villages, towns and cities, in other
countries. People like us, but not always exactly like us.

Because we can speak and understand the speech of others, we can learn. It is
certainly a miracle!

A Language to Love (C2):

If we stop and think about the wonderful language we have, we begin to understand the amazing things we can do with it. Your language is worthy of your
love!

We should get to know the language we love. We should know what makes it so beautiful, and so useful.

> Words are like flowers. Good writing is like a garden. One cannot make a flower beautiful, though one can plant a garden using beautiful flowers. But, to make a garden one must know something about the flowers, and about gardens, and about the soil the flowers grow in.

When you write something in your language you cannot make the words beautiful. They have always been beautiful. Nevertheless, you can put them into lovely sentences where each word makes the other more beautiful. However, you cannot do this, until you know something about words, about language, and about the people who give it life.

Your Language (C3):

Let us begin by telling you something about your language. It may seem foolish for someone who does not know your language to try to tell you something about it. That is true. We do not know your language. However, we know some things that are true about all languages in the world, and therefore, true of yours.

> *All languages are difficult.* Your own language will seem easiest because you learned it as a child. However, children in all parts of the world learn to speak at about the same age, and so the people who study languages (linguists) say that one language is as difficult to learn as another. Of course, much depends on the person. Burmese people might find Mandarin easier to learn than Tamil. However, a Hindi-speaking person might find Tamil less difficult than Mandarin.
> *All languages are wonderful.* They all have very fine ways of expressing the thoughts and hopes and desires of people. Every language has many ways of saying things, a large variety of words and phrases that can be used in very exciting ways.
> *Languages spring out of the lives of the people who use them.* By studying a language, you can learn very much about the habits and the thoughts of the people who use it. In fact, the life of the people would be impossible without their language.
> *The language we speak makes a difference to the way we think.* People think of things in different ways, partly because their languages are not the same.

This is one reason why people from different parts of the world sometimes misunderstand each other.

All languages are changing. This is because people are always changing. Languages change fastest when they meet with other languages, and begin to borrow words and phrases. Now that we have so much travelling from one part of the world to another, and so many movies, books, and radio programmes going from one country to another, languages are changing very fast.

Your language is changing. As new ideas and new experiences come into the lives of your people, they develop new words to talk about them. Some of the words come from other languages. Other new words come when old words are changed or given a new meaning. This is the way languages grow. They have always grown in this way, and they will continue to grow in this way.

This means that you must know *how* your language is growing. You cannot write radio programmes in the language your people used several years ago; and you cannot write in the kind of language they may use in the future. You must write the way people are speaking today.

Studying Your Language (C4):

There are several things you should do to become familiar with your own language. They will help you to know even more about it, and this will help you to write better programmes.

Do not say, "Never mind, I already know my language. After all, I have spoken it since I was a child!" A good writer never stops studying his own language, even if he already can speak it and write it better than most people.

Assignment One (C5):

Gather together a group of four or five people from your studio, or some of your friends. These should be people who know your language well. Ask them to help you answer these questions.

What kind of words would these people use if they were turning down an invitation to come to your house: a truck driver?
                              a school teacher?
                              a bank clerk?
                              a farmer?

If you were riding a bicycle and you bumped into each of these people, what would each say and what kind of words would be used?

If each of these people came to you to borrow some money, what would each say and what kind of words would be used?

Talk about these things in your group, and try to find out what differences there are in the way people in your country talk. Write a few paragraphs describing these differences. They should go into your research file after they have been seen by your supervisor.

Listening to Your Language (C6):

Try to make a habit of listening to the way people speak. When you are in the market, riding a bus, or visiting with friends, listen to their speech. Each person has his own way or style of talking. You will not only find it interesting, but very useful to discover what these differences are. Whenever you hear an interesting word or phrase, put it in your notebook.

Looking for a Linguist (C7):

There may be scholars in your country who are making a scientific study of your language. You might find such a scholar at a university. Perhaps the university may be able to tell you if there is someone near by studying your language.

If there is a Bible House in your city, someone there may be able to arrange an interview with a person who has studied your language in order to translate the Bible.

Such a person should know at least something about linguistics, the scientific study of language. Try to visit him if you can, or at least talk to him on the telephone. You may not be able to find such a person, but if you can it will be well worth the time.

If you cannot find a linguist, try to find someone else who has worked with your language. Perhaps a writer, a language teacher, or an actor.

Here are some questions you could ask:

What different dialects do we have in our country? (A dialect is a slightly different way of speaking the same language.)

What is the most important dialect in our country? Why is this?

How should we decide which dialect to use in our radio programmes?

Sometimes we try to explain things in our language, but we cannot find the right words. How can we overcome this problem?

Are there any books or magazine articles I can find to read, which would help me to understand our language?

There may be other questions you could ask. Write down the answers, and place them in your research file, along with the information you gathered in *Projects A* and *B*.

Consult a Foreigner (C8):

It may seem strange, but a foreigner who has tried to learn your language may be able to tell you some interesting things. He certainly will not be able to speak as well as you do, but because he has been forced to study the language in order to learn it, he may see some things that you have not noticed.

> In the same way, you may know some things about English that I do not know, because you have had to study it in order to learn it. I learned English as a child. I did not study it.

The next step in your language study will be to find out what makes your language such a useful thing. We would like you to discover the ways in which your language can be used to express ideas powerfully, beautifully, angrily, sadly, happily, sorrowfully, or lovingly.

Assignment Two (C9):

Try to find three or four good poems in your language. You may need to ask your supervisor to help you with this. Perhaps there are books of poetry you could look for. Most certainly there are folk-songs. The words of folk-songs are usually good poetry. Try to find three or four different kinds of poems. Perhaps a folk-song, a classical poem, and a modern poem. Read the poems several times. As you read them, find the answers to these questions, and write them down.

> Do any of these poems use the same words or phrases over and over again? Does this help to make the poem strong? Why is this?
> Are the sentences short or long? In what way does this help the poem?
> Are there certain words used very well in the poem? Which words are these? Why do you think they are used well?
> Can you find places in the poems where several words have the same sort of sound? (such as the three "s" sounds above). Does this help give us the feeling of the poem?
> Do any of the poems help you to *feel* a certain way? Do they sometimes

give you a *feeling*, even when they do not give you a *meaning*? How do they do this?

What other ways are used in the poems to make it a strong or a beautiful poem?

Do you think you could translate any of these poems into another language and keep all of the beauty and meaning? Why? Why not?

Assignment Three (C10):

This assignment will make you laugh. It is a simple little trick that you might wish to use at a party some time.

Here is a short story. Translate this into your own language. Then give your translation to a friend and ask him to translate it from your language back into English. Do not let him see this book, or tell him what the English was like here. Then compare his English translation with the story that follows.

"The Rabbit and the Turtle" (C11):

The rabbit was boasting to the other animals about his speed. "I can run faster than any of you," he said. "I challenge you to a race!"

A turtle spoke up. "I can win a race against you."

The rabbit laughed. "I can dance around you all the way," he said.

"Don't boast until you've won," replied the turtle.

So the race began. Almost at once the rabbit ran far ahead of the turtle. To show his contempt he lay down under a bush and went to sleep.

The turtle walked on and on. Slowly, slowly, he moved closer to the finish. Just as the turtle was almost at the end, the rabbit woke up. He ran as fast as he could but it was too late. The turtle had WON.

Then the turtle said, "Slow and steady wins the race!"

by AESOP

It will be amusing to compare the two translations. It will be even more amusing if you ask another person who has not seen your first translation, to change it again into your language. Then you can compare the two English stories, and the two in your own language.

This amusing trick tells us about a very difficult problem, the problem of translation. We will tell you more about this later. At the moment, however, take all three assignments to your supervisor.

From One Language to Another (C12):   PART TWO

The last assignment (translating the little story from English to your language, then back to English, then into your language again) tells us two very important things:

> Translation is not easy.
> The story changes when it is translated.

Translation is not easy, for many reasons:

> One must understand two languages well to do it.
> One cannot translate word by word, because usually one cannot find a word in one language that means exactly the same thing as a word in another language. Sometimes one has to use a whole phrase or sentence in one language to say a single word from another language.
> Different languages have different *idioms*. An *idiom* is a word or a phrase that has come to mean something more or even different from what it actually says. For instance, sometimes in English we say, "He was cut to the heart." This does not mean that the person had been cut with a knife. It means that his feelings were hurt, or that he was deeply insulted. If you translated those *words* into Palau, they would mean, "He had to decide between two possibilities."
> Languages use a different *syntax. Syntax* is the order in which the words follow each other in a sentence. I'm sure you have humorous examples of foreigners who have used words in the wrong order when speaking your language. For instance, in some Nilotic languages, you would never say, "He went to town." Instead your word order would be, "The town was gone to by him." In Luganda, you would not say, "I have lost your book." That would mean that you intended to lose it. Rather you would say, "Your book has lost me."
> However, it is not the sentences that give us most of the trouble. It is the whole story. People from other countries tell the parts of a story in different orders too. The same story would begin, proceed and end differently if it were told by a Micronesian, than it would if it were told by a Ugandan. A man making a public speech would begin, proceed, and end differently, depending on the language he spoke.
> You must know what the differences are, between the language you are translating from, and your own language.

Languages have different ways of emphasising; that is, making a phrase strong. In English, if we want to make a strong statement, we repeat ourselves. For instance, I might say, "Truly, truly," thinking that if I say it twice it will be stronger. However, in many Philippine languages, if you say it twice, that makes it weaker. Some Filipinos would only say "Truly, truly", if they weren't very sure it was true.

Adaptation (C13):

There is a difference between a translation and an adaptation.

The translation: When doing this we try to be as true to the first language as possible. This would be so if you were translating a magazine article or a book. You would not only try to get the facts right, but would also try to put as much of the author's style of writing into your translation as possible.

The adaptation: This is where we are more interested in giving our listener the idea or information. It really means that we use the idea or information to write our own story. Even though you are changing something from one language to another it is not a translation, but an adaptation. You change much of the story to fit your programme and your people.

Assignment Four (C14):

Here is a short story. We chose it, because it sounds very "Western". We did that because most of the people using this manual will be working in other than "Western" nations. Here are some suggestions on the way to proceed with your adaptation:

Read the story just once, very quickly.

Write down, in your own language, what you think is the most important *idea* of the story.

Make an outline of the story which you will write from this idea, telling it the way your own people would tell the story.

Write your own story based on the outline. Make sure it is *your* story, using only the *idea* from the one in this manual.

Now read the story again, perhaps two or three times. Are there any other ideas, besides the important one, that you should put into your story? Is there anything else in the English story that would make yours richer? If so, put it in, but only if it fits.

Now do your first editing, your rewriting, and your second editing.

Here is the story.

"Young Eyes" (C15):

The other day, I drove past the town where I was born. It's a pretty small place. It hurt me a little to see just how small. In fact, I hadn't realised how terribly small until I went back.

When I was a young boy, it seemed pretty big. The house we lived in then seemed big too and very nice. Now it looked small and dirty and run-down.

The school house seemed so close by! I used to think it was a long way from our house to school. Now, I wondered if they had moved the school closer.

They hadn't. *I* had moved.

My son was beside me in the car. He's just the age I was when we moved away from that house and that town. "Boy, that's a swell house," he said, "and big! Did you live in that house, Daddy?"

"Yes, son, I did."

Our car roared down the paved highway. It had been a dirt road once.

"Boy!" he said, suddenly. "You sure must be old!"

I looked at the boy's eyes – eyes that had seen a "big" house, a "swell" house.

"Yes, son. Old! Very old!"

Check-list for an Adaptation (C16):

1. Is the story interesting to your listener? Yes ____ No ____
2. Is the story useful to your listener? Yes ____ No ____
3. Have you made sure that the story does not sound "foreign" in any way? Yes ____ No ____
4. Is it told in the way one of your people would tell the story? Yes ____ No ____

If you cannot answer "yes" to all of these questions, then go back and change those parts that are wrong. It may even be necessary for you to rewrite your adaptation again.

You will see that we did not ask you if your story gave the same information as the English story. The important thing is that you found a good thought, and used it in your own story. You did not really use the story at all, but only the "idea".

Translation (C17):

A translation is like an adaptation in many ways.

> You must still tell the story in a way that is interesting and useful to your listener.
>
> You must tell the story in the manner that one of your own people would tell it.
>
> Your idioms and syntax must be changed to fit your language.

In a translation, however, there are other things you must do as well.

> You must find out exactly what the writer means, and then put this as clearly as possible in your language. Often you will need to do some research. You will need to look up words in a dictionary to be sure what they mean. You may need to discuss the item you are translating with someone else who has read it, to get another point of view. You may need to read other things by the same author, to become familiar with his way of thinking.
>
> You must attempt to understand the spirit and the style of the writing, and then put this into your translation. This will mean reading the item many times and studying it very carefully before you begin.

Assignment Five (C18):

Here is a news item from "The Voice of Ethiopia" which we would like you to translate. When you are finished, there should be two good news items containing the same information. Yours should be in the style best suited for your country.

You will probably need to write and edit, and then rewrite your news item a number of times before you are satisfied with it. Look at the check-list for the adaptation *(C16)*. Use it for this news story, along with the questions in the check-list.

World Food

The world food situation is more precarious today than
at any time since the end of the second World War, according
to the latest report issued by the Food and Agriculture Organisation (FAO) the UN Specialised Agency with headquarters in Rome.

Food production in the year 1965/66 was no higher than
in the preceding years while the world population increased
by about 70 millions. Concern felt at the poor harvests was
heightened by the running down, during this period of
world stocks of grain reserves.

Food production per head of the population in Africa
and Latin America was down by 4 to 5%, in North America
it was up 4%, in Western Europe by 1% while in the Soviet
Union and Eastern Europe it declined slightly.

Until recently the grain reserves, established chiefly in
North America during the 50s, had seemed to be an adequate
precaution against serious need.

Large shipments of such grain last year had made it possible for India and other countries which suffered from
drought to avoid a catastrophic famine.

However these shipments and the sales of grain to the
Soviet Union and China, together with the efforts of the
United States Government to limit grain production at home
had reduced grain reserves to their lowest level for more than
a decade.

All this merely serves to emphasise the well known fact
that the world is heading for catastrophe unless something
is done to establish a balance between the growth of popula-
tions and the production of food. Up to now there has been
more talk on this subject than action.

Voice of Ethiopia, November 1, 1966.

Check-list for a Translation (C19):

1. Does my translated news story have the same informa-
   tion as the one in English?   Yes ____ No ____
2. Have I chosen my words so that the listener can under-
   stand easily?   Yes ____ No ____
3. Did I avoid using foreign words even when it was not
   easy to find words that meant the same thing in my
   language?   Yes ____ No ____

If you can answer "yes" to at least six of the seven questions, then you probably have a good translation. If not, go over your news item again, and try to
improve the places that are weak. When you feel you have the best translation
you can make, take it along with your adaptation, to your supervisor.

E

PROJECT D

Research, Spot Announcements and Your Voice

Things a Broadcaster Must Know (D1): PART ONE

What must you know to be a good radio broadcaster? If you are an educational broadcaster of any kind there are three things you must know.

A successful broadcaster must know his subject.

One cannot very well be a successful agricultural broadcaster unless one knows something about agriculture. Neither can one be a successful religious broadcaster unless one knows something about one's own faith.

A successful broadcaster must understand the technique of radio.

We are trying to teach you some of this in this manual.

A successful broadcaster must understand his audience.

We cannot describe your audience for you, because audiences are different in every part of the world. You must find out for yourself.

Audience Research Continued (D2):

In *Projects A* and *B* you did some work on a research file. You began to find out something about your audience. In this project we hope you will find out even more.

As you gather this information, be sure to put it in your research file so that you will have it to look at later.

The question you must answer in *Project D* is:

"What does my listener know about this?"

If you are an agriculturalist, ask: "What does my listener know about farming, and what are his traditional farming customs?"

If you are a medical man, ask: "What does my listener know about medicine and hygiene, and what are his traditional beliefs about health and medicine?"

If you are a religious broadcaster, ask: "What does my listener know about my faith, and what are his traditional religious beliefs? What are his doubts? His problems? His misunderstandings?"

Whatever field of broadcasting you may be in, you must try to find out what your listener already knows about the matter, and what his traditions are about it.

Where is My Listener? (D3):

There is a very good reason why you must know this. In any radio programme, you must *begin where the listener is!*

This means that you must begin any programme by talking about the things your listener already knows, believes, and enjoys. Only after you have made your listener feel confident in you, can you begin to lead him to something new.

However, you cannot talk about what the listener already knows and believes and enjoys, until you find out what these things are.

If you have more education than your listener, and if you earn more money, then you probably think differently than he does. You will need to go and find out more about what your listener is like, so that you will know in what way his thinking is different from yours.

Research in Libraries (D4):

In *Project B* you should have found out what libraries are available to you, and which of your friends have useful books.

Try to find out what these libraries may have that will help you understand your listener. You may find a whole book that will help, or perhaps a chapter that is useful. Talk to the person in charge of the library. He may be able to suggest some books or magazines.

Read everything you can find that will help you understand something about your listener. Even something about another country can often help you understand the listener in your own area.

Make notes about all the important things you find out from the books and magazines. You will need to show these to your supervisor later.

Research Through People (D5):

Now try to find somebody who has really worked with people like your listener. It may be a person in your own organisation who often goes out to talk and work with the people you are trying to reach.

If you can find such a person, be sure you become his friend. He may be able to tell you many useful things about your listener.

Whether there is such a person in your own organisation, or whether you find him somewhere else, it is important that you do your best to find such a man or woman. Ask him the questions, "What does my listener know?" and "What are his traditional beliefs?"

If this person doesn't give you full answers, ask more questions so that he will tell you more. Write down his answers in your notebook.

Finding out from the Listener (D6):

Even if you have a great deal of information already, you must go back to your listener. Find out from him!

You talked to some people when you did your research in *Project A*.

Read over those research notes. Then think of the ways you can use to get this new information from these listeners.

One of the ways you can do this is to use a *questionnaire*. This is a list of the questions you want to ask your listener, but it is a list that is difficult to make. Your questions must be very carefully prepared, or you may not get the information you need.

Asking Questions (D7):

There are three things to remember about talking to (interviewing) your listeners:

Always ask a question the listener can easily understand and answer.

If you want his opinion or viewpoint on something, ask what others think. What he tells you is usually his own viewpoint.

Do not make your questions so that the listener will answer the way he thinks you want him to.

In the Philippine Islands a radio station asked many listeners the question, "Do you always listen to our station?" Most of them said, "Yes." Before that, they had asked, "What radio station do you like to listen to?" Most of the listeners named another radio station.

Before you can go to your listener to find out what you must know, make a questionnaire. Write down all the questions you think you should ask. Then write down other ways of asking the same questions. Mark the questions that you think best, but do not remove the others from your paper. You may need to ask the same question several different ways before you get a full answer.

Do not put your questions on a piece of paper and then ask people to write in their answers. This method would be successful only with people who have many years of formal education.

It may be best if you do not even hold a piece of paper in your hand when you talk to these listeners. Have the questions in your mind. Remember the answers to write down as soon as possible afterwards.

If you can, talk about interviewing with someone who has had experience in doing this kind of work. He may be able to give you some good suggestions. He will certainly tell you that it is important to make friends with your listener first. You should talk to your listener about his family, his farm, his home, and try to make him feel that you can be trusted. If he is afraid of you for some reason, he will not want to give you very much information.

Assignment One (D8):

Work out a questionnaire to be used in interviewing some of the people who might listen to your programmes. As you do this, keep in mind the same kind of people as those you studied in *Project A*. Plan to interview about ten to fifteen people.

When you have made your questionnaire, take it to your supervisor before you go out to do your interviews. Ask your supervisor if he has any suggestions to help you make better questions. He may suggest some questions that should be asked, or tell you about some that should not be asked. He might suggest a better way to ask the same question.

Be sure you keep all the notes you make during your interviews. They should be put into your research file, where you will find them very useful as you make programmes later on.

When you return from your interviews, write a report. This should tell what you found out in your interviews. Use the information from your reading, from the talks you had with people experienced in working with your listeners, and from your interviews.

Make some suggestions in your report about the ways you think you can make the listener have confidence in your radio broadcasts.

Try to describe how you can:

> make the listener feel you understand him,
> make the listener enjoy your programme, and
> best tell him the things you want to say.

When you have finished your report, take it to your supervisor.

PART TWO

In this part of *Project D*, we would like to help you make some *spot announcements*. Spot announcements are very short. They are from ten seconds, to a minute and thirty seconds long.

Attention Span (D9):

Spot announcements are very useful because radio listeners have a very short *attention span*.

Attention span is the length of time someone will remain interested and listening. A person has a much shorter attention span when he is listening to the radio than when he is listening to a friend talking, or watching a moving picture at the cinema.

Radio broadcasters have learned that the attention span is not the same for all people.

They have learned that:

> The attention span of children is much shorter than it is for grown people. (It grows longer as children grow older.)
> The attention span of an educated person is longer than that of the uneducated person. (The more education a person has, the longer he can listen to one thing.)
> If someone is already interested in what is being said, he will listen longer than if he is not already interested. (A politician will listen to a programme about the government longer than a person who is not concerned about politics.)

This means that a spot announcement is very useful for reaching people who:

are not usually interested in the subject,
do not have very much education, and
who are not very old.

Of course there are some cases where this is not so. There are some young listeners and some uneducated listeners who will listen for a long time. What we have said is *usually* true, but you may find people in your audience who are quite different. The important thing is that you must always keep the listeners' attention span in mind as you prepare programmes.

Spot Announcements (D10):

Spot announcements are also useful for many other reasons:

They can reach a large audience because they do not need a long attention span.
The listener hears the message before he has a chance to become bored.
Spot announcements can be repeated many times, and so may be remembered more easily.
A short item can have a lot of power if it is done well, since it speaks of only one subject.
Spot announcements can easily be put in between programmes or used when only a little time is available.
Radio stations can often find a space for a spot announcement when they cannot find time for a whole programme.
Spot announcements usually cost less to make.

What Spot Announcements Can Do (D11):

In countries where stations have advertising, the spot announcement is used to sell things to the listener. Although we are not going to talk about radio advertising in this manual, what we say about spot announcements is useful whether you are working in public service broadcasting or commercial broadcasting.

In fact, a great deal has been learned about how to use spot announcements from those radio stations where they have been used for advertising.

Here are a few of the ways in which they have been used by public service broadcasters. Spot announcements have been used:

to tell listeners about important events or programmes that will take place,
to tell them where they can find information they may need,
to talk about programmes that will be heard at another time on the radio station, and
to convince people of the truth of a certain viewpoint or policy.

It is sometimes hard to tell the difference between a spot announcement and a short talk. Here are some of the things that usually make a spot announcement different.

Spot announcements:

are often repeated many times by a radio station, and can sometimes reach a large audience because of this,
often do not have any real connection to the programmes in which they are used, and are often used between programmes,
often have no opening or closing announcements but simply give the message without even telling the name of the speaker,
can be read by announcers who may not have any opinions or feelings on the subject of the spot announcement,
are often written in fast-moving style.

What Spot Announcements Cannot Do (D12):

There is a danger in using spot announcements. They may be able to give simple information easily. They may be able to "sell" things, such as a certain kind of tooth-paste. However, they cannot really change the lives of people. To reach deep down into the life of a listener, you must touch his imagination, his emotion, and his intelligence. This can hardly be done in one little spot announcement.

Writing a Spot Announcement (D13):

Later in Assignment Two, we will ask you to write two spot announcements. One should be one minute long and the other should be fifteen seconds long. Both of them should be about the same subject.

First of all, go back and read over quickly what was said in *Project A*. Secondly, read your notes from the first part of *Project D*.

What would you like to write about in your spots? It should be something that is easy to talk about, something specific. It should be something your listener will find interesting and useful.

Here is a suggested subject which you may use for your spots:

> Your organisation would like to help farmers grow a better kind of rice.
> Your organisation has a man who will go and visit the farmers to tell them about the new rice.
> Give the name and address of your organisation so people can write in and ask the man to visit them. ....

Write spot announcements with this information, or choose any other subject.

> Talk about only one subject in each spot.
> Be sure your information is clear, simple and interesting.

The Outline (D14):

Here is how to make your outline:

> *Attention-catcher:* You must begin your spot with a sentence or two to make the listener interested. From your research in the first part of the project you should have some ideas about ways you can do this with your listener.
> *Information:* Give your information in a bright and interesting way. Make it sound important, but not more important than it really is.
> *Motivation:* One motivates a person by giving him reasons or ideas that make him want to do something. In the last few sentences of your spot, try to encourage (motivate) your listener to do a certain thing, such as write to the radio station, or go to a certain place.

Keep going back to your research as you make the outline for your spot announcement, especially when you are doing the part on motivation. Keep asking the question, "How will my listener respond to this?"

When you are writing your 15-second announcement, you will only be able to have perhaps one line for each part. When you are writing the one-minute spot announcement, you will be able to devote more time to each section, but you will still need to move very rapidly from one part to the next.

Spot Examples (D15):

Here are samples of 15-second and 60-second announcements about the same subject matter.

15-SECOND SPOT

Does the world of politics make you scratch your head?
Well, Jose del Santos has a helpful programme about politics
and people every evening at eight o'clock on this station.
Listen to his programme. Jose del Santos will help make
things clear to you. (forty-three words)

60-SECOND SPOT

A friend of mine told me yesterday he was very puzzled
by politics. Often he switched off his radio when the
news came on, "Because," he said, "I don't think it
worth while listening if I don't know what it is all
about anyway."
I told this man about Jose del Santos. Mr. del Santos
is a well-known barrister in our city. He has spent a
great deal of time studying politics, and because of
this he can help both you and me. Mr. del Santos has a
programme every evening at eight o'clock. It's an
interesting programme about the meaning of political
events, and about the interesting people who make
politics.
Very often Mr. del Santos invites important men from
the government to come on the programme and answer the
questions you would like to ask.
So if you're puzzled about politics, then I have a
suggestion. Listen to Mr. Jose del Santos, every
evening at eight o'clock on this station. That's at eight
o'clock this evening for Mr. Jose del Santos. (160 words)

As you work on the outline for your spots be sure that what you want to say will be interesting and useful to the kind of listener you are trying to reach.

Learn by Listening (D16):

Before you begin writing, however, spend about half an hour with a radio receiver. Try to see if you can hear some spot announcements on any station.

> Listen to the way the announcer gets the listener interested. Does he do it well or badly? Why?
> Does he give the important information without trying to say too much?
> Did he make the listener want to do something when the spot was over?

Make notes on what you hear, so you can see at a later time what you have discovered about spot announcements. Also, show these notes to your supervisor when you have finished Part Two.

Timing the Spot (D17):

Here is a suggestion to help you make your spot announcements the right length:

> When I speak on the radio, I say 160 words a minute. This means that a one-minute announcement for *me* must be 160 words. A 15-second announcement must be one-quarter of that, or forty words.
> When I type, I usually put an *average* of ten words on a line. Some lines have a few more words, and some have a few less. So if I want to write a 15-second spot, I know I must write four lines. If I want a one-minute spot, I must write sixteen lines.

Find out how fast you read. Find out how many words you read in one minute, when you are doing a radio programme. It may be 115 words a minute or 180. If you do this, and if you find out how many words you usually type on one line and on one page, you will be able to tell quickly *about* how long your talk will last without using a stop-watch.

Each person speaks at his own speed. The right speed for one person may be too fast for another. If you are writing talks for someone else to read, find out how many words *he* speaks in a minute. He may speak faster or slower than you do.

Assignment Two (D18):

Write two spot announcements, one fifteen seconds long, the other sixty seconds. Please write your first draft very quickly, leaving plenty of space on your page. Then edit your first draft very carefully being certain to follow the suggestions in *Project A*. Then write and edit your second draft.

Make your words as bright and lively as you can. Try to make the listener understand and enjoy what you are saying.

Check-list for Spot Announcements (D19):

After you have written your second draft, use this check-list to see if it is of high quality.

1. Did I talk only about one subject in this spot announcement?   Yes ____ No ____
2. Did I tell about something my listeners would find use-ful?   Yes ____ No ____
3. Did I use bright words and phrases that show move-ment in my spot?   Yes ____ No ____
4. Would my first sentences get the listener's attention and interest?   Yes ____ No ____
5. Was the information in the middle part of the announcements clear and easy to understand?   Yes ____ No ____
6. Did the last sentences in the announcement make the listener want to do something?   Yes ____ No ____
7. Will my spots be the right length?   Yes ____ No ____

If all of the seven questions can be answered "yes", then you should take your spots to your supervisor. If any of them were answered "no", go back and do a third draft of your announcements, correcting the mistakes.

One Last Word (D20):

We have told you how to prepare the most simple kind of announcements. However, you will discover there are even more interesting and exciting ways of making them.

Spot announcements can use music, sound effects, or several voices in a short drama. You will learn how these things are done as you move on to the work in other parts of the manual.

You will also learn more things about writing, speaking, and about your audience which will help you write better spot announcements.

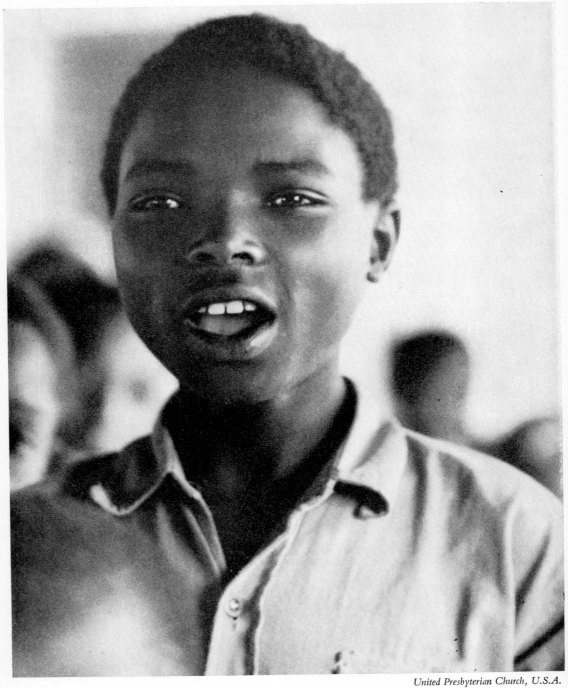

Your language is a beautiful, living thing.

The Spoken Language (D21):

If you and your supervisor have agreed that your spots are satisfactory, then you should record them.

Read again the part of *Project A* which tells how to prepare yourself to read your talk or spot announcement into the microphone.

There is something else you should know about language. Language is something that is *spoken.* When you write on a page, you make some marks which stand for the sounds you make with your mouth.

The Sound of Language (D22):

No matter how good your system of writing may be, you can only put down *some* of the sounds that make your language a living thing. Some languages have a better writing system than others, but most of them cannot be put down on paper:

mood – the feeling in your voice which makes it sound happy or sad, angry or
    cheerful, hopeful, dull or bright;
texture – the quality of your voice, which makes it sound harsh or pleasant,
    rough or smooth;
intonation – the musical part of your speaking (when your voice moves higher
    or lower);
stress – the ways in which you make some words more important than others;
pacing – saying some words faster or slower than others;
speed – the rate at which you speak;
accent – the stress or change in tone that you give to part of a word, making it
    different from the other parts of the word;
tone – making one part of the word higher or lower than another part. In some
    languages, the writing tells what tone or accent there should be. English
    does not.

All of these things add meaning to the speaking voice. We all know that people can say very nice words, but we know by the sound of their voice that they are not sincere. We also have friends who may pretend to be very angry sometimes, but we know by their voices that they are only joking.

Your listener will decide what kind of a person you are by the sound of your voice, by its mood, texture, intonation, stress, tone, accent, pacing and speed.

By practising your radio speaking over and over again, you will learn to control all of these things, so that you can make the listener feel you are a nice person.

Marking Copy (D23):

The most important things to work on at the beginning are stress and pacing. To help you do this, put various marks on your paper, so that you can decide before you go on the air what kind of stress and pacing you will use.

The kind of marks you use doesn't matter very much, as long as you can easily understand them. One good way is to put one line (/) for a short pause, two lines (//) for a long pause, and three lines (///) for a very long pause. One can also draw lines between words like this (tie⌢your⌢words) when you should say them quickly. Finally, you could underline the important words in every sentence.

Sample of Marked Script (D24):

If you do this, your script will look like this:

```
Does the world of politics make you
scratch your head?//Our station has a
programme that can help you.//Jose del
Santos is on the air every evening,/with
up⌢to⌢the⌢minute news reports,/and
interesting comments about people and
politics.///
```

Think about each sentence carefully as you mark your script. Where should you pause to make a word or a sentence sound more important? Which words should be said quickly because they are not important? Try to put variety into your pacing by saying some words and some sentences more slowly, and others more quickly. This will help make your speaking more lively.

Which words should be underlined, so that you will remember to give them more stress? You may wish to put one line under <u>important</u> words, and two lines under <u>very</u> important words.

You should learn to mark your copy so that you can decide before you go on the air how you will use your voice. You should also develop other marks to help you read effectively.

While you are practising and marking your copy, you may find some words or sentences that are hard to say. You may find phrases that seemed fine on the paper, but don't sound too well when spoken out loud. If so, change the words so that they can be said easily, and so that they sound right. Remember, it does not matter what the word looks like on paper. The important thing is the way it *sounds* to the listener.

When you have marked your copy and read it over out loud at least six or seven times, go to your studio to record your spot announcements.

Check-list for Radio Speaking (D25):

After they are recorded, use this check-list to see how well you did:

1. Did I smile as I spoke?   Yes ____ No ____
2. Did my voice sound natural, as if I were talking to a friend sitting beside me?   Yes ____ No ____
3. Was there variety in my pacing to make the talk interesting and alive?   Yes ____ No ____
4. Did I put the right stress on the important words?   Yes ____ No ____
5. Did I pause in the right places?   Yes ____ No ____
6. Were my spot announcements exactly fifteen seconds and sixty seconds long?   Yes ____ No ____

Listen to the tape-recording of your announcements several times to be sure that you have answered these questions well. If you were not able to answer "yes" to all of them, then practise your talk some more and record it a second and even a third time.

Improve Your Speaking (D26):

There is hardly anyone who cannot improve his speaking voice. One of the best things to do is sing. Some radio-speakers take singing lessons even though they do not want to be singers. Others join choirs. All of them find that singing helps their speaking. However, you must do more than sing. You must practise speaking.

> An athlete must practise if he is to win in his competition. He must not only learn how to jump or run or swim, but he must also make his muscles strong to do these things. Your tongue, your lips, and your throat must be trained, just as an athlete trains his arms and legs. Anyone can run, but an athlete must know how to run well and fast. Anyone can talk, but a radio-broadcaster must be able to do it better, more clearly, and much more beautifully.

Here are some questions you should ask about your voice. To do this, it would be best to sit down with someone who has experience in speaking. This may be an actor, a public speaker, a minister or a priest. Have him listen to a tape-recording of your voice, and ask him to help you answer these questions.

Clear Speech (D27):

Is my speech clear and easy to understand? Do I say all the sounds that are important in each word, or are some parts of the word hard to understand?

If you are talking to a friend, and he asks, "What did you say?" then it probably means that your speech was not clear. To speak well, you must use your tongue, lips and teeth.

Each day, try to spend at least fifteen minutes in front of a mirror. Say the letters in your alphabet, or say a poem that you know well. As you do this, make all the sounds in every word much bigger than you ever would do in front of a microphone. You should move your lips and your tongue so hard, that at the end they are feeling a little tired.

Next, spend five minutes talking to the mirror, but keep your teeth closed and try to make the sounds clear by using your lips only. Spend another five minutes whistling. If you don't know how, find someone to teach you. Whistle any song you wish, but whistle quite loud.

Do all these exercises every day. They will help you to build the muscles in your lips and your tongue. They will help you to speak more clearly. We do not mean that you should speak in such a way that your words sound strange. Your voice should sound natural and relaxed. Remember, however, that a listener cannot see your face or your lips. This makes you more difficult to understand. That is why a radio-speaker must speak more clearly than other speakers.

Speech Texture (D29):

> Is my speech harsh?
> Is my voice unpleasant?
> Should I improve the texture of my voice?

Unpleasant voices are sometimes caused by tight muscles in the throat. This tightness can most often be heard in women's voices, although almost everyone has a little bit of tightness. It is worst when you are afraid, nervous, or tired. That is why a person just beginning in radio work sometimes finds his voice is not as pleasant as he would like it to be. When you are nervous, the muscles in your throat get tight and change the texture or sound of your voice.

To relax your throat, make your body limp and let it fall forward in the chair a little. Let your head drop, let your jaw hang open, and your arms hang loosely by your sides. Slowly and gently, roll your head in a circle. Do this three or four times. Yawn a few times, and open your mouth wide. Say words like "clock", "saw", "gong", and "paw". Then practise talking gently, as if you were speaking to a small baby.

If you have trouble with a harsh voice, do this several times each day. Always spend five minutes doing this just before you are going to speak on the radio.

Speech Colour (D29):

> Is my speech lifeless?
> Does it lack colour?
> Does it sound uninteresting?

One of the best suggestions is to find people who really enjoy life. Talk to them. Listen to them. Do not try to imitate their speech, but try to feel the spirit that makes them enjoy life. People who enjoy living, who enjoy other people, often speak in a colourful way. Perhaps if you enjoy life more, your speech will show that joy.

You can also do an exercise that will help you make your voice more lively. Learn to laugh out loud, using the musical scale. Go up and down the scale singing, "ho", then "ha", "he", and "who". Do this slowly at first, then practise each day doing it faster and faster. Sing these from the very lowest note you can sound to the very highest, then down to the lowest again.

A musician must practise his music. An athlete must work hard at his sport. A good speaker must work and practise just as hard, if he wishes to use his voice well.

Glossary Assignment (D30):

Look up these words in the glossary and translate the meanings of the words into your own language.

CUE   TAPE

SPOT ANNOUNCEMENTS   TIMING

When you have finished this assignment, take it to your supervisor and ask him to help you make some improvements.

PROJECT E

Interviews: Section One

Why Study Interviews? (E1):   PART ONE

In this project and *Project F* which follows, we will help you learn how to do interviews. This seems like a very easy thing. After all, it is just two people talking to each other.

It is true that an interview *seems* very easy. In fact, the more skilfully it is done, the easier it will seem to the listener. Nevertheless, an interview is a very difficult thing to do well.

> Anyone can fill a programme with talking. Only the skilled interviewer can fill it with interest and purpose.

As you do the assignments in *Projects E* and *F*, you will learn some of the things that will help you become a better interviewer. To become a highly skilled interviewer, however, you will need a great deal of practice and hard work.

The Art of Description (E2):

Some countries such as the Philippines have a tradition in which people make up beautiful speeches or poems. They do not write their speeches or poems first. Because they have really mastered their language, they can compose their poetry as they speak. They speak *extemporaneously*.

If your country has such a tradition of extemporaneous speaking then you are very fortunate. You would be wise to learn this art, since there may be many times when you could use some parts of it on a radio programme.

Even though you will prepare scripts for most of the programmes you make, you will need to speak well extemporaneously:

during discussion programmes,
when doing an interview,
when doing an *actuality* broadcast (see Glossary),

on some music programmes, and
on some news commentary programmes.

There are four things you should do to learn the art of extemporaneous or impromptu speaking. You should:

learn to use your language well, *(C7)*
develop your ability to see and hear interesting things, *(B3)* and
know your people and country well. *(A8)*

Even after you have done these four things, you will still need a great deal of practice before you will learn this art.

Assignment One (E3):

The exercises in this assignment will help you learn the art of description. Tape record each exercise several times, until you are able to make a smooth description that is interesting, lively, accurate, and without long pauses. Do not stop the tape-recorder until each description is finished.

1. Find an interesting picture or painting that shows people doing something. Take the picture into a studio with you and describe it completely. Do not stop talking until you really feel there is nothing more that can be said about it. Tell who the people in the picture are, what they are doing, how they are doing it, why they are doing it, what they did before the activity shown in the picture, and what they will do after that activity. It does not matter if you may not know anything about the picture or the people in it. You should use your imagination, and make up ideas in your mind.

2. On a piece of paper write down the name of a friend or a member of your family. Take this paper into the studio and begin to describe this person. Tell who he is, what he looks like, what he does, how he acts, how he speaks, how he thinks, where he lives, what he will do in the future, and any other things that are interesting about him.

3. Take your notebook and pencil. Go to the street corner in your town, and make notes about the things you see. Do not write out long descriptions, but just one or two words to help you remember the things you saw on that street corner. Now go back to the studio. With your notes before you, describe the street corner as if you were really there at that moment.

In each case, do your description two or three or more times, until you feel it is of high quality.

A student broadcaster practising the art of description.

Check-list for Description (E4):

Here is a check-list to use to find out if your descriptions are as good as they should be.

1. Did I describe the most important things?   Yes _____ No _____
2. Did I use colourful words?   Yes _____ No _____
3. Was the description interesting and lively?   Yes _____ No _____
4. Was the description smooth, without long pauses?   Yes _____ No _____
5. Was I able to find the right words easily without stopping to think of them?   Yes _____ No _____
6. Did I avoid repeating myself?   Yes _____ No _____

If you can answer "yes" to all of these questions then you are indeed a remarkable person, for it is difficult to do such descriptions well until you have had a great deal of practice. If you could answer "yes" to four of the six questions, then you are ready to move on to the next assignment. If not, then do the descriptions again until they are satisfactory.

Practise Description Any Time (E5):

You can practise the art of description any time and at any place. You do not need a tape-recorder or any other equipment. When you are riding in a bus, or walking along the street, or waiting at a street corner, describe the scene in your imagination. In your mind think of the words you would use if you were doing a programme at that moment. Look for the things you would describe.

If you describe things in your mind in this way, you will not only gain a lot of practice in the art of description, but you will find also that your bus rides, your walks, the times you spend waiting for someone, become very enjoyable and exciting. You will also train your eye and your mind to see things you have never noticed before.

Now take the recordings of your descriptions to your supervisor.

People Like People (E6):   PART TWO

People like to listen to people. They like it even better when they can listen to people talking to each other. That is why an interview is usually a better programme than a talk by just one person.

People are always curious to know how others live, what they do, what they think and what kind of people they are. An interview is simply two people talking to each other. Two voices are always more interesting than one.

Almost everyone has an interesting personality. Nearly every person can be the subject of an interesting interview. Of course, it is much easier to interview some people than others.

A good interview is always spontaneous. The answers are not written out or memorised beforehand. The best interview is like an ordinary conversation. If the answers are practised or written down beforehand the programme will sound dull and lifeless.

Preparing an Interview (E7):

This does not mean that there is no preparation for an interview. Good interviews need a great deal of hard work.

The following method will help you make a good interview programme.

After you have decided whom you wish to interview, and have made arrangements to do so, find out as much as you can about the person who will be your guest on the interview programme.

There may be books or magazine articles about your guest. Read any you can find. Perhaps there have been items in the newspaper about him recently. He may have written some books or articles. Talk to others who know your guest. They may be able to tell you interesting things, and they may also be able to tell you where to look for valuable information. Make notes on all you read, and make a list of questions you might possibly ask.

Perhaps the person is not well known. In that case, there must have been other good reasons why you asked him to come for an interview. Write down those reasons. They should help you make a list of questions which your guest would be able to answer in an interesting and informative way.

Perhaps you may be interviewing someone to get more information, or an opinion, concerning an event that happened recently. In this case, you must be familiar with the details of the event, as well as knowing something about the person you are questioning. You will not find this difficult if you have read newspapers and magazines day by day.

What Would the Listener Ask? (E8):

Some people say you should ask the questions which the listener would like to ask of your guest. It is probably better to say that you should ask the questions the listener at home wished he had *thought of* asking.

Some very good broadcasters will go to the market or out in the country, and talk to people about the person they will interview. In this way they try to find out what these people are thinking, and what sort of things they would like to know, or ought to know. It is not necessary to go far for this kind of information. The man who sweeps your studio might tell you what he feels about the person you will interview. Perhaps the bus driver on your way to work each morning may give you some ideas.

Such information can be very helpful to a broadcaster who really wants to serve his people. He tries to think of his listener's interest (not his own) when he works out his questions.

Preparing the Guest (E9):

Invite your guest to the studio well before the time you should begin recording your interview. If you are going to make a 15-minute programme then he should come *at least* half an hour ahead of time. If it is a half-hour programme then have him come *at least* an hour before.

Take your guest directly into the studio where you will record. It will help him become familiar with his surroundings and he will not be as nervous when the time for recording comes.

The Interview Rehearsal (E10):

Do not say, "I will ask you these questions." Rather, talk to him informally, chatting about unimportant things until he is more relaxed. Then you can begin to discuss some of the things you would like to talk about on the programme. Once again, be informal and relaxed. For instance you might say, "Mr. Nhaywa, I've been very interested in the literacy project you've been working on." In this way, Mr. Nhaywa will tell you about the project before your interview begins. You can then decide whether what he says is interesting or dull, and whether you should ask more questions on that subject, or change to another.

If you are concerned that a certain question may cause your guest some embarrassment, you should ask him directly whether it should be asked. Also, if you are going to ask him a question that will need to be answered with exact numbers or names, you should warn him first so that he can have time to write this information on a piece of paper.

Try to keep your guest from writing out his answers. They will not sound natural if he does this. However, encourage him to make a few notes about difficult subjects so that he will not need to search his mind for the information.

If you have done your preparation well, you will really have given your guest an informal kind of rehearsal. Because you talked to him about the matters you will discuss later on your programme, he will have thought about the answers and will be more ready to discuss them when you begin recording.

At the same time, you have not told him exactly what you will ask and he will not answer in quite the same way. The programme will still sound fresh and interesting.

A Flexible Plan (E11):

While you are talking to your guest before the programme, you should be planning the way in which you will do the interview. You should write down all the questions that seem to be worth asking, and you should decide in what order you will probably ask them.

However, do not make your plan too firm. Your guest will not answer exactly the same way as he did during your rehearsal. His answer to one question may lead unexpectedly into another subject, and in this case you should change your order and ask the question that fits best at that moment.

In other words, you must be flexible. You must be able to change your plans as you go along.

Introducing the Guest (E12):

If you did not find out during your first research, then be sure you find out during your preparation the proper way in which to address the person you are interviewing. You must be sure you have his name right, as well as his position and title.

There are many ways to write the opening announcements for an interview. It is usually best, however, to write your opening and closing announcements after you have finished the interview. Another announcer would then introduce you, possibly in this way.

ANNCR: Great progress has been made in our nation's literacy campaign. To find out just how much progress, Moses Ogatu talked to Mr. Joseph Nhaywa, the Director of the National Literacy Campaign.

TAPE: OGATU–NHAYWA INTERVIEW 4:15
(END CUE: ". . . in the very fine work that is being done in so many places.")

ANNCR: That was Moses Ogatu speaking to Mr. Joseph Nhaywa, Director of the National Literacy Campaign.

Some broadcasters prefer to introduce the guest themselves, even though this may make the guest a little nervous.

OGATU: This evening we have with us Mr. Joseph Nhaywa, the Director of the National Literacy Campaign. Mr. Nhaywa has been working in the rural areas of our nation, in an effort to teach more of our people to read and write. Mr. Nhaywa, would you tell us . . . etc.

Be Polite (E13):

Remember that you must change that introduction to fit the customs of your own country. Listen to some of the radio stations in your country. How do they introduce a guest when he is to be interviewed? Do you think they do it the right way? Why? If you were introducing an important man to a friend, how would you do it? Do you think you could do it the same way on a radio programme? Why?

Move Along Quickly (E14):

When you are doing your programme, be sure to ask each question just as your guest has finished answering the last one. It is better usually not to make any comment on what your guest has said, unless you are sure it is something very worthwhile. Do not say something like, "Oh yes, I see," or "That's very nice," or "Thank you," after each answer. These little remarks do not do any good, and they will certainly slow down the movement of the programme. Thank your guest at the end of the programme. Do not say anything that does not really help the programme stay lively and interesting.

Use your guest's name from time to time during the interview, and also mention the subject you are discussing. Your listener may have tuned in late, or he may have forgotten the name of your guest.

Assignment Two (E15):

We would like you to do two interviews with people you know well. They could be people who work in your studio. You might ask your supervisor to suggest someone, or you might ask a friend who lives or works nearby. They should be people who are willing to spend a little time at this, since you will probably need to do each interview several times before you are pleased with it.

Do one interview that is about three minutes long, and another that is five minutes long.

Do the 3-minute interview twice, one right after the other, before you use the check-list to see if one of them is satisfactory.

Asking for Criticism (E16):

After you have finished recording, ask the person you are interviewing for his criticisms. Since he is a friend, he will be willing to help if you tell him you really are very anxious to learn. If you are a mature person, you will not be offended by sincere criticism.

Here are some of the questions you should ask him:

> Did you feel nervous when I interviewed you? What could I have done to make you feel more at ease?
> Did I make any mistakes in the way that I spoke to you?
> Did I ask important questions, or were there others that would have been better?
> What would you have done to make this a better interview?
> Which of the two recordings did you think was better? Why?

Listen carefully to what your friend has to say, but remember that he may not have very much knowledge about how to do radio interviews. Do not follow the suggestions if you think they are wrong.

Check-list for a Short Interview (E17):

Now use this check-list to see if your interview was of high quality.

1. Was I able to make my guest feel at ease?	Yes ____	No ____
2. Did I ask interesting questions?	Yes ____	No ____
3. Did I ask important questions?	Yes ____	No ____
4. Was I able to go from one question to the next without bad pauses or awkward sentences?	Yes ____	No ____
5. Was my interview the right length?	Yes ____	No ____

If you can answer "yes" to four of these five questions, then you have done well and may move on to the next interview. Be sure you listen to both your 3-minute interviews several times, to be sure that you have answered the questions in the check-list very carefully. If you have answered "no" to more than one, then do another 3-minute interview.

Keep on doing these 3-minute interviews until you have done one that is satisfactory. You need save only the best one for your supervisor.

Now move on to the 5-minute interview. Do the same research and preparation as you did for your 3-minute interview. You will need to do more of it, however, since you are attempting a longer programme. When you have finished your interview, again ask your friend for his comments and suggestions.

Use the same check-list to find out how well you did. You will probably also need to do this interview several times before it is satisfactory. When it is, take it to your supervisor along with your 3-minute interview.

Project F will also deal with interviews. This is because in *Project E* you learned only some of the things you should know about this kind of programme and only about one kind of interview. There are many different kinds of interviews, and we would like to tell you about each one.

Glossary Assignment (E18):

Look up these words in the glossary and translate the meanings into your own language.

AD–LIB	CONTROL DESK
CONTINUITY ROOM	CONTROL ROOM
CONTINUITY STUDIO	

When you have finished this assignment, take it to your supervisor and ask him to help you make some improvements. Remember to keep all of your glossary assignments, so that you will be able to make your own glossary when you have finished the manual.

PROJECT F

Interviews: Section Two

Practice Makes Perfect (F1):   PART ONE

In *Project E*, we talked about some of the things you need to know in order to do a good interview. This project will deal with interviews again, this time telling you some of the different ways this kind of programme can be done.

Please remember that there is a great deal of difference between knowing all the rules about an interview, and being able to do a good interview. There is an old saying: "Practice makes perfect." This is true of interviews, as it is true of all radio programmes, and that is why you will need to make many such programmes before you can begin to feel that you have learned the art.

Three Kinds of Interviews (F2):

Many people feel that you cannot make a list of the different kinds of interviews. They are right, because it is impossible to say that one interview is this kind, and another is that.

The best way to learn about different types of interviews is to think in terms of the reason *why* we do the interview, or the *objective* of the interview.

Objective

CELEBRITY INTERVIEW

To find out more about a famous person – someone who is well known. Your questions would be about the thing that made him famous. If your guest is a famous singer, you would ask him questions about his music and his songs. If your guest is a politician, you would talk with him about government and politics.

PERSONALITY INTERVIEW

To let your listeners hear a personality – an interesting kind of person. Your questions would be intended to bring out the unusual or interesting ways your guest sees various things. Every interview is a personality interview in some ways, because whenever a person speaks on the radio, the listener learns a little about the kind of person he is.

INFORMATIONAL INTERVIEW

To bring information to your listener. Your questions would be intended to allow your guest to tell people about a certain subject. Every interview is an informational interview in some ways, since each time a guest speaks he usually has some information to give, even if it is only telling us about his own opinion.

As you can see, you can have all three objectives in one programme. One could easily do an interview with an important person who had an interesting personality and who has some important information to offer.

It is always wise to begin planning your programme by spending a few moments writing down the reasons *why* you should do this interview. You will probably have one *main* reason, and several *smaller* reasons; but, unless you have these reasons clearly in your mind before you begin, you are likely to waste time in your research and to have an interview that seems to be without purpose.

Interview Formats (F3):

There is another way you can make a list of the different kinds of interviews. This list will help you to see how many kinds of programmes you can make from interviews.

One-time Interviews (F4):

A "one-time" interview is used in a special programme, or included in another programme. It is not a usual part of the programme, and is done simply because the guest was important or interesting enough to make the station set aside some time for the interview.

This is the kind of programme we most often think of when we speak of an interview, but it is only one of many kinds. It is most often used because an important person has come to the city and is willing to be interviewed. It would be wise to tell your listeners many times during the days before you have a special interview, so that they will turn on their radios to hear it. You can do this by using a series of spot announcements about the interview on other programmes or between programmes.

Serial Interviews (F5):

These are interviews done on a series of programmes. They must then fit into the theme of the series. For instance, you might have a programme called, "They Serve Our Nation." On each programme you would have one or two interviews with people who in some way are helping your country.

This kind of programme can be very effective. Because it is heard regularly, people will make a habit of listening, and the size of your audience may grow. Such a series could be done with important people if enough of them visit your city. It could also be done by interviewing ordinary people who have an interesting viewpoint. There is no end to the list of subjects you could use for such a series. Here are just a few ideas:

"New Life on the Farm" . . . interviews with farmers who are using new ways to grow better crops and animals.

"Sounds of our City" . . . interviews with the exciting personalities who make up a city, to find out how they are trying to solve the problems of city life.

"Adventure in Faith" . . . interview with people who have had real problems in their lives, and whose faith in the love of God has helped them in these problems.

"Around our Nation" . . . interview with people coming from different regions of your nation, to help your listeners learn more about their country.

Perhaps you will have even better ideas more suited to your country. It is important, before you begin such a programme, to decide how many programmes you will do, and if there are enough interesting people to fill all the programmes. If you use all your best interviews in the first two or three programmes, you will find that the series gets weaker and weaker. Make a list of the materials you will use before you begin. Such planning is important to any kind of programme.

Spot Interviews (F6):

Spot interviews are very short, usually not more than three minutes long. They are used in much the same way as spot announcements.

Because the attention span of many listeners is very short, the spot interview can sometimes be very effective. Some stations use it in between the musical selections. In this way, these stations have made a lively popular programme that is able to bring a great deal of important information and education to the listeners. Such programmes can deal with a very wide variety of subjects.

When preparing a guest for such spot interviews, it is best to explain to him the way in which you will use them, and why you are making them so short. Otherwise he may feel you do not think he is worth a long interview. Since most interviews are recorded, it is easy to do three or four, or even more such interviews at one time. Each interview must be on one subject only, and there should be only one or two questions during each one. The opening and closing must be very short. Here is an example:

ANNCR: Crowded city life is a real problem. Dr. Otto Ort, of the Urban Renewal Centre is here with us. Dr. Ort, what is your Centre trying to do to solve the problem?

DR. ORT ANSWERS IN ABOUT 2½ MINUTES. (END CUE: ". . . To make life richer!"

ANNCR: Thank you very much, Dr. Otto Ort, of the Urban Renewal Centre.

Explain to your guest that his interviews will be at different times and on different days, in order to reach as many people as possible with his important message. He may be more pleased at having been interviewed many times, than he would be if you had just done one long interview.

News Interviews (F7):

These are intended for use on a news programme. One would ask several questions of the guest, then use only a short portion of the interview on the news programme.

Interviews and comments by people who are doing important things can make your news programme much more interesting. The portion used on the programme should be short, and is usually introduced by the man making the newscast.

NEWS ANNCR: In the northern part of our city today, crowds swarmed around the Rice Centre protesting against the recent price increase. Although there was no violence, there were angry outbursts of shouting and police feared a riot would result. The cause of the price increase was explained by the head of the Rice Centre, Mr. Chellandurai.

TAPE: CHELLANDURAI: (IN CUE: "The situation we see . . .") (. . . END CUE: ". . . assure the citizens they have nothing to fear and that the problem will be solved.") (31 sec.)

NEWS ANNCR: Mr. Chellandurai went on to say that . . . etc.

We will talk a great deal more about this method of making a news programme more interesting, when we get to *Project M.*

Special Event Interviews (F8):

Such interviews are done during a broadcast of a special occasion or important event such as a sports day or a conference. The whole programme may be made up of interviews with people involved, or there may be other things that make up most of the programme, and the interviews are used to add a little interest and variety.

The interviews on such a programme can be very exciting, especially when they are heard with the sound of activity in *the background.* They should usually be short, although there will be occasions when a longer interview is necessary. Such interviews can be used to help the listener see the events through another person's eyes, as well as to get the feeling of the kinds of personalities which are at the event. Look up the word BACKGROUND in the glossary.

Always be Ready (F9):

The "special event" interview does not usually give you any time for preparation or planning. This can be true of the news interview as well.

There are two things you can do so that you are always ready for this type of programme:

Be sure you have had plenty of experience doing interviews of the kind where you *can* prepare ahead.

Keep your eyes and ears open to all the life that is going on around you. Read widely.

The impromptu interview is very difficult to do well. You do not know what subject will come up in the interview, so you must be ready to talk about *all* subjects at any time.

There are so many ways an interview can be used, that it would be impossible to talk about all of them. Many new kinds have been developed, especially in places where television stations now have taken drama and variety programme audiences away from radio stations.

Assignment One (F10):

This is a study of the interviews which are being heard now by listeners in your area.

If there are radio stations in your area that have interview programmes, try to have some of these programmes recorded on tape. Your supervisor may be able to help you with this, or perhaps he may have some tape-recordings of interviews which he would allow you to use. Listen carefully to as many different kinds of interviews as you can find. Those done in your own country are best to listen to, but those produced in other countries would be useful also.

Write down a short description of each programme. Be sure to tell what *you* think and feel. In your description mention:

    the type of programme on which the interview was used,
    the kind of person being interviewed,
    the type of questions asked by the interviewer, and
    the quality of the interview.

To help you decide on the quality, use check-list *E17*. Instead of using it to judge yourself, use it to judge the interviewers on the programmes to which you listened.

Take your report on these programmes to your supervisor.

The Common People (F11):   PART TWO

Because it is now possible for most radio stations to send people anywhere quickly, many have discovered that one of the best ways to find materials for programmes is to interview ordinary people.

Some radio stations interview only important people. Others feel that their listeners are also interested in common people. Find out what your studio director thinks about this.

One energetic young broadcaster decided to find out if this was true. He took a portable tape-recorder, and began talking to ordinary people. He sat and recorded the conversation that took place where the people gathered to talk in the evenings. He went to the market-place and talked to the people buying and selling. He went with the fishermen in their boats and walked with the farmers behind their ploughs.

Then he went back to the studio. From the things he had recorded, he carefully chose those parts which were exciting or interesting, and put them together into a programme. Not only did the audience enjoy the programme, but he was able to help people to think deeply about many important problems and ideas.

Alertness and Other Qualities (F12):

This young man had the most important quality of a good interviewer. This is *alertness*. He was wide awake to the needs of his listeners, and very much aware of the possibilities of the people he was interviewing. His mind was alert enough to know that even the most uneducated person may have something valuable to say, and he recognised this value when he heard it.

This alertness is important whether you are interviewing the most important man in your country or the most simple person.

In addition to alertness, you must have some other qualities if you are hoping to be a good interviewer.

Be responsive: You should be interested in your guest. All of us have good qualities and bad qualities. Look for the good qualities in your guest and try to bring them to your listener through the interview. However, do not be afraid to let your guest show his bad qualities too. An interview should help the listener know what kind of a person your guest really is.

Be respectful: Even if you do not agree with the things your guest is saying, you should be willing to let him present his viewpoint to your listeners. You will serve your listeners best if you bring many viewpoints to your programmes, so that the listener can make up his own mind on the matter. This means that you must also have respect for your listener and treat him as an intelligent person even though he may not be educated. However, do not be so respectful that you only ask the questions your guest wants to answer. There are times when a broadcaster feels he must ask questions the guest will find embarrassing.

Be interested in the subject: If you are not interested, then your listener will probably not be either. Your guest will not give his best, because he will sense that you do not really care what he says. It is hard to be interested in a subject unless you know something about it. This is another reason why a broadcaster must read widely, and keep his eyes and ears open all the time.

Enjoy it: Interviewing can be exciting. It can be fun! If you do your preparation well, you can do the programme without being worried about it. You can relax and enjoy the conversation with your guest. Your listener will sense this. Your guest will sense it. Both of them will like it better if you enjoy your work.

Be flexible: We mentioned this in *Project E,* but it is well to say it again. Unexpected things always make programmes more interesting. Sometimes they can spoil a programme, but usually they add life and sparkle to it. If you are flexible, if you are able to change your plan in the middle of an interview and talk about something unexpected, this will make your programme that much better instead of spoiling it. This also means that you must be flexible enough to interview different people in different ways. If you are flexible, you might interview three people on exactly the same subject, but you would ask your questions differently in each case.

All of these things bring us back to that word, *alertness.* You cannot be responsive, respectful, interested, flexible, and you will not enjoy yourself, unless you are alert. You will not be alert unless you are willing to take the time and to do the work to fill your mind with the life and colour of the world around you.

The Art of Asking (F13):

There is an art to asking questions in an interview. Part of the success of your questions will lie in the preparation you have done. If you know the person you are talking to, and what he is talking about, then your questions will probably be good questions. As you gain more experience and learn more about people, you will find that your questions change a little to fit the kind of person you are talking to, and the mood of the interview.

You will also learn that a question, when it is said in one way gets a poor answer, and when it is said in another way gets a better answer. There is no rule we can give you. It is something that can be learned only by doing many interviews.

However, there are some things we can say about asking questions. Some of these things may not be true in *your* language and *your* country. If not, make a note about it, so that you can explain it to your supervisor.

Three Ways of Asking (F14):

One can get a reply from a guest in three ways:

By asking a question: "How many people are working here?"

Very often an interview is just one question after another, and the guest can do little more than answer "yes" or "no". This is very dull. Try to make your questions so that the guest must answer with a statement or an explanation. Sometimes you can do this by putting two questions into one:

"How many people are working here, and where did they come from?"

Be careful that you do not confuse your guest and your listener by putting too many questions together. Keep your questions simple and direct, but keep them interesting.

By making a statement: "There are thirty people working here. That sounds like a lot!"

A statement like this in an interview is like a challenge. You are inviting your guest to agree or disagree with you, and so his reply might be more interesting than if you just asked a question. You might also find a statement about the subject or the guest in a newspaper or a magazine. Read a short part of it and ask your guest to say what he thinks about it. It might be a statement by someone who disagrees with your guest. You then give your guest the chance to give his viewpoint.

By a contradiction: "In spite of what you say, I don't think it's necessary to have thirty men working here."

The first thing we must say about this is . . . *be careful!* When you tell your guest he is wrong, you may turn your interview into a quarrel. You may also offend your guest. There are some interviewers who have done some very good interviews using contradictions. However, these are people who have had very much experience and who are certain they know what they are doing. *Do not try this until you have done many, many interviews!*

There is another kind of contradiction, however, that you can use without making your guest angry. Sometimes you can say you are surprised by your guest's reply. He may then explain things a little more. Sometimes you might be able to say, "As you know, some people have been saying that you are wrong. How do you feel about this?"

In this way you can have your guest defend himself against those who disagree with him, but you do not need to disagree with him yourself.

If there are good arguments against the viewpoint of your guest, you should try to make your guest answer these arguments. Then your listener can decide who is right – your guest, or those who criticize him.

Keep Control (F15):

There is a problem that sometimes develops when a young broadcaster interviews an older and very important person. Because he does not feel he is the equal of the guest, he loses control of his interview. Instead, the guest takes over and directs the interview the way he wants it.

Your guest may be a very fine and a very important person. You, however, are the one who should know more about broadcasting. Your guest may have more education and may know many things, but he may not know as much about broadcasting as you do.

It is difficult to keep control of an interview in such a case, but it is most necessary. Because you have studied your listeners, you know the kinds of questions you must ask. Because you have ideas about why you are serving your nation and your community, you know there is certain information that should be broadcast.

Be polite, but be firm! If your guest tries to lead you into a subject that is not important or not interesting, ask him a direct question that will bring him back to the subject. If necessary, repeat the question. There even may be times when you will have to interrupt your guest, although you should do this only when there is no other way.

It is not usually a good idea to say to your guest, "Is there anything else you would like to say to our listeners?"

If you do this, your guest will probably take control of the interview, and you will find it very difficult to make him stop talking. Secondly, your programme has changed from a conversation between two people, into a speech by one person.

Instead, ask your guest before you begin if there is something he would like very much to tell your listeners. If you feel that your listeners should hear this, then ask your guest a question that will give him a chance to say it. If you do not think it is important or interesting, then you simply do not ask the question.

It Depends on You (F16):

Keep your interview moving. Talk about things that have value. Do not become dull or uninteresting. If an interview is not good, it is usually the broadcaster's fault. It is his job to draw interesting answers from the guest, and to keep the programme constantly alive with sharp questions.

One broadcaster in Africa had this outline for the questions in an interview:

What is it all about?
How did it come about?
Why?
What will happen now?
How will this happen?

That is a good outline, if you are careful not to follow it too closely. Every interview is different, and each one must be done differently. There are no rules for doing an interview. There are good ideas that help, but you must try each idea several times before you know if it is good for your country and your kind of broadcasting.

The most important thing is that your interviews:

are honest and sincere,
provide your listeners with true information,
help your listeners to gain a better life, and
are interesting and lively.

The Studio Interview (F17):

Before you begin your interviews, there are some technical things you should know that will help you with your interviews.

Try to make your guest as comfortable as possible when you take him into your studio. It is best for you and your guest to sit on opposite sides of a small table, with the microphone in between you but very slightly off to one side. A good table would be between 60 and 90 centimetres (24 to 36 inches) wide. You and your guest should sit close to the table, sitting up straight with your arms on the table in front of you. The microphone should be about half-way between the two of you, and about 10 to 15 centimetres (3 to 6 inches) to one side.

It is important that speakers be exactly the right distance from the microphone.

It may be that your voice is stronger than your guest's. If so, move the microphone a little closer to his side of the table, or have him move a little closer to the microphone. If your voice is lighter, then you must be closer. You cannot decide this in the studio. The man at the CONTROL DESK (see glossary) must listen and then tell you where you should move the microphone and how far. Look up the word BALANCE in the glossary.

If possible, place the microphone so that you can see your guest easily. If it is a BOOM MICROPHONE (see glossary) hanging from above, it should be just above the level of your eyes. This is important, because you must look directly at your guest to show that you are interested. This will also help your guest to forget the microphone, and to talk with *you*.

Using a Microphone Outside (F18):

You will usually use a portable tape-recorder for this kind of interview. Be sure you are completely familiar with the way the tape-machine works, if you are the one who must operate the controls. If not, ask a technician to explain it to you.

The microphone must be held in your hand. Never put it down on anything when you are recording. You should stand or sit quite close to your guest, with your heads about 50 to 75 centimetres (20 to 30 inches) apart. Most microphones should be held about midway between you and your guest, although you will have to learn to judge if one of the voices is louder or softer, and then hold the microphone so that both voices have about the same VOLUME (see glossary) on the tape-recorder. Never let your guest hold the microphone. He does not know about microphones and will probably hold it in the wrong place and spoil the interview. If he reaches out his hand for it, just hold on to it firmly. You must keep control of the interview *and* the microphone.

If you happen to be doing an interview in a very noisy place, then ask your guest to stand very close to you, so that you can both have the microphone close to your mouths.

It is possible that you might be using a "close-talking" microphone, one that must be held very close to the mouth. Check with your engineer to find out. If it is such a microphone, then you will need to move it back and forth from your guest's mouth to yours as you speak. Try not to use a "close-talking" microphone unless you are in a very noisy place.

If there is a wind blowing, it may make a bad noise on your recording. If you cannot move to a place where there is no wind, wrap a piece of cotton cloth over the microphone (a handkerchief will do). Some microphones have a round shield over them, which helps keep out the wind noise. Such a shield or a piece of cloth will protect the microphone from a light wind. If there is a strong wind, you simply must move to a quiet place, or be prepared to accept a low unpleasant sound on your tape.

Before you go any further, turn to the glossary and look up the following words. If you do not understand the meanings clearly, ask your engineer or your supervisor to explain.

ACTUALITY	OUTSIDE BROADCASTS
BACKGROUND	PEAK PROGRAMME METER
BLASTING	VOLUME CONTROL
GAIN	

Wrong!

Wrong!

Right!

Editing an Interview (F19):

It is often necessary to make changes in an interview after it is recorded. This is called EDITING. In Projects *A* and *B* we told you how to edit a script. When an interview is finished, you must sometimes edit the tape. Look up the word *editing* in the glossary.

Editing may be needed on an interview:

if the guest was very nervous and kept repeating himself,
if someone said something that should not be broadcast,
if the interview is too long, or
if part of the interview is very uninteresting or of no value to the listener.

Dangers of Editing (F20):

There is a danger in editing an interview. In one radio station, the workers played a joke on the manager. They took a tape of a programme he had made in which he talked about the government and the wages of government workers. Working all night long, they took one piece of tape from here and one piece from there, and changed the tape around so that the meaning was much different. Then when the people of the radio station had a gathering, they surprised the manager by playing the tape for all to hear. The manager was heard on the tape saying that the wages of all the radio station workers would be increased by 600 per cent. It was a good joke and everyone, even the manager, laughed.

This story shows us how easy it is to change the meaning of what a guest has said. Any broadcaster who tries to change the *meaning* of what his guest has said should not be allowed to do interviews.

If something a guest says goes against the policy of your studio, then you should not use the interview at all.

It is good manners and simple honesty to explain to your guest if you plan to make any big changes in the interview. Most people are very reasonable, and if you explain the problem they usually agree.

However, be sure you never use editing to change a tape, so that your guest is saying something he did not intend to say.

Studios have different rules about tape-machines and the use of tapes. Find out what rules your studio follows. If you are allowed to do your own editing, then you should practise until you know how. If this must be done by a technician, read the instructions on dubbing and splicing, and then ask a technician to do these while you watch. You should know what can be done in this way, even if you are not able to do it yourself.

Dubbing (F21):

The easiest way of editing a tape-recording is to DUB. Look for that word in the glossary. It takes a little practice, but you will soon learn to take the parts of the interview that you want to use, and *dub* them on to another tape. Talk to your engineer about this. Dubbing is not possible in some studios because a "click" or noise goes on your tape each time you stop and start. In this case, you can only edit by splicing.

When dubbing, you can stop or start only at the end of a sentence, or at a natural pause in the talking. You cannot stop or start at a place where the speaker sounds as if he is going to continue his sentence.

Splicing (F22):

The most difficult kind of editing is done by cutting and SPLICING the tape. Look for the word *splicing* in the glossary. Practise cutting and splicing until you can do it easily, quickly and neatly.

It is possible to remove even half of a word from a tape through cutting and splicing. It is sometimes necessary to do this when a few words in the middle of a sentence, or just one word, or sometimes even half a word can make the difference between a poor interview and a good one.

Here are the steps to use to remove a very short part of a tape. Do not be surprised if you are not successful the first time you try. In fact, you will need to try this many times before you will be able to do it right.

> Listen over and over again to the part of the tape where you want to cut. Move the tape through the machine by turning the reels with your hand, so that you hear the voice speaking slowly. Do this several times so that you can move the tape very slowly and still find the places where each word begins and ends. Listen for the beginning and the end of the part that you want to remove.
>
> Take a marking crayon, a felt pen with a fine tip, or even a ball-point pen. Move your tape by hand so that the beginning of the part you want to remove is exactly over the PLAYBACK HEAD. Ask your engineer or your

supervisor to tell you where this is. Put a small mark on the shiny side of the tape in this place, as shown in this picture.

Move the tape so that the end of the part you want to remove is exactly over the *playback head*. Mark this spot also.

Cut the tape somewhere between those two marks, then splice your tape together, so that the two ends are joined exactly at the places where you had the two marks.

Do not be content to read about this. You will not know how to cut, splice and edit until you have practised many times.

There is a lot of work in these assignments. Remember that each one is important, and each one should be done carefully and well.

Glossary (F23):

Look up these words in the glossary and translate the meanings into your own language.

ACTUALITY	OUTSIDE BROADCASTS
BACKGROUND	PEAK PROGRAMME METER
BLASTING	SPLICE (tell how splice is made)
DUBBING	VOLUME CONTROL
GAIN	

Assignment Two (F24):

Ask your supervisor for an old tape which can be used to practise splicing and tape editing. On this tape record a short talk or a short interview. Cut the talk or interview in half, by editing.

Check-list for Tape Editing (F25):

1. Are all the splices neat, without any spaces between the ends of the tape, and without overlapping of one end on to the other?   Yes ____ No ____
2. Does the talk or interview still sound natural and complete?   Yes ____ No ____

If you can answer "yes" to both those questions, then you have finished Assignment Two. You will probably need to do this a number of times until it is satisfactory. Practise until you can make a splice fairly quickly. When you have finished Assignment Two and the Glossary Assignment, take them to your supervisor.

Assignment Three (F26):

Ask your supervisor to help you arrange an interview with someone in your community who is doing important work. If possible, it should be someone you do not know personally. Do all of the research and preparation as suggested in *Projects E* and *F*, and try to make the programme of high quality. This interview should be done in the studio and should be five minutes long. The check-list for this assignment follows Assignment Four.

Assignment Four (F27):

If your studio has a portable tape-recorder, make arrangements to do one of these programmes:

> Go to a meeting, convention or other gathering that may be going on in your community. Find out all you can about the gathering, then interview two or three of the important people right at the place where the gathering is held.

Choose an organisation or an agency that is working to help your community. Find out all you can about the organisation, then interview two or three of the important people in the organisation. If possible, interview them at the place where they are doing their work.

In each case, the interviews should tell the listener what is happening, why it is happening, what will happen in the future, who is helping it happen, and what the person you are interviewing does and thinks about what is happening. Each interview should be from three to five minutes long.

Check-list for an Interview (F28):

1. Did I spend a few moments before beginning my research and preparation to list the reasons why I was doing the interview?   Yes ____ No ____
2. Did the interview show that I was alert?   Yes ____ No ____
3. Did the interview show that I was responsive?   Yes ____ No ____
4. Did I respect the opinions and ideas of my guest even if I did not agree with them?   Yes ____ No ____
5. Was I interested in the things my guest was saying?   Yes ____ No ____
6. Did I enjoy the interview?   Yes ____ No ____
7. Was I flexible enough to change my plans when the things my guest said made this the best thing to do? Yes ____ No ____
8. Did I ask many different kinds of questions?   Yes ____ No ____
9. Did I keep control of my interview at all times?   Yes ____ No ____
10. Did I keep the interview moving by giving my next question as soon as the guest had finished his reply? Yes ____ No ____
11. Did I keep from making little comments or saying unnecessary words that would not help the broadcast?   Yes ____ No ____
12. Was my microphone balance good?   Yes ____ No ____
13. Was the interview of value to my listener?   Yes ____ No ____
14. Did it provide the listener with true information?   Yes ____ No ____
15. Was the subject interesting to the listener?   Yes ____ No ____

If you can answer "yes" to ten of these questions, you have done well, and you should take your programmes to your supervisor. If not, then read *Project E* and *F* again, and ask your supervisor for another assignment which will help you learn more about interviewing. Do not be disappointed if these interviews are not as good as you had hoped. Interviewing is difficult to do well, and most students will need to have several extra assignments before they can feel they have begun to learn.

If you are alert, you will discover that you never completely learn the art of interviewing. The more interviews you do, the more you talk to your fellow broadcasters about this art, the more you will realise how much there is to learn.

PROJECT G

The Panel Discussion

Why a Panel Discussion? (G1):

Three or four people sitting around a microphone and talking, can make an excellent programme or a very poor one. It might be a great success or a complete failure.

Such a programme is called a ROUND TABLE, PANEL DISCUSSION, or RADIO FORUM. Look up the words *panel discussion* in the glossary.

Why have a panel discussion? Why not simply ask each person to write a short speech? Then they wouldn't waste time in argument!

It is certainly true that a good one-voice speech is far better than a badly done panel discussion. If there is poor preparation, the panel members (those taking part in the discussion) may spend most of their time trying to think of something to say, and then saying it very badly. That kind of a panel discussion is worse than none at all.

A good panel discussion can:

present important questions in an interesting way,
help listeners think about different viewpoints,
help the panellists really talk about the problem instead of just making a fancy speech, and
present several minds working together to find a solution to a problem.

In *Projects E* and *F*, we talked about interviewing. Many of the things you have learned in those two projects are important when making a panel discussion. Look back, whenever you find it necessary, to those projects to help yourself remember.

What is the Topic? (G2):

One of the hardest things about a panel discussion is choosing the topic, or subject matter. This seems fairly easy to do for one or two programmes, but if you are making a programme each week, you may find that you soon have trouble finding a useful and interesting topic.

Many broadcasters have found it helpful to have a committee or an advisory board for such a programme. In fact, such a committee can be very helpful for any important type of programme.

If you can form such a committee it should be asked to do three things:

> evaluate or judge the last programme,
> help you decide on the best *idea* for the coming programmes, and
> help you decide on the best *people* for these programmes.

Of course, you will not be able to organise such a committee for your assignments in this project.

However, here is a list of questions that may help you choose the right topic or subject. You will need to look at your research file to answer some of the questions. Make a list of ideas for topics, then ask the following:

> Is it recent? Is the subject about something that happened a short while ago? The more recent the event to be talked about, the more interesting your audience will find it.
> Does it concern your listener? The more your listener can say, "This is important to *me*", the more he will listen.
> Is there some struggle or conflict in the topic? Is there something the speakers can express different ideas about? An exchange of different viewpoints makes a panel discussion more interesting, and helps the listener think more clearly about the subject.
> Is it something new and interesting? Will it bring out ideas or information that the listener hasn't heard before?
> Does it fill a need for the listener? The panel discussion programme and all radio programmes must try to do something that the listener finds useful in some way. The *listener* must find the programme helpful, or it has no value.

A great deal of your success will depend on the way you think of your listener. Can you think of your listener as a real person who deserves your respect? If so, then you will probably find the best way to meet his needs.

Your listener is a thinking person. Through a panel discussion, you can help him hear some lively talk by honest and well-informed people. The listener can become a part of the thinking. He can share in the struggle to overcome the problems which the panel is discussing, and may learn to explore his own mind and his own thinking.

The Moderator (G3):

The MODERATOR, or LEADER (or CHAIRMAN) of a panel discussion is the most important person in the discussion. He should not say as much as the guests, but his work will usually make the difference between a bad discussion and a good one. Look up the word *moderator* in the glossary.

On some programmes you produce, you may be the moderator yourself. On others, you may invite someone else (perhaps someone who knows a great deal about the subject you will discuss) to be the moderator. In this project, however, we ask you to think of yourself as the moderator.

As the moderator of a panel discussion, you must:

decide how much time will be given to each part of the subject,

be sure that each person on your panel is treated equally, and that each has *about* the same amount of time to speak,

keep order and balance (if someone is rude or unfriendly, the moderator must use his best manners to make that person behave properly),

help to find the opinions and ideas of all panel members by asking good questions or inviting them to comment on what someone else has said,

lead the panel members through the subjects you have decided to discuss, and bring them to a satisfactory ending.

We spent some time in *Projects E* and *F* telling you how important it was to be alert and flexible. This is just as important for the moderator of a panel discussion, as it is for the interviewer.

One of the reasons why a panel discussion is more interesting to the listener than just a talk, is because he feels that the people are talking naturally, just as they do in ordinary conversation. Sometimes unexpected things happen. When they do, the moderator should be ready to use them to make the programme better. If he doesn't, the same unexpected things may spoil the programme.

Choosing the Panel (G4):

If you have a committee to help you choose the panel members, then your task will be much easier.

As you discuss each possible person, the committee members can say what they know or think about him. After you have the information and opinions of the committee members, try to guide them into a wise choice. A person is sometimes chosen for a panel because he is a close friend to a committee member, but not because he has any knowledge or ability to give to the programme. In the same way, a person who would make an excellent panel member has not been chosen because there is someone on the committee who does not like him. Help the committee to see that its main concern should be the *listener* and *his needs*.

If you do not have a committee, then make a list of some possible panel members and show the list to other people on your staff. Ask them to comment on your list, and to make other suggestions. Even if your fellow staff member does not have any good ideas, he may at least help you to think about your list in a different way.

Here are some questions to ask about possible panel members that may help you choose the best people:

> Does he know the subject? This does not mean that he must be an expert. He must know enough, however, to ask good questions and to bring some ideas and information to the programme.
>
> Is he able to speak well? He does not need to be a person who is able to make speeches in front of many people, but he should be able to find words fairly easily to say the things he means.
>
> Is he a person who is concerned about your listeners and would like to help them? That should be the purpose of your programme, and so your panel members must also have that purpose.
>
> If he is an expert on the subject, can he talk about it in such a way that your listener will understand what he means? No matter how well a person knows his subject, it does not help the listener at all if he uses big words and difficult explanations that will not be understood.

Try to find different kinds of people for each panel. For instance, if you were planning a discussion called "Health in the Home", you might include a doctor, a housewife, and a teacher. If you were going to have a discussion called "The Village Churches", you might have a pastor, a church member, and someone who is against the church. In this way you will have many different viewpoints from people who can see many sides of the same problems.

Never have more than four people plus the moderator on a programme. The listener will be confused if there are too many different voices. A panel of three people is much better. Two panellists plus a moderator are not too few.

Preparing the Discussion (G5):

Before you begin to work with the members of your panel, you must begin by preparing yourself. This is very much like preparing for an interview.

Read as much as you can about the subject. You do not need to be an expert, but you cannot lead a good panel discussion, unless you know what kind of questions to ask, and what the important things are that your panel should discuss.

Find out as much as you can about the panel members. You may have done this already before you chose your panel. In any case, make a few notes about each person. Be sure you know their names and positions. Try to find out a few interesting things about each member that will help your listener feel he knows the man who is speaking. It always makes the panel discussion (or the interview) a little brighter, if you can say something like this:

MODERATOR: We also have with us, Mr. Jonathan Scojavit, the head of the Plant Research Department. Mr. Scojavit is smiling today because his first child, a son, was born just a week ago. Congratulations, Mr. Scojavit.

Make a first draft of your plan for your panel discussion. You will probably change this plan later when you begin to work with your panel, but if you have some ideas on paper before you begin, you will save a great deal of time later on.

Here are some ideas that may help you make your plan:

Decide what is the most important information your panel members can bring to your listener.

Decide what other things might be interesting and useful to your listener. Make a list of these subjects, so that they follow one another in a way that seems right. In other words, you should arrange them so that one subject leads easily and naturally into the other. Try to have your most interesting and important subject just before the end.

Rehearsal (G6):

About an hour or so before you want to record your panel discussion, have your panel members meet with you to talk about the programme. Allow a little time for them to get to know each other, unless of course they know each other well already.

Some radio people have found it helps to give the panel members some coffee, tea or other light refreshment, to help them relax and to get to know the other panel members. One moderator even invites his panel members to eat a meal with him before they do the programme. The important thing is to make them feel they are friends, because friends always talk more easily to each other than strangers do.

The next step is to sit down with your panel members to prepare them for the programme. There are three things you should try to do with your panel members at this time.

> Help them to plan the programme with you.
> Teach them some of the things which will help make the programme a little better.
> Prepare the comments and questions.

As you begin, give them each a few sheets of paper on which to make notes.

Planning with the Panel (G7):

As we said earlier, you should already have a first draft of a plan prepared before you meet with your panel. If your programme is part of a series which has a pattern or FORMAT (see glossary) that is used each time, then you must explain this to the panel.

If possible, give them the outline of the *format* typed on a sheet of paper.

If you are able to choose among the various kinds of formats (which we will explain later in this project) then help your panel decide which is the best one. Since you are the person who will probably know radio programming better than any member of your panel, you should have thought about the matter beforehand, so that you can give them some good advice. Usually you should be the one to decide what format to use after you have gathered the ideas of your panel.

Preparing the Panel Members (G8):

You should decide with your panel, who is going to say the most about one subject, and who is going to talk the most about another subject. You have already made a list of some of the suggested topics, and this will help you. Be prepared to change the list if any panel member has a good reason for wanting to do so. Be as firm as you need to be if someone wants to change something that you have a good reason to think should not be changed.

Suggest to your panel members that they should practise the discussion before they record it. This kind of practice should be quite short. You do not want to spoil the liveliness of the discussion by having each member know exactly what the other is going to say. Rather this kind of practice should simply give the members and the moderator some *ideas* of what the others will say. For instance, if you are doing a 15-minute discussion, your practice should not be more than five minutes, unless you are talking about a very difficult subject.

Encourage your panel to make notes on the things to be discussed. The panel members should be asked to write down any important names or numbers that they might forget. Except where something must be said in exactly a certain way, ask your panel members not to write out their comments.

The moderator should also be making notes. He should be preparing to take part in the discussion acting as a guide, but not usually as an expert. In other words, he should certainly make comments that will help keep the programme interesting and lively, and ask questions that will help it move on to the next subject. However, he should never take the main part of the programme away from his panel members.

The Moderator's Summary (G9):

The moderator must also be making his notes for his *summary*. This *summary* should be just a few words at the end of the programme, which will bring it to a satisfactory closing. It should not repeat what the panel has said, although it may remind the listeners of the most important things that were talked about. It may also tell in what way this conversation might be important to the listener. Such a summary should be quite short, usually not more than a minute or two in length.

Suggestions to the Panel (G10):

Here is a list of some suggestions that can help make a panel discussion better. As a moderator, you must decide how much of this you can tell your panel in the little time you have with them. You may decide that it is not necessary to tell them all of these things. Certainly you must be sure they understand the purpose of the interview and the kind of audience for which it is meant.

All the panel members should take part in the discussion, but none of them should take more than their share of the time. As much as possible, the conversation should move back and forth quickly among the speakers. Although there are times when a panel member should speak longer, he should *usually* talk for only a minute or two, before giving another speaker a chance.

The conversation in a panel discussion should be as close as possible to the kind of conversation the panel members would have if they happened to meet in somebody's home. Normal conversation means that people some-times interrupt each other; they make little short comments when someone is talking; sometimes there are jokes and laughter. A panel discussion is not the place for a speech. It would be like people having an informal conversa-tion at home, but it must be more orderly. It must also be much shorter. Joking and laughter are good, but there must be only a little.

Jokes are like spice in food. A little makes it tasty. Too much can make it unpleasant.

Use names when you are speaking to each other. Your listener will easily forget who is on the panel, and may have a hard time knowing the voices. Do not say, "Sir, what do you think about this?" Rather say, "Mr. Sihkwa, what do you think about this?" Then the listener will know who is going to speak.

Talk to each other directly. When you have a question or a comment, say it to someone in the group rather than to the group as a whole. Do not say, "Well, I have something I'd like to mention." Rather say, "I have some-thing I'd like to say to Mr. Sihkwa about this."

Everyone should keep his elbows on the table.

There are two reasons for this:

It helps people to stay the same distance from the microphone. The moderator and the technician must find out which voices are loud and which are soft, and then move the speakers back and forth so that they all have the same volume at the control desk. If the speakers move back and forth, this *microphone balance* will be gone.

It helps keep the elbows away from the chest, and so the speaker can breath and speak more easily. The moderator may explain this to his panel and then say, "If you happen to forget during the recording, I will point to my elbow to remind you to put your elbows on the table."

"Elbows on the table" by the way, is also a good rule when you are speaking into a microphone yourself, or when you have a guest in your studios for an interview.

The panel members should talk from personal experience as much as possible. Ask them to tell a little story to show what they mean. Remember that your listeners do not know as much about the subject as your panel does. The panel must help them understand by speaking clearly and simply. Mention the topic or subject three or four times during the interview. Many listeners may have turned on their radios after the programme has started. They will want to know what you are talking about. The panel members can mention the topic, but if they do not, the moderator must be sure that *he* does. All the panel members and the moderator should co-operate to keep the programme interesting and lively. If the discussion seems to slow down, the moderator must move quickly to a new subject, or one of the panel members should bring in a new idea. Panel members could show that they have something they wish to say by simply raising their hands. Then the moderator can say, "I wonder if Mr. Sihkwa has anything to add," and Mr. Sihkwa would be ready.

The programme must end on time. Tell the panel members that you will give them a signal to tell them certain things. For instance, if you want one member to stop and allow another to speak, you might simply hold up one finger. If the programme is coming to an end and you wish to begin your summary, then hold up one hand to tell the member to stop. Sometimes you may even have to interrupt someone in order to make the programme finish on time. It usually helps to explain to the panel before you begin, why it is important that the programme must end exactly at a certain time.

Be polite to each other. Observe good manners, but be as informal as you can.

Assignment One (G11):

Find two or three panel discussion programmes on the radio, or ask your supervisor if he has some tape-recordings of panel discussions. Write a short description (about 200 words) of each programme. In your description, tell what was good and what was bad about the programme. Also answer these questions in your description.

Was the programme interesting and lively? Explain.

What kind of an audience do you think the programme was intended for? Describe the audience.

Did it provide helpful and understandable information to this audience? Explain.

What kind of format was used? Was it a good format? Why?

The check-list at the end of Assignment Two (G18) will also help you judge these programmes. When you have done this, bring your description to your supervisor.

A Panel that Disagrees (G12):

People with different ideas can make an exciting panel discussion. However, one of the hardest things for many panel members to do, is to encourage other speakers to present another viewpoint. It is easiest for a person to speak as if he thinks, "I am completely right! Everyone who disagrees with me is completely wrong!" When a man says that, or acts as if that is what he is thinking, it is almost certain that he is not sure he is right. He becomes angry when someone disagrees with him because he is unsure of himself.

The kind of person who will do well on a panel is one who is not afraid to say, "Although I do not agree with you completely, Mr. Sihkwa, I think there is much truth in what you say. Can you explain it some more for me?" Such men are hard to find, but you should constantly look for them.

Be sure that your panel disagrees only about important things. When a panel argues about little things, the listener soon becomes dissatisfied and turns off his radio.

A Panel that Searches (G13):

This kind of panel is not always as exciting as the panel that disagrees, but it is often more useful. In this kind of a programme, the panel members will do what they can to find solutions to a problem, or perhaps simply try to see the problem more clearly. There need be no real disagreement. Each panel member tries to bring his best thoughts to the discussion, and also tries to understand what the other panel members mean. They act as a team looking for the best answers or the best ideas.

However, you cannot usually say that one panel searches and that another panel disagrees. One panel may often do both, and this is good. A good panel will usually spend most of the time searching together. But its members will not be afraid to disagree sometimes, if there is good reason for it.

Panel Discussion Formats (G14):

If you have not done so, look up the word *format* in the glossary. Here are just a few suggestions on ways to organise the format of a panel discussion or round table. There are many other ways, of course, and you should be constantly looking for new ways that fit your audience better.

> Three or four people, including the moderator, simply talk about the topic or subject. This is the most common kind of panel discussion, but not always the best.

Two persons carry on a conversation between them, each one giving as much information and as many ideas as the other. There is no moderator. This can be very good, but it needs people who know their subjects well and have had some radio experience.

Each panel member gives a short talk on his viewpoint. Then the moderator begins the conversation or discussion.

A short drama or talk is given, bringing to the listener and the panel a problem with which its members are all concerned. The panel then discusses the problem presented in the talk or drama.

Following a panel discussion on any of the formats which we have just mentioned, discussion groups in towns and villages talk about the matter themselves. Sometimes their ideas are sent to the radio studio, and are used on a later programme. Such programmes have been used very successfully in India, Ghana and other countries.

A Panel Discussion Series (G15):

If you are planning to have a series of panel discussions, be sure you make a general plan for all the programmes before you begin the first one. You should make a list of all the topics you might discuss, and also a list of the people who might be your panel members. List some extra people for each programme, because the first person you ask may not be able to take part.

This does not mean that you cannot change your first plan if you have a better idea later on, or if something important happens that you should discuss on your programmes.

It is like gathering wood for a fire. You should have enough wood *before* you light the fire, otherwise the fire will die while you are away looking for more wood.

Scripted Panel Discussions (G16):

Sometimes it may happen that it is necessary to have a script for a panel discussion. There may be certain people who will not talk without a script. Perhaps someone will insist that his subject is so difficult, that he must have a script for the programme. The easiest way is simply to ask your panel members to sit down and to write out their own scripts. That is the *easiest*, but it is not the *best* way to do it.

The best way is to bring your panel members into the studio and record the discussion without scripts. Then listen to the tape and write out everything that is said. Give this rough script to your panel members and have them change anything they feel is necessary. In this way, the interview will sound a little more like a conversation. It will be more natural, but of course, it is a great deal of work!

Try to avoid scripts for a panel discussion or an interview. People usually sound very uninteresting when they are reading. Try to explain to them that they will sound much more natural and convincing without scripts. Most people speak quite well if they are talking about something they understand and enjoy. You should not have a script for a panel discussion or an interview unless there is no other way. *A scripted panel discussion is almost never an interesting one!*

Assignment Two (G17):

With the help of your supervisor, make a 10- or a 15-minute panel discussion programme. Look at your research notes again to find out what topic your audience would find most interesting and useful. Make a list of some of the subjects you think would be good; then discuss them with your supervisor.

After you have chosen your topic, make a list of some of the people you could ask to be members of your panel. If possible, they should be people who would not mind doing the programme several times. Talk to your supervisor, and ask him to help you choose three people. You should be the moderator for this panel discussion.

Follow the suggestions for your planning and preparation which we have told you about in this project. Then record your panel discussion.

Check-list for a Panel Discussion (G18):

1. Was the subject interesting to the listener?   Yes ____ No ____
2. Was the subject useful or helpful to the listener?   Yes ____ No ____
3. Did the moderator make sure that each of the panel members had about the same amount of time to speak?   Yes ____ No ____
4. Did the moderator help to find the opinions and ideas of all the panel members, by asking good questions and by asking them to comment on what someone else had said?   Yes ____ No ____

5. Did the moderator bring the programme to a good ending with a short but interesting summary?   Yes ____ No ____

6. Did the panel members know enough about the subject to talk about it in an intelligent and interesting way?   Yes ____ No ____

7. Did the panel members talk in a simple way so that the listener could understand the subject?   Yes ____ No ____

8. Did the panel members and the moderator talk as if they were in someone's home having a friendly conversation?   Yes ____ No ____

9. Did the panel members and the moderator use each other's names?   Yes ____ No ____

10. Did the discussion move along from one idea to the next in an interesting and lively way without any bad pauses?   Yes ____ No ____

11. Was the microphone balance good?   Yes ____ No ____

If you can answer "yes" to nine of the questions in the check-list, then you have a good programme. If not, then record the same panel discussion over again or if you wish, find a new topic and a new panel and do another programme. When you have a programme that is satisfactory take it to your supervisor.

Remember, however, that like the interview (and all radio programmes) you will not really know how a panel discussion is done just by making one or two programmes. You must keep on doing such programmes, and each time you do, ask yourself, "How could I make it better?" Only in this way will you continue to become a really fine broadcaster.

Glossary Assignment (G19):

In your own words, and in your own language, explain the *meaning* of these words.

FORMAT

HEADPHONES

LIVE

MODERATOR (What does he do?)

PANEL DISCUSSION (What kind of a programme is it?)

REBROADCAST

These Lebanese broadcasters carefully study and answer each letter that comes from their listeners.

PROJECT H

Audience Studies

In *Projects A, B,* and *D* we told you some things about audience research. In *Project C* we talked about language and how it is used.

I'm sure you will know by now, that audience research is one of the most important parts of your work as a broadcaster. This does not mean that you must become a *sociologist*; that is, a scientist who studies the way groups of people live and act and think. It does mean though, that you must know enough about this science to be able to *find* the information you need.

Many broadcasters feel that when you are planning programmes, you must begin with the listener. You must know what *he* needs, and what *he* would like in a radio programme. Then you must fill *his* need by making a programme that *he* would like.

Other broadcasters say that it is more helpful to think of it like this:

All broadcasters agree that you must consider the listeners very carefully when planning a programme. You cannot reach a listener until you understand him, and to understand him takes a great deal of work and study.

I have heard people say, "Foreigners come to our country to study our people. We know our own people. We do not need to study them."

However, these foreigners also study their own people in their own countries, because they know how hard it is to get to understand any group of people, even one's own people. Some even say that this is harder.

If you are on top of a mountain, you know many things about it because you have climbed all the way. You know the trees on the mountainside, and the sharp rocks that cut your feet. But you cannot see the whole shape or the real beauty of a mountain, until you stand far away and look at it.

Because we are so much a part of our own people, we know many things about them. We know that most of the people are good and kind, and that a few are not so good. We know them as individual people, but because we are one of them, we sometimes fail to notice very important things.

If we can pretend for just a little while that we are from some other country, and look at our people from a distance, we may see them as a nation. We may see a beauty and a richness we had not known before. We may also see some problems we had not noticed.

You may not agree that it is harder to understand some things about your own people, but you should agree that you can learn *more* about them.

Culture (H2):

There is one word you will find often in the next few pages. It is *culture*. We are using the word here the way sociologists use it, not to mean music or art, but to mean "the kind of society in which people live".

To understand a culture, you must understand the things which people do and think and feel when they live their ordinary day-to-day lives. How do they plant, plough, water the ground and harvest? How do they feel and act when one of their numbers does something they think is wrong? What are their traditions when they get married, have children, and what happens when they die? What kind of God or gods do they believe in, and how do they worship? What things do they think are right, and what things are wrong? These and many more are the questions a sociologist asks when he studies a culture. The answers are not always easy to find.

We cannot tell you about your own culture in this manual. However, we can tell you some things that will help *you find out* about it. If you do the research and the assignments that we suggest, you will certainly learn more about the life of your people. You will learn that your culture is rich and beautiful, and that it should be in the heart of all your programmes.

It is important that you understand this listener's culture, before you begin to make programmes for him.

However, we want to warn you of a very big danger. The danger is that when you have finished this project, you will feel you know all about sociology and the culture you live in. Please remember that this manual can do nothing more than introduce you to a very small part of a very big subject. There is much, much more to learn.

What Has Already Been Done? (H3):

The first thing to do is to try and find out what information is already available. There is no use working hard to find information, if someone has done so already. Learn where the information is, so that when you need to know something you can say, "I do not have the information in my mind, but I do know where I can find it." Knowing where to find information is sometimes more important than having it in your head. There is far more than one person can learn anyway.

In *Project B* we asked you to find out whether there were any libraries near by that you could use. Check your notes on *Project B* to see if there are any other places you could add to your list.

UNESCO (H4):

Some information about your country may be available from UNESCO. Your supervisor will find the address in his guide.

UNESCO now has offices in very many countries. There is probably one in your country. It would be very useful to write or visit this office to find out what information it has. If you do not know where to find the closest office, write to Paris and ask. Other information sources are listed in Appendix *S11*.

Your supervisor probably knows of some places where you can find useful information about your culture. Ask him to help you locate the information you will be asked to find in this project.

Also ask other people if there are persons in your area who might have some information in their minds or in their own libraries. Your government may have done some studies that will be helpful. Find out, if possible, what is available there.

Background Information (H5):

Many broadcasters find it very useful to make several maps of the area in which their stations or their programme is heard. We would like you to make such maps, in order that you can see more clearly the problems you face in your broadcasting.

Draw seven or eight maps of your listening area. You do not need to put in every little village or river, but be sure you include the important cities, mountains, boundaries, etc. Do not draw this map from memory. Find a good map to copy from.

If you can use a duplicating or a mimeograph machine, you might need to draw only one map and then make as many copies as necessary.

If possible, use coloured pens or pencils to put in the information you will be asked to find. Each colour would represent different information. Of course, you could also use different symbols or signs. The language map *(H7)* uses different marks to show the different languages and dialects.

You may not be able to make all the maps we suggest in this project, but make as many as you can. At least make the *language* and *population* maps.

Here are the maps you should make:

Population (H6):

How many people are there in your listening area? Do more people live in some places than in others? If you can find detailed information, mark your map by putting one dot for each 10,000 people (or one dot for each 1,000, 5,000, or even 50,000 people, depending on your country) at the places where they live. Show on your map how many live in cities, how many in towns, and how many in small villages. You will see why this map is useful when we talk about other maps.

Language (H7):

Read through *Project C* once again. Try to find out more about the various dialects and languages that are spoken. Try to put on your map the areas where these are used. Different shades of blue might show one language and its dialects, while different shades of red might show another. If you compare this with your population map, you will be able to see easily where people of different dialects live and about how many speak each one.

SOUTHERN   INDIA

American Bible Society.

Economics (H8):

How do people earn their livelihood? Find out what kinds of crops are grown and in what areas. Is there some manufacturing in your country? Where is this done? Show this on your map with different colours or symbols, then compare it with your population and language maps. Then you will be able to see where people live, what they do, and what languages or dialects they speak.

Culture (H9):

In some places, there are groups within the country that have customs and ideas different from others near by. They may be called groups, tribes, clans or minorities. A map showing this might look a little like your language map. Compare this with your other maps and you may be able to answer a question something like this: "How many people are there in this tribe, where do they live, what language do they speak and how do they earn their living?"

Religion (H10):

The religion of people has something to do with everything else in their lives. Therefore you should know something about the religion of your people no matter what kind of broadcasting you are doing. It may not always be possible to draw a map of the religions, but you should try to find as much information as possible. Here are the questions to ask:

How many people belong to each religion?
Do some belong to more than one religion?
What do these religions teach?

Radio Placement (H11):

There are many places in the world where it would be very hard to find out how many radios there are, and who owns them. This information is very valuable, however, and you should do everything possible to find out. It seems only reasonable to make programmes for those people who have radios, but you cannot do this until you find out who they are.

For instance, a magazine article about radio in one African nation said that out of almost 6,000 radios:

4,000 were owned by Europeans
1,700 were owned by Asians
50 were owned by Africans

If this were your country, you would need to think about this very carefully before making plans for programmes, remembering that programmes need not always be made for the largest number of people. You may decide to make programmes for those who have the greatest need, rather than for those who have the most radios. Whatever group you make programmes for, you should do so with your eyes open and with the facts in your mind.

Get as much detailed information about radio sets as you can. Copy this and keep it near by. You should look at this often.

Education (H12):

This is another very important thing to know. You would certainly make a programme differently if it were for villagers with no education, than you would for people with two or three years of school. And you would make a programme for people with ten years of school differently again. Very often the broadcaster is making programmes for those who have much less education than he has. It is difficult to keep this in mind, and sometimes the broadcaster makes the mistake of writing as if his audience knows the same things as he does, or enjoys the same things he does.

It may not be possible to make a map of the education people have, but you should try to get as much information as you can. How many people have a university education? How many have ten years? Five years? One year? None at all?

In some cases, you will find that those with the most education also have the most money and are most likely to have radios. However, in some places it has been found that university graduates listen to the radio less than those who have five to ten years of education.

New Information (H13):

All of this information can help you decide on the kind of programmes you are going to do. Each year, more and more such information is becoming available, and you should be constantly watching for it.

For that reason, you will need to keep changing your maps from time to time as you receive new information.

You will also find a good deal of information that you cannot put on maps. Put this information down in such a way that it is easy to understand and interpret.

Assignment One (H14):

Begin work on a notebook or a file containing the information and the maps on population, language, economics, culture, religion, radio placement and education. Put this together carefully, leaving plenty of room to add new information when it can be found. At the end of each of the seven parts, write one or two paragraphs which tell either:

what effect this information will have on your radio programmes,

or, (if you were not able to find very much information)

what problems you may find because you do not have this information.

Leave space in your notebook or file since other items from this project should be added later. There may be other things you find in your research that would be useful to add. Bring your notebook and your paragraphs to your supervisor when you have done this.

Analysing Cultural Groups (H15):

The information you have been gathering so far will be very helpful to you but it is not all you need. If you go back to your notes from *Projects A, B* and *D* you will see that it is even more important to know the culture within a family group or within a village or tribe. It is not as easy to find this out, since you cannot write down the information in numbers and very much of it is hard to put into words.

Those of you who are using this manual will have had an education. Some of you may be highly educated. Because of this, you have learned to think in new ways, and to act differently in some ways from people in your country who have less education.

A Filipino doctor once told me, "I am not happy in my barrio (village) any more. I have been educated away from my people. I talk differently, I act differently, I think differently. I find it very hard to help the people in the barrio where I was born, because I am no longer one of them."

We are not trying to say if this is bad or good. That is not the reason for this manual. However, those who wish to serve their people must know if they have become different from their own people, and if so, *in what ways.*

Cultures and Sub-cultures (H16):

At the beginning of this project *(H3)* we asked you to find out what information was available about the cultures of your country. Before you continue, read as much of that as you can. If possible, go and talk to a sociologist and ask him to tell you about the different cultures in your country.

There is no such thing as one culture for each country. There are often many different cultures, and each one has small groups within it that are called sub-cultures.

For instance, if there are different clans or tribes in your country, then each of them has a culture of its own. However, the people in a cultural group are not all exactly the same. Certain people from one tribe may have moved away to the city where they now work in a factory. They would still be part of the culture from which they came, but because their habits have changed in the city, they would be a little different. They would belong to a sub-culture.

You may have belonged to the culture of a village or a tribe. Then you went to school and now you are probably working in a city. If that is the case, then you are a member of a sub-culture.

It is important that you begin to understand the things that are different between the various cultures and sub-cultures in your country. Only then will you be able to make successful programmes for the people in these cultures.

Assignment Two (H17):

Ask your supervisor to help you make a list of the different cultures and sub-cultures you find in your country. You probably do not have names for them, but a short description of each will be enough. As an example, here is one of the Philippine cultures and a list of its sub-cultures.

Culture:	*Sub-cultures:*
Tagalog Speakers.	Those living on farms.
	Those living in small towns.
	Workers in the city.
	Educated people in the city.

Choose three or four of the most important groups in your country. If possible, include a group of foreigners. Below is a list of questions. Try to find at least one person (two or three would be better) from each group, and ask him to help you find the answers to these questions.

Write the answers just the way they are given, even if you think they may not be correct. Write these answers on small cards or pieces of paper about half the size of this page. When you have finished, arrange your cards or papers so that all the answers to question one are together, and all the answers to question two are together, and so on.

Write a short paragraph about each question telling what was the same in all the groups, and what things were different. Keep these cards in your research file. You will want to look at them often when you are preparing programmes.

Cultural Questions for Assignment Two (H18):

1. *Parents:* Who decides things in the family? The father? The mother? Does the father decide some things and the mother other things? Do they decide anything together?
2. *Family:* Why is the family important? Does the family own property together and work together? Does the family work in different places?
3. *Family Group:* How large is the family? Does the family include many relatives? Is this good? Why?
4. *Children:* Are children usually punished for their mistakes? How are they punished? Is this good? Are children expected to obey their parents? Do the parents listen to what the children have to say? What is the biggest problem that parents have in raising their children?
5. *Marriage:* Are marriages arranged by the family? Are they decided by the boy and girl? Do they "fall in love"? Must the parents agree to the wedding? Why is this so?
6. *Courtship:* Can the boy and girl meet freely? Is there a third person around when they meet? What things can they do and what must they not do before they are married? Why?
7. *Sex:* Are a boy and girl allowed to have sexual relationships before marriage? Are men allowed more freedom than women? Why?
8. *Divorce:* What happens if a man and a woman do not want to be married any more? Can they get a divorce? Why? What problems come up when a man and a woman do not want to be married any more?

There are, of course, other important questions you could ask about these cultures. If possible, you should also ask similar questions about religion, farming, medicine, the life in the community, and all of the things that make up culture.

Even when you have done this assignment, remember that it does not mean you really understand the cultures in your country. We hope, however, that it will make you curious enough to want to study your country and your people much more. You will find this kind of study very interesting, and it will be a great help to you when you are trying to reach the people of your country with important ideas and information.

Not Knowing is Expensive (H19):

It is important for a broadcaster to find out as much as possible about the culture into which he is broadcasting. For instance:

> In one Asian nation, a series of programmes to help people in villages grow better rice and have better health did not seem to be succeeding. A sociologist who studied the culture of the villages, found that the people had certain "authorities", or people who the villagers thought knew the most about certain things. A certain woman might be considered the one who knew the most about keeping healthy. The workers could not hope to persuade the other people in the village to do things about health until she agreed. In the same way, one man would be thought to know more about farming, and so he would have to be persuaded first. Knowing this, the workers visited the "authorities" first. When *they* agreed to the idea, then the radio programmes could be used to keep the people interested, and to help them gain a better understanding of *why* they should do this or that.

There could be many stories told of how radio-programme producers (and many others) failed because they did not really understand their audiences. Such failures have happened to foreigners making broadcasts to another country, but they have happened just as often to those making programmes for their own people.

When you have finished this assignment, bring all your notes and paragraphs to your supervisor.

How to Find Out (H20):   PART TWO

Read again those parts of *Projects A, B* and *D* that tell you about research. Study the notes you made about your audience.

You should keep on building your research file, even after you have finished your work on this manual. Your audience will change as the situation in your country changes. Sociologists will be finding out more things about your people.

Your government and other agencies in your country will be finding more information. Always keep looking for new information about your audience.

There is one thing that no other agency will find out for you. This is, "Who is listening to our programmes, and how effective are they?"

> Unless you can find some answers to those two questions, you will be like a man shouting in the dark. He does not know if there is anyone listening. There may be three people. There may be thousands. *But he doesn't know.* Even if there are people hearing his voice, a man in the dark does not know if they are interested in what he is saying, or whether they believe the things he is talking about.

What Do You Think? (H21):

It is important that a broadcaster know something about himself. Everyone believes that the things *he* says are important. Everyone believes that the things *he* says are interesting. It is natural for a broadcaster to think this. *He* finds his programme interesting and important, and thinks the *listener* will also find it that way.

> Have you ever heard a radio programme that was very dull? You probably have. Did the man who prepared that programme think it was interesting? He probably did.

This can happen to *you*! A programme you think is very interesting might be very dull for others.

Your Friends Might Not Help (H22):

Every broadcaster has had people come to him and say, "Yes, I liked your programme very much." Or someone might introduce you to another by saying, "This is Mr. ____. He makes a radio programme called "Life in Our Land". Then you would hear the reply, "Oh yes . . . of course . . . yes . . . I always listen to your programme!"

A broadcaster must understand enough about people and about his friends to know when they are just being kind to him, and when they are really talking about his programmes. You will probably find, if you stop to think about it, that many of the people who tell you how much they enjoy your programme, are really only paying you a compliment. They really mean, "I want to say something kind to you, because I am your friend."

Of course, there are also many of your friends who will listen to your programme and make comments that are very useful.

The people you are friends with, or those you meet most often, are people who are like you in many ways. They probably have about the same education as you have, and probably are interested in many of the same things. There is nothing wrong in that.

The question is, "Do they think about my programme in the same way as the rest of my audience?"

> One radio station in Asia is built on the grounds of a fine university. Most of the people who live and work at the university have a good education. The people who work at the radio station also have a good education. They have many friends among the university people.
>
> However, the radio station is making programmes for people in the villages who have very little education. A man from that station once said, "One of the university professors just told me he liked my programme. If he likes it, then I don't think the people in the villages will like it. Perhaps I should change my programme!"

What Does a Comment Mean? (H23):

We do not mean that you should not listen to the comments of your friends. Listen to them and consider them carefully. However, ask three important questions before you decide if the comment is useful to you.

> What did this person *really* mean by what he said? Does he really listen to the programme, or was he trying to make me feel happy?
>
> What is his education? Social standing? How wealthy is he? Does he belong to the same group as my listener?
>
> Now that I have considered these things, what does this mean for my programme?

Many broadcasters keep notes on the comments they receive. Whenever they hear something about their programmes, they write down what they think the comments mean. In this way, they can wait until they have a large number of comments, and can see each one in relation to the others.

If you do this, be careful! You might collect a large number of comments which say that your programme is good. This does not always mean that your programme *is* good. It may only mean that those who thought it was bad were too polite to say so.

Letters (H24):

Almost every radio studio or station receives letters from its listeners. Many stations try very hard to encourage the listeners to write letters. If you study your letters they can help you learn a great deal about your audience. They can also give a lot of false information.

There are three things you should know about letters:

One letter can represent only *one* listener. No matter what he may say, he is still giving the opinion of only *one* person. His opinion may be just like the opinion of many others, or it may be completely unlike any others.

Even though a programme gets many letters, that does not mean it has more listeners than a programme that gets few letters. Some programmes, especially if the station is giving something away free, will receive many letters. A news programme, even though it has many listeners, might never receive a letter.

Letters tell you only about those listeners who wrote the letters. There may be far more listeners who did not write. People do not write because:

They do not know how to write.
Postage stamps cost too much.
The post office is too far away.
They have nothing to say.
They are too lazy.
They do not like the programme and have stopped listening.

So you can see that judging a programme by the letters is *very difficult*, and sometimes impossible. However, if you develop a good system for studying letters, and use the system always, you can get some important information from letters.

Here is a chart for analysing letters which one station used. The information it gives will not be useful for your country, but it may help you to make your own chart. Then you can make it fit your own kind of broadcasting and your own audience. Study it carefully.

LISTENER LETTER ANALYSIS 162 letters	EDUCATION			SEX		RELIGION				LOCATION			TARGET AUDIENCE		TOTALS
	1-5 yrs school	5-10 yrs school	10 plus school	Male	Female	Roman Catholic	Protestant	Muslim	Not Known	Small Village	Town	City	Member of Target	Not Member	
Requested listener reception report without comment	10	35	5	45	5	2	15	3	30	1	23	26	11	39	50
Complaint about programme	—	1	4	5	—	-	6	-	-	-	3	2	-	5	5
Praising the programme	5	29	6	32	8	4	6	20	10	2	31	7	12	28	40
Question about the topic of the programme	-	-	2	2	-	-	-	-	2	-	-	2	-	2	2
Request for free gift	5	38	2	19	26	16	5	10	14	5	29	11	5	40	45
Request for a music selection	2	14	4	9	11	6	2	4	8	2	14	4	6	14	20
TOTALS	22	11	23	112	50	28	33	37	64	10	100	52	34	128	162

From: March 16/66
To: April 16/66

Audience Target: Villagers with little or no education.

Purpose of Programme: Teach new ways to keep clean and healthy.

Before we discuss the information which the chart gives us, let us think about the way we find the information to put on the chart.

Analysing Letters (H25):

It is not hard to keep such a chart. Each time you read a letter, put the information it gives you on a chart. At the end of each week or each month, count the marks and then put all the information together on a sheet like this.

How often you put all the information together depends on how many letters you get. If there are at least 150 letters a week, then do it once a week. If not, then do it once a month. It is helpful to put several weeks or several months of results together on one sheet after you have looked at them week by week or month by month.

Education: The problem comes when you try and find information the letter writer doesn't actually put into words. How do you know how much education the writer has if he does not tell you? Very often you must make a guess. The words he uses and the way he writes often tell *about* how much education the writer has.

Sex: Finding out if the writer is a man or a woman will be very easy in some places, and hard in others. In many places the name tells you whether it is a man or a woman. For instance, in many parts of Latin America, a name ending in "o" is usually a man, and one ending in "a" is a woman. In some places it is impossible to find this out.

Religion: A man's attitude to almost everything is determined by his religion. That is why you should try to find out the religion of the writer from his letters. Often a certain word will tell you he represents one faith, or a particular style of writing may tell you something else. Sometimes his name will tell you. Often, of course, you cannot tell, but it is worth while finding out as often as you can.

Location: The postmark on the letter will often tell you where it came from. Sometimes the writer gives his address inside the letter. It is important to know what size of town, village or city the writer comes from. Village people often must be considered differently from city people.

Target Audience: It is important to try and determine if the letter writer is a member of your target audience. The target audience is that group of people you have decided should be contantly kept in mind as you make your programme.

It sometimes happens that a radio programme catches the interest of a group of people for whom it was not intended. What happens more often is that it catches the attention of a very small group of people for whom it was not intended, and none of the group for which it *was* intended. Your letter chart may possibly give you this information.

What Does the Chart Say? (H26):

The chart (which is just an example) says some very interesting things. It gives some true information, and it also gives some information that is *false* if taken all by itself. Here are some of the things that can be learned from this chart – things we might not know otherwise. Notice, however, that it tells us only about the *people who wrote*. It says *nothing* about those who did not write.

Most of the people who wrote are *men* who have had from *five to ten* years in school, and who live in a *town*.

Most of the people who wrote to this programme were *not* within the target audience which the producers of the programme had chosen.

Women wrote more letters for free gifts and for music than the men.

There was not enough difference in the numbers under *religion* to tell us very much, except that for some reason the *Moslems* praised the programme more than others.

People will write more often to *praise* than to *complain*. They will also write if given a free gift, or if they can choose a music selection.

What Does the Chart Not Say? (H27):

It does *not* say that the programme is not hitting its target audience. The target audience in this example is "men and women in villages with little or no education". How could they write? Most of them probably do not know how, and many would not be in the habit of writing letters.

So the chart tells us only about the kind of person who writes letters to the radio station. One would need to use another method to find out if the programme was really reaching the target audience.

A letter chart would be *more* useful if the target audience was a class of people who could write. It would still only give us part of the information, however, because only certain *kinds* of people will take the trouble to write letters to radio stations. These are usually people with strong ideas and opinions which they like to make known. Many quiet people may listen and learn from your programme, even though you do not hear from them.

Audience Survey (H28):

The only way really to be certain how your programme or radio station is doing, is to undertake a major audience survey. There isn't enough space to say very much about that here, except that you should have it supervised by someone who has been trained for such work. It is often expensive and quite difficult. It is very worthwhile for those who can do it.

However, a scientific audience study is probably the only way you can really find reliable information about the way in which people receive your programmes. Some stations and studios have worked in co-operation with universities in making such studies. They not only received help from the professors and teachers who had training in this kind of research, but also they were able to use the students to do some of the work.

Bicycle Survey (H29):

In most tropical countries, and in many countries in the summer time, windows and doors are left open. Radios are often turned up quite loud. It is quite easy to ride by on a bicycle (or walk) and hear whether the people in the house are listening to your station or another. Go through the wealthy places in your area, the middle-class places, and the poor places. When you hear a radio, listen for a moment. Write down the name of the station or programme, and also the kind of house you see. The house will give you some idea of the class of people who are listening to the radio. If people might be afraid to see someone writing things down in front of their home, then simply go by slowly and keep the information in your mind. As soon as you get to a place where you can, write it down.

Such a survey is impossible in many places, of course. Also the information would be only about those people close enough to reach by bicycle. In fact, there are many reasons why a bicycle survey often does not give very reliable information. It should only be used when no better method is possible.

Assignment Three (H30):

If you are working at a station or studio that is already producing programmes, then ask your supervisor if you may have about fifty letters, so that you may make a Listener Letter Analysis. Make a chart to fit your programmes and your country, then analyse the fifty letters. Make your chart in such a way that you can place it in your booklet or file. What information does the chart give you? What information does it *not* give you? Write a few paragraphs answering these two questions.

When you have completed Assignment Three, take the chart and the letters to your supervisor.

In *Project H* we have tried to show you how important audience research is for successful radio broadcasting. It is easier to do a programme that simply entertains, than to make a programme that is enjoyable and at the same time helps your audience find a better way of life. You will never be able to do this kind of educational broadcasting unless you get to know your audience.

Drums are an ancient and useful means of communication.

PROJECT I

Communication

Media and Communication (I1)

The mass media are now being used all over the world. Because of this, many good people are trying to find out how mass communication can be used to help mankind rather than destroy him. We hope this project will help you understand more about how communication takes place, and the ways in which the mass media can help your country.

First of all, we must understand those two terms: *mass media* and *mass communication*.

The word "mass", as we use it here, means large numbers of people listening or watching one thing. One person talking to ten or twenty people is not speaking to a mass audience. One person talking to 500 people over a loudspeaker, or writing a newspaper story which many will read, is addressing a mass audience.

Media are the things we use to reach the mass. We may use one *medium* (singular) or several *media* (plural). When we talk on a radio programme, then radio is our *medium*. If we write a book, then printing is our *medium*. Radio, television, movies, filmstrips, newspapers, books, magazines, pamphlets are all *mass media*.

There are other media that are not used to reach the mass. If you talk on the telephone to a friend, the *telephone* is your medium. If we talk to him in the same room your *voice* is the medium.

Of course, we use our voices when talking on the radio too, and the listener uses his ears to hear the sound from his radio. Your voice, your ears, your eyes, your nose, your fingers are all media of communication. You may use many media at one time.

Five Parts of Communication (I2):

Communication means getting an idea, a thought or some information from one person to another. However, we must say more about communication than just that, otherwise we would be telling you only part of the story.

There are five things needed for communication to take place:

1. a sender,
2. a message,
3. a medium,
4. a receiver, and
5. a response.

Let us see what happens when you have a conversation with a friend.

The things you wish to say are formed in your mind. In other words, you are the *sender*, and you make the *message* in your mind which you then put into words. The words then become the *medium*. When your friend hears your words he becomes the *receiver*.

Just hearing the words, however, does not mean that there has been communication. There must also be a *response*. This means that the *receiver* understands the *message*, or *does* something because of the message. Your friend may *respond* by thinking, "What a silly thing to say!" He may laugh or cry. He may walk away or do something else. He may respond by simply thinking about what you have said. He may say something back to you.

If he does, then his words are not only a *response*, but also the first part of a new communication. He then becomes the *sender*, you become the *receiver*, and so the communication flows back and forth.

Of course, you and your friend can both be a sender and a receiver at the same time. Perhaps as you are talking, you see a smile on your friend's face. This means that while you are the sender using words as your medium, your friend is also a sender, using the expression on his face as a medium. One might say that the communication goes in a circle, each person sending out messages and getting reactions in return.

You can often use more than one medium at a time. If you wave your hands or point your fingers while you speak, you will be communicating more than what your words are saying. The tone or sound of your voice may also communicate more than what your words mean by themselves.

Encoding and Decoding (13):

When a person decides what he is going to say, he chooses the words and ideas in his mind that he thinks are best, and then speaks them. This is called *encoding*.

You are changing your thoughts into a *code*, or vocal sounds that your listener can understand. Your listener must know your code (your language) if he is to understand what you are trying to communicate.

When your friend hears your message he must *decode* it. He hears your code (words) and interprets its meaning.

You could draw a picture of the *communications* process like this:

Distortion (14):

When you listen to the radio, especially to short-wave radio, you often hear a voice become thin and squeaky, or the words become muffled so that you cannot understand. The sound has changed from the time it left the mouth of the speaker at the radio station till the time you heard it on your radio set. This is called *distortion*.

Distortion happens in all kinds of communication, not always to the sound but to the message itself.

Distortion in your message can happen even when you are talking to a friend, usually when you are encoding or decoding.

Here is what we mean. Have you ever had a problem finding the right words to express the things you were thinking? Everyone has this problem. We know what we want to communicate, but the right words don't seem to come out. This is distortion in encoding. It happens even more often when we are not aware of it, because the words (code) we use never quite tell *all* that is in our minds. Your friend cannot hear your thoughts. He can hear only your words. So when the words leave your mouth there is already distortion in your communication.

Supposing you use a word like "religion". What the word "religion" means to you depends on what religion you belong to. It depends on whether you think religion is good or bad. It depends on whether you are a religious person or not religious. However, you spoke only the *word* "religion". It means so many things to you, things you feel and things you think.

What about your friend, the receiver? The word "religion" may mean something quite different to him. He may belong to a different faith. He may belong to none at all. He may have different feelings and different thoughts than you do.

So when you encode the word "religion" it stands for many things. When your receiver decodes the word, he may understand something very different. This is distortion.

Distortion happens at all times in communication. It happens when you are talking to a friend. It happens even more when you are talking to a radio audience, where each listener will encode something slightly different from your words.

A radio station engineer knows there is always *some* distortion in the signal before it reaches the listener's radio. He tries to make this distortion as little as possible by being certain that all his equipment is working well.

The programme writer or producer also knows that everything he says will be only partly understood, and some of it may be completely misunderstood. Nevertheless, he does all he can to be sure there is as little distortion as possible when he communicates his message to the listener.

Feedback (I5):

Mass communication has greater problems with distortion than person-to-person communication. When you are talking to a friend, he can ask you a question if he does not understand. He can tell you he agrees or disagrees. He can show you with a frown or smile how he feels about the things you are saying. He is sending you his *feedback*.

Feedback is another word for the response you get from your listener. Communication works best when there is plenty of feedback. When you are talking to a small group of people, you can adjust your message as you go along. If you see puzzled faces, you explain your idea a little more.

It is hard to get feedback in radio broadcasting. In *Project H* we talked about surveys and about analysing personal comments and letters. These are different kinds of feedback from a radio audience, but they don't tell as much as we would like to know.

Mass communication is useful only because it can reach very many people at one time. It is not as effective as talking to each person by himself. This is partly because we do not get very much feedback from a radio audience.

That is why we have been asking you over and over again to study your audience. Only by studying and knowing your audience can you remove most of the distortion from your message, and know where to look for feedback.

Field of Experience (16):

Only by studying and knowing your audience can you discover its *field of experience*. We have talked about this before in *Project B*, when we said, "Speak of something your listener knows and understands." The things a person knows and understands, the things he has done, the places he has gone to, the education he has had, the suffering he has undergone – these are all part of a person's field of experience.

People become friends because they *share* experiences together. They may be only little experiences (a cup of coffee, or a ride on the bus), or they may be big experiences (fighting together in a war or worshipping together).

Friendships also grow when people have had *similar* experiences.

> In Kenya I met a young broadcaster from India. We discovered that he and I both knew an Indian broadcaster in Jabalpur. Our friendship began because we both knew the same man, and we were both broadcasters. We shared a field of experience.

You have a field of experience. Your listener does too. What experiences do you share with this listener? There are many! How about love, hope, worry, fear, joy, pride, sickness, health, death, birth, and many others?

Your listener must accept *you* before he will believe anything you *say*. He must think of you as someone he can trust and someone he enjoys having in his home. Communication cannot take place unless there is this kind of a relationship. You can build such a relationship just as you can build a friendship, on this shared field of experience.

Interference (I7):

We spoke a few moments ago about an engineer doing his best to remove the distortion from his radio signal. An engineer also worries about interference. Sometimes another station may move into part of his frequency, so that the listener hears two programmes at one time.

A programme producer has problems of interference also. This interference usually comes from other things that are happening in the places where people are listening to their radios. Perhaps the dogs are barking, or the children crying. Somebody else may be talking or there may be cars and motor-cycles going by outside.

You must be aware of this interference when making your programme. It is no good thinking that most people are all by themselves giving all of their attention to their radios. There may be a few such people, but most of your listeners will find many things to take their attention away from your message.

This must be remembered when planning any programme. Your script should be written so that even if some interference happens right in the middle of it, the listener will not lose all of the message.

Assignment One (I8):

In your own language explain what is meant by these words. Most of these words are not in the glossary.

DECODING	FIELD OF EXPERIENCE
DISTORTION	INTERFERENCE
ENCODING	MASS COMMUNICATION
FEEDBACK	MASS MEDIA (or MEDIUM)

Assignment Two (I9):

Make a list of twenty words (in your language) which might suffer from distortion when used in communication. Some English examples are: religion, loyalty, politician, democracy, etc.

Assignment Three (I10):

List four different subjects which you think would make helpful programmes for your listener. Tell what kind of programme it should be (the format) and describe a field of experience you and your listener have in common, which you could use for each programme.

Assignment Four (I11):

In a few paragraphs, describe the type of interference listeners might find in the places where they listen to the radio. Describe as many different classes or groups as you can. In another paragraph indicate some ways you might overcome this interference when you make your programmes for each group of listeners.

When you have finished these assignments, take them to your supervisor. You may want to use Assignments Two, Three and Four again, when you are preparing programmes. We would suggest that you put them into your research file. In fact, throughout this manual, you should be looking for things that will be useful later on, and which should become part of your research file or your idea file.

Bringing Change Through Radio (I12):   PART TWO

Radio is used for many purposes in almost all nations of the world. In this manual we are thinking of those broadcasters who use radio in some way to help their people to a better life. Some of you may be working in education, some in community development, some in religion. All of you are trying to bring change to your nation.

If we are going to change some of the habits and practices of our people, we must know how these changes happen. It will not help just to make more programmes, or to put more radio sets among the people, or to have more people listen to our programmes. These things may help, but they cannot bring change by themselves.

Dr. Schramm's Book (I13):

Dr. Wilbur Schramm, working with the United Nations Educational, Cultural and Scientific Organisation (UNESCO) has written a very excellent book called *Mass Media and National Development*. Part of this book has been reprinted in a pamphlet called "The Role of Information in National Development". You should certainly get this pamphlet from UNESCO and study it carefully.

We would like to tell you about some of the ideas Dr. Schramm gives in the chapter called, "What Mass Communications Can Do, and What It Can *Help Do*, in National Development."*

Dr. Schramm tells us that changes in a culture come about when:

> one culture has contact with another culture for a long period of time,
> a conqueror or a ruler forces people to change, or when
> better information and better education makes people *want* to change.

We are trying to bring about the third kind of change with our radio programmes. To do that, we must make our people aware that they need something which they do not now have. Then when they know of this need, they must invent or borrow some way of meeting that need.

That is very easy to say, but it is very difficult to do. There are many things which cause problems when you are trying to bring about changes in the habits and thoughts of people.

A Culture is Tied Together (I14):

One of the reasons why it is hard to change an old custom is because all of the parts of a culture are tied together. If you change one part of a culture, it will change many other parts also.

> In some parts of the world, if you were going to help people improve their health by killing the flies that carry diseases, you would also have to change a part of their religion. Some religions do not allow the killing of any living thing.

Many organisations have found big problems with the culture when they tried to change the ways in which people farm. Farming, in many areas, is not

---

* UNESCO, Paris, 1964. Many of the ideas expressed in the following pages are gleaned from pages 115 to 145 of this book.

just a matter of growing food. The farmers have religious practices which they use when they plant and harvest. The life of the farmer's whole family is related to the way in which he earns his living. When you change some of his farming methods, you will also be changing part of his religion and some of his family patterns. This is one of the reasons why people often do not accept the changes we try to bring to them. They cannot bear to see something they have loved and lived by, changed overnight.

What we must do then is to think of the *whole culture* when we are trying to introduce a change. We must try to bring the new idea in such a way that the whole culture of the listener works toward helping the change, rather than working against it. This is easy to say, difficult to do, but very necessary for success in broadcasting.

People Live in Groups (I15):

Dr. Schramm tells us that another reason why we find problems in bringing change to our people, is that we think of them too much as individuals. It is true that a society or culture cannot change until the individual person changes, but these individual people live in groups. They work and play in groups. They feel very close to their clan, or group, or family or tribe. It is very hard for one person to go against the ideas of the people with whom he lives and works. He must usually change the ideas of everyone, or find another group to become a member of.

This means that if we can change things in a way that everyone will approve of, then change will be much easier. However, very often the things that need so much to be changed, are just those ideas which the group thinks are very important.

There are some ways broadcasters have found to help a whole group to change. Most often this happens when the tribe or clan is given some information about the problem, talks about it, and then *decides*, as a group, what to do. The people are *not told* what they must do. They think about the problem, and perhaps with a little help are able to find a solution that fits their community.

The Radio Forum (I16):

A good example of this is the "Radio Forum". In *Project G* we told you about panel discussions presenting the problems and facts to the listeners. The listeners then talked about these in discussion groups in their own towns and villages. They not only decided what they would do themselves, but they sent their decisions in letters to the radio stations. In this way they had a small part in helping the whole country make the right choices.

We told you about another way of working with a group in *Project H*. We said that you could begin to work through that person in the group or community who seemed to be the "authority" on a certain matter. In one Indian village, agricultural workers made the mistake of working with the political leaders. The political authorities were very co-operative, but they had very little influence on the way the farmers did their work. The farming leaders were different people, and the agricultural workers only began to make progress when they started working with the right "authorities".

The Use of Mass Media (I17):

Dr. Schramm tells us there are two important things we can learn from all of this:

> The mass media can fail to do the work they should. In fact, they can even do the opposite of what we intend, if we do not know enough about the culture we are working with. Time after time, people have failed in their use of the mass media, because they did not understand the people they were trying to help.
>
> There are some things the mass media can do, and other things they can only *help* to do. On radio we can only *tell* a farmer how to plant rice. Even if we were using television and could *show* the farmer how to plant, that still would not be as good as getting into the rice paddy and working *with* him.

The mass media cannot *make* people decide to do a certain thing. They can help by giving the group the information it needs, and by encouraging people to talk about the problem. The mass media cannot *do* the deciding, nor take action once the decision has been made.

This simply means that before we decide to use radio programmes for a certain reason, we should first ask ,"Is radio the best way to do this? Should we use another of the mass media? Can we use the mass media at all? Should we use the mass media *as well as* workers who will go out and talk with the people personally?"

Frank Palomares, DYSR, Philippines.

Radio can only tell this farmer how to plant rice. It cannot show him.

In most cases, it has been found that the last question should be answered "yes". As a rule, you should try to use all the media which the people are able to receive, *plus* workers who visit the people and work with them. Of course, we wouldn't use radio programmes to reach people who have no radios, just as we wouldn't use books or pamphlets to reach people who cannot read.

The most successful work has been done where radio was looked upon as just one tool among many. The agency, organisation or church looked at its work and found out what tools could best be used to get it done. Radio programmes were not done separately. They were done as part of a much larger scheme using many different methods of reaching people.

What the Mass Media Can Do (I18):

We have said that the mass media can do some things well, but other things not so well. Here are some of the things the mass media *can* do.

A wise African once told Dr. Schramm that the mass media are like magic "because they can take a man up to a hill higher than any we can see on the horizon and let him look beyond". At I17 you can see a picture of a farmer riding a water buffalo. When that photograph was taken, he was listening to a translated broadcast of two spacemen circling the earth in a satellite.

Certainly the mass media can let a man listen to things he could never hear otherwise, and know people he can never meet. They can bring far away things close, and make people in a distant village a part of the life of the nation and the world.

This is important, because people are helped to understand their countrymen in another part of their nation. The listener learns to know about people of other countries. Then when they meet, they are not total strangers. Everybody gets along more easily, because they were introduced by the mass media.

Telling Us What is Important (I19):

So much of what we learn about things outside of our own home comes from the mass media. For most of us, the things we know about our country's politics, its development, its people, come to us through newspapers, radio and books. Because of this, our ideas as to who is important, and what is important, are shaped by these media. The Prime Minister of my country may not be the most important man in my nation. However, I think of him as being most important, because every day I hear about him on the radio and read about him in the news-papers.

We all know that a politician has very little chance in an election unless he uses the mass media well. The more developed the mass media are, the more this is true. This is because the mass media can call people's attention to the politician just as the mass media can call attention to many other matters.

This is important because it means that through the mass media, attention can be kept on the things that will help your people the most. Constantly keeping your listeners aware that there are better ways of farming, or that other import-ant things need changing, can help a great deal in bringing these things about.

Making People Want Things (120):

We can learn something from those radio stations that have commercial advertising. These stations try to make people *want* or desire the things that are advertised.

When people learn of new things and of the changes that are happening in other places, they may also learn that things *can* be changed for the better in their own villages. They may learn that as people and as a nation they *can* work together for a better life; that life can be better because of the things they do.

There is a danger in this. People should not be taught to want things they have no hope of getting. Otherwise, they will simply become unhappy. It is not right to encourage your listeners to desire motor-bikes, when they could not and should not be buying them.

Once again this means that radio cannot work by itself. For instance, if you are making programmes that will make people want a better rice harvest, then there must be workers who go into the villages to show people better ways of farming. Better seed and fertiliser must also be made available.

Helping People Decide (121):

We often think the mass media are more powerful than they really are. Because we speak very strongly against this idea or that practice, we feel people will listen and will change. This does not usually happen, unless the listeners already agree with most of the things we say.

The mass media are not very effective for changing strong ideas or customs. People have come to believe in these ideas and customs because they have

L

worked very well in the past. The people are members of a group. Because the group holds these ideas and customs, it is very hard for one person to go against them. He might lose his family and his friends if he did so.

Our minds work in strange ways. When we believe something very strongly, we may do three things:

> We look for ideas and arguments among our friends and in the mass media that will support our beliefs.
> We turn away from arguments that go against the things we believe.
> Sometimes we turn the arguments around, so that they support what we believe, even though that may not have been the intention of the speaker. We are not aware that we do this, but all of us do it none the less.

Changes of ideas and customs usually come about from within a group. We think the way most of the others in our group think, because we enjoy the friendship and the togetherness of that group. Our happiest times are when we are with our families, or with the people in our churches or clubs, and we learn to act and think the way the other people in this group do. It is the same with people everywhere.

This means that if we are going to change ideas and customs through the use of the mass media, we must use a carefully thought-out method.

Person-to-person Communication (I22):

A radio programme can be used very well to "feed" the communication that takes place between people in the groups. We can broadcast information and ideas that are interesting to talk about. This information and these suggestions will gradually help people decide for themselves what they should do or how they should decide. We can also try to reach the leaders or "authorities" which we have mentioned several times. As Dr. Schramm says:

> "When agricultural information is carried in the mass media, there is a very high chance that this same information will be picked up and repeated by the agricultural 'influentials'. When information on child care is carried, there is a good chance that the woman whose advice on child care is important will pick the information up and repeat it.".

Of course, this will not happen if these leaders do not have radios, or if they are strongly against the ideas being broadcast. But if they have radios, and do not disagree too much, there is a good chance that your radio programmes can "feed" them with ideas that will help bring the changes.

Changing Ideas a Little (I23):

We have said that the mass media do not work very well for directly changing strong cultural habits or strong ideas. However, the mass media can change customs and ideas that the listener does not feel very strongly about. The mass media can also change new ideas and customs that have not yet become a very important part of the culture. For instance, if you can make the farmers feel that the new way of planting rice is just a *very small* change from the way they have been doing it for many years, the farmers will be able to accept the change much more easily.

Also, if people have already agreed that it is good to learn how to read, then it is much easier to persuade them to attend a certain class that will teach them, or to listen to a radio programme that will help them learn reading.

Making a Leader Important (I24):

We all like to hear our names on the radio or read about ourselves in the newspaper. This is because it helps us to feel important. It also makes our friends and the people in our community think of us as important.

The mass media can be very useful in building the leadership of those who are trying to help the community. By telling your listener about the good work a nurse is doing in a certain village, or the help which a minister or priest is giving, we make them important in the eyes of those they work with. It also helps the workers themselves feel their work is worth while.

The mass media can also help a certain person gain the respect of his neighbours, if the good things he has done are talked about on the radio.

Helping People Learn to Enjoy Things (I25):

People learn to like what they see and hear. That is not completely true, of course, but it does happen a great deal in music and art. In many countries, a new song will not become well-known until it is heard on radio. It also happens that a new song is rejected simply because it is unfamiliar. If you use music in your radio programmes (and you certainly should) you will have a part in shaping the musical taste of your listeners.

This is important in a new country where people in one area do not know very much about their countrymen from another part of the nation. Music, poetry, stories, and legends can form a bridge between one group and another. As people learn to enjoy these arts, they will soon have a shared field of experience which will help them to understand each other and to work together. So music, legends, drama, and poetry can be very useful to any radio studio which is trying to build a sense of "nationhood" among its listeners.

Radio in the Schools (126):

In many nations, the mass media are used a great deal for education. Whenever you make a programme that tries to help people, you are doing an educational programme, even though it may not have anything to do with a school.

However, the mass media are also being used more and more in the classrooms. In the schools, however, the mass media can only *help*. A radio programme cannot take the place of the teacher, just as you cannot give someone a book and expect that he will learn to read.

A radio programme can be very useful to a teacher. It can bring dramas, music, talks, and important people to the classroom. These are things that the teacher might not be able to give to the class. It can help the teacher do things he could not do by himself.

In a few cases, radio broadcasts must be used because there are not enough teachers, or because the teachers do not have enough training. This is not as effective as when the teacher uses a radio broadcast as a *tool* to aid his own instruction.

We said earlier in this project that in a village, the best results come when a worker goes to the villagers, talks to them, answers their questions, works with them, and uses a radio broadcast to help his work. In a classroom, person-to-person communication also works best. There can be excellent results when a good teacher uses a good radio programme in the classroom.

What Radio Cannot Do (127):

Radio is not magic. It cannot change a nation overnight. A radio programme is not going to make everyone agree with you or decide to help you. Radio can do some things, but only *some* things.

We have all heard stories of how wonderfully powerful some radio programmes have been, and how they have swayed the minds of a whole nation. Many of these stories are true, but we must remember that these things often happened under unusual circumstances.

When a government can control *all* the media of information: radio, news-papers, books, schools, and even what people say to each other; then it is some-times possible to control the minds of people. Fortunately, this does not happen very often.

Most broadcasters find there are many media trying to catch the attention of people. Even the most powerful broadcasts reach only some of the people, and these people often have many other sources of information, news and ideas. None of the mass media are as powerful as person-to-person communication, except that they can reach more people at one time.

Radio broadcasts can do many things when used well. Remember, however, that they cannot do more than what we have talked about in Part Two of this project, and they can do that only, when a broadcaster uses the best skill and the best knowledge to make his programmes.

Programme Targets (128):

Why does your studio make radio programmes? It would probably take a long explanation to answer that question. Some of you might not be able to answer. Some of you may be working in studios that have their reasons (or objectives) very clearly thought out and written down. Others may work at studios where no one really quite knows why they are making programmes, except that money comes from somewhere to pay the salaries and so they continue working.

> If you are hoping to hit a target with a gun or an arrow, you must know *where* that target is, and you must be able to *see* it. A radio studio is not going to do a good job if it does not know exactly what that job is. It will not fulfil its purpose if it does not know what that purpose is.

The objectives in each studio may be somewhat different. Find out if you can, what these objectives are and study them carefully.

Assignment Five (129):

Do *one* of these:

> If your studio has a well-developed list of objectives, study them carefully, and then answer each of the questions in the list below.

If your studio has only a partly-developed list of objectives, or none at all, use these questions to help you make a list of objectives for your studio.

In each case, be sure you tell *why* you think the way you do.

Whom are we trying to help? What groups of people? Which is the group we must help most?

Why do we want to help them? What is the *real* reason we spend time and money for these broadcasts? This is the most important question.

Do these people want our help? What do they think about us? How do they feel about the changes we want to make?

What other groups or agencies are helping us? In what way is our work related to theirs?

In what ways can radio be used to reach these people? In what ways should it not be used?

Be careful not to give quick easy answers, especially to the second question, "Why do we want to help them?" Do not hesitate to talk to as many people in the studio as you can, to get their ideas. Be sure to talk to your supervisor and ask for his suggestions. If there are other ideas that should go into your objectives put them down, but be sure you tell *why* you included them.

Assignment Six (I30):

Ask your supervisor for tape-recordings of three different kinds of programmes used in your country. They should be programmes between ten and thirty minutes long, which were intended to help the people of your country in some way. Your supervisor may ask you to choose three different kinds of programmes that are being broadcast in your area. If possible, have these recorded on tape so that you can listen to each one several times.

As you listen to each programme, answer the following questions. In each case explain *why* you gave the answer that you did. You may need to go back to your research file to help you remember certain things about the culture you are concerned with.

What kind of an audience do you think the programme is aimed at?

What kind of change is it trying to bring to this audience?

In what way will this programme help (or not help) the audience make this change?

Did this programme make good use of the radio medium, or was it trying to do something radio could not do well?

In which of the following ways did the programme try to help its audience? Did it try to help:

by bringing the world to people through information and entertainment,

by calling the attention of the listener to the idea or information,

by making people want something new,

by helping people decide by "feeding" the leaders with ideas and information,

by changing old ideas or customs just a little,

by changing new ideas that have not yet become an important part of the culture,

by making a leader seem important,

by helping with education in schools,

by some other method we have not talked about?

Do you think the programme was successful? Why? In what ways do you think it could have been improved?

Listen to the programmes as many times as you need to, but be sure there is good reasoning behind the answers you give. When you feel you have thought through all your answers carefully, take them to your supervisor, along with the work you did for Assignment Five.

A Venezuelan harpist.

PROJECT J

Music Programmes

If we were to ask the question, "What kind of programmes are used by almost every radio station in the world?" the answer would be, "Music programmes." There are several reasons for this:

> Almost everyone enjoys listening to music, since it is part of every culture. Music is well-suited to radio broadcasting.
> A music programme usually takes less time to produce, especially where gramophone records can be bought. In many places it also costs less.

Radio stations have different reasons for producing music programmes. Here are some of them:

> to encourage more people to listen to the radio station,
> to provide pleasure for the listener,
> to help the listener learn to enjoy and appreciate a certain kind of music,
> to help the listeners feel a certain way; that is, to create a mood,
> to provide information or education, and
> to communicate a message through the music.

Of course, there may be other reasons, and a music programme may be produced for several of these at one time. It is important to know what your reasons are before you begin making any programme. However, there are several things you must find out about your audience and your music before you can answer the question, "Why am I making this programme?"

What is Music? (J2):

That is a very difficult question. Music comes in so many forms in so many parts of the world. We can say that most music is made up of rhythm (the beat or pulse of the music), melody (the tune), and usually harmony (several notes together which make a pleasant sound).

We can also say that people like music because it appeals to their emotions; it can make them happy, sad, angry. Music can comfort them when they are sad and it can make them feel like fighting. Music is used by lovers and warriors, and in fact, by people in almost every kind of situation, to express every kind of feeling.

People find different emotions in music. Music that makes me feel one way may make you feel a different way.

> Three young Asians from different countries were listening to some music. One said, "It makes me feel like dancing." Another said, "It makes me feel sad." The third man said, "It reminds me of a war dance." They were all listening to a piece of Western music called "The Flight of the Bumblebee".

This does not show that any of the young men were wrong. It simply shows us that because they came from different parts of the world, each one got a different feeling from the music.

Music and Emotions (J3):

The people of your country have learned to love certain kinds of music. They react to this music the way they do, because your people have heard certain songs at certain times.

> If they have heard a song very often at a funeral, they may feel sad when they hear it again, even if there is no funeral. If they heard a song many times at a wedding, they may feel joyful whenever they hear that song again.

People have eyelids to close their eyes, but there is no way they can close their ears. Our ears are always open. Sound means much to us, and music is a pleasing sound; therefore music is one the easiest forms of art to enjoy.

Doctors tell us that music can help people work harder, or feel less tired. Music can help us bear pain, or sometimes make us feel pain.

Since music can do so many things to our emotions or feelings, we should be careful how we use it. We must try to consider the ways in which people will feel when they hear a song. We must try to be sure that the feeling the music gives will not be harmful.

Many Kinds of Music (J4):

Since there are so many different kinds of music in the world, we cannot say very much that will help you make good decisions about what music to use. Nevertheless, you must make such decisions, if you are going to produce good programmes.

Here are some questions you could ask about any piece of music. They may help you judge each music selection before you use it.

Is this music of high quality? Are the musicians doing their best?

Does this music have a clear pleasing sound? Is the recording of good quality?

How will our listeners feel when they hear this music?

Will our listeners understand this music? Will our listeners enjoy this music?

Do the words of the song tell about something that will benefit our listeners?

The Record Library (J5):

One of the most important places in any studio or station is the record library, the room where the gramophone records are kept. Some radio stations have thousands of records, and some have only a few. If you have many records to choose from when making your programmes, you will find it much easier to make music programmes which will really serve your listener. You should do everything you can to encourage and help your studio add good recordings to the library. However, it is possible to produce excellent music programmes from even a small library, if the selections in that library have been well chosen.

The first thing you must do is to become familiar with the record library.

Learn enough about the records in the library to have a general idea of what you might find. Listen to as many as you can.

Become very familiar with the way in which the catalogue or listing of records works. You should know how to find any record quickly and easily.

Learn the rules of the library. If you have a person in charge of the library, ask him to explain everything about it.

Look up the words GRAMOPHONE, GRAMOPHONE NEEDLE, and GRAMOPHONE RECORD in the glossary, and read what it says carefully. Practise taking a record out of the cover, placing it on the gramophone, and putting it back into the cover again. It is important that you learn this, otherwise you may cause damage to the records. The glossary tells you how to do this.

Kinds of Music Programmes (J6):

There is almost no end to the variety of ways you can do a music programme. Each programme is different from the next depending on the person who prepares the programme, the audience for which it is prepared, the station on which it is broadcast, the music that is used, etc.

However, there are three basic kinds of music programmes. These are as follows:

The formal programme has a special script written for it and the programme follows a certain set pattern.

The informal programme is also known in some places as a "disc-jockey" programme. Here the announcer speaks without a script: that is, he "AD-LIBS" everything he says. The pattern of this type of programme is very loose. Look up the word *"ad-lib"* in the glossary.

The programme where music has a minor part sometimes just gives the listener a little rest from the talking; sometimes it helps give the programme a certain mood; sometimes it makes a bridge from one subject to another.

Planning a Music Programme (J7):

Before you can decide which music to use, or what kind of a programme it will be, you must think first about your listener. What audience do you hope to reach? If necessary, go back to your research notes to help you decide.

Next you should ask, "What is the purpose of this programme? In what way will this programme be useful?" Then by keeping in mind your audience, and the purpose of your programme, you can begin to plan the music.

There is a very old rule that we can use for all art, including music programmes:

Variety within Unity

By unity, we mean that the programme sticks together. There is something about all the music selections and the talking that makes the listener feel they belong on the same programme. Each piece of music must be related to the other in some way. It may be that:

the style of music is similar,
the same performer does each selection,
all the pieces tell about the same subject, or
all the selections come from the same place.

There are many things that can tie a programme together to give it unity.

However, a programme that has only unity is dull. There must also be variety. There must be enough difference from one piece of music to the next, so that the listener stays interested.

Arranging the Order of the Music (J8):

The first selection of music should help the listener to know what kind of a programme it is going to be. It should set the mood of your programme, but it should also help to make the listener interested. This first selection should please as many listeners as possible. Therefore, it should be one that most of your listeners know quite well.

Next you must decide what your closing selection will be. In many ways it should be like your opening music. It should be something that will make your listener want to hear the programme again next time it is on the air.

Arrange the rest of your selections so that they flow smoothly from one piece to the other. Do not put all your lively melodies together, nor all your quiet ones. The mood of the programme should change a little from one selection to the next. There are many ways this can be done, depending on the kind of music and the programme. At *J28* we have an example of a script of Philippine folk-songs, called "Bayanihan". The mood of this programme could be put into a picture like this.

Because the selections in this programme are mostly dances, the mood is mostly in the rhythm. The "Pukol" is the liveliest of the dances and so it is placed last. The first selection, the "Tinikling", is the next liveliest, followed by "Magtanim", and so forth down to the slowest one, the "Sagayan". There is unity in this programme because all of the songs are Philippine dances which must be performed in groups, and most are played by a Filipino band called "rondalla". Variety is found not only because there are different rhythms, but because the "Kalinga Dance" and the "Sagayan" come from groups within the Philippines that might be called "minorities". The "Kalinga Dance" and "Sagayan" are dances most Filipinos do not hear very often, which is why they are presented between dances that are already very popular.

When you introduce new music, do it a little at a time. Try to make your listener interested by saying something he might like to know about the music or the performer. If it is a long selection, see if it is possible to play only a part of it. You might play it again the following programme just to remind your listener. If so, do not use it again for several programmes, but do play it from time to time until it has become familiar.

Making Selections Shorter (J9):

Some pieces of music are very long. Remember that the problem of attention span bothers us in music also. The more unfamiliar the music, the shorter the attention span.

Many countries have very long folk-songs that tell a story. You will have to decide for yourself whether it is wise to play the whole song, or just a part of it. Sometimes there may not be enough time to play it all, even if the audience would like to hear it. You can make it shorter by playing the first part of the song, telling the story yourself in your own words, and then playing the very last part of the song.

Try to avoid repeating the same music over and over again, even if a selection is very popular and you receive many letters asking for it. Even though many may like it, many will also soon find it very boring.

Children like to listen to the same song over and over again. However, if you are doing a children's programme, remember that older people may be listening also.

Writing a Music Programme Script (J10):

The purpose of your script should be the same as the general purpose of your programme. Your script should be written for the same kind of audience as the one for which you chose your music. It should be written to help the music reach the purpose of the programme. It can do this by:

saying interesting things about the music,
providing information about the music,
building little "bridges" between the pieces of music,
presenting a message or other information that fits in with the music, or by
making the mood of the programme stronger.

If the music is the most important part of your programme, then the "talking" or the script should be as short as possible. Too much talking on a programme, unless it is very well done, may make the listener lose interest and turn off his radio.

Of course, there are many excellent programmes where the music is not the most important thing. In these programmes, the writer or producer knows that because the attention span of listeners is very short, he can give his information a little bit at a time, and then can let the listener rest a little and enjoy some music.

Many people find it hard to listen to fifteen minutes of talking. If the same information can be broken up into little pieces about two minutes long, and if music can be found that fits the listener and the information, a half-hour programme of music and information might be much more effective and popular.

Resources (J11):

People who write radio programmes often seem to be saying the same things in the same way each time.

If the writer or the announcer searches his language for new ideas he can avoid this. You and your studio should make a constant search for new information about the music in your record library. Some studios fasten this information on the record covers. Others have a file in which they put newspaper items, magazine articles and all other information about the music and musicians. They also have a number of good books about music. Although these things are very useful, they may not be possible for every studio. Even so, no opportunity should be lost to gather useful information and put it together in such a way that it can easily be used by everyone in the studio.

The script for the programme "Bayanihan" at the end of this project (*J28*) is an example of one kind of script. Look at it and see if you think it is a good example or a bad one.

Music Cues (*J12*):

Look up the word CUE in the glossary. You will find that the second meaning given has to do with the length of time between one part of a programme and another. In a music programme, the length of time is important:

> between the announcer and the beginning of the music, and
> between the end of the music and the announcer.

It is one of the things that gives a programme "pace", or a feeling of movement. We cannot say that the length of time should be one second, or three seconds or ten seconds. This is something for which you must listen; it is something you must learn to *feel*. It depends so much on the music and the audience.

Generally speaking, the faster the music, the faster the cues. The most important thing, however, is that the announcer and the technician know their equipment well enough so that they can make the cue the exact length they feel is right for the programme. They will usually not look at a clock to do this, but will try to feel what is right for the mood of their programme. Cues must not be left to chance.

Assignment One (*J13*):

Here is an assignment to help you learn a little more about music in your country.

Find out as much as you can about the music of your country. Find out if there are any books or magazines that have useful information, and if there are any people who might be able to tell you something helpful. Talk to some of the musicians in your area, to find out more about the kind of music they play. There may also be someone (perhaps at a university) who is studying or teaching music. If so, try to talk to him. Here are some of the questions to which you should try to find answers:

> What kind of music is enjoyed by most people in my country?
> Is this music similar to music from any other places? If so, what place, and in what ways?

What kinds of foreign music can be used in your country?

Do different groups of people in our country have different kinds of music?

Are there other kinds of music enjoyed in my country? What kinds?

Are the people of my country beginning to like music from other places? (For instance, the music of the Congo and West Africa is spreading to the rest of Africa.) How much do people like it? What other kinds of foreign music do they like?

Is there a new kind of music developing which is bringing together my own national music and the foreign music? If so, is this resulting in a good kind of music? Why?

Write as much of this information as possible and put it in your research file; then prepare a full report for your supervisor, giving as much of this information as you feel will help your programming.

Assignment Two (J14):

Select three different kinds of music programmes that are being heard by listeners in your area. At least one should be a popular music programme. You may choose these from one of the radio stations in your country, and if so, try to have them tape-recorded. You will need these again for Assignment Three. Your studio may have some tapes to which you could listen. Write a few paragraphs on each programme, answering the following questions:

What seemed to be the purpose of the programme?

What kind of music was used? Did it fit in with the purpose of the programme?

What kind of an audience would have found this programme most useful and enjoyable?

In what way would it have been useful?

Was the music of high quality? Were there any selections you feel should not have been included?

Did the programme have "variety within unity"? In what way? Could it have been improved?

Was the music arranged in an interesting order?

What was good about the arrangement? What was not good?

Did the script fit in with the purpose of the programme? Was it an interesting script? How could it have been improved?

Were there new words and phrases that made the programme fresh and lively?

When you have finished Assignments One and Two, take them to your supervisor.

Programme Series (J15):   PART TWO

All of the suggestions given in the rest of this project are important when making music programmes. However, they are just as important for any kind of programme you may wish to do.

If you are planning a programme series, remember that the idea of "variety within unity" should be used for the whole series as well as for each individual programme. There should be a "theme" or an "idea" that is found in all the programmes, and yet each programme should be a little different from the others.

It is wise to make a plan for all the programmes in a series, so that you are certain you have enough material and ideas for all of them.

Choosing a Name (J16):

There are a few things to remember when deciding on a name for any programme. The name (or title) should:

be short enough to be remembered easily,
be short enough to be put into a printed programme list,
give the listener an idea of what he can expect on the programme (it should not be misleading),
be "ear-catching"; that is, it should sound interesting, and it should be a good clear use of your language.

Opening and Closing Announcements (J17):

There are many ways of making opening or closing announcements. Sometimes they are very simple. For instance:

A programme might begin like this:
"Hello, this is Kim Lee talking about market day."
It might close simply by saying:
"Thank you. Good night."

Other programmes may have openings and closings with music and sound effects. However, they all do much the same three things.
A programme opening:

answers the question "who?". When someone telephones you the first thing you ask is, "Who is speaking?" The radio listener wants to know that also. Sometimes just a name is enough. However, if a person is talking because he is an official of an organisation, then you must also include his title in your introduction. If the speaker is famous for another reason, you must let the listener know what it is.
Ask yourself, "What does the listener want to know about this person?" Be polite, but use as few words as possible.

answers the question "what?". The listener wants to know what kind of a programme it is going to be and what it is about. You should somehow tell the listener that it is going to be a drama, or a talk, or a music programme. Also tell him what the subject is.

answers the question "why?". If there is a special reason for presenting a programme, the listener should be told. If you are speaking for a certain organisation, then the listener has a right to know this. Sometimes it would be easier to hide your purpose from the listener, but it would be dishonest. Your listener would find out in any case, and then would consider you untruthful because you hid the real purpose.

Here is an example of an opening and closing announcement. Does it answer the three questions?

ANNCR: Are the people of our nation really learning to read? Here is Mr. David Bhotilai, President of the National Literacy Committee, to tell us what progress we are making.

TALK: MR. BHOTILAI. . . .   4' 12"

ANNCR: Thank you, sir. Mr. David Bhotilai, President of the National Literacy Committee, has told us about the progress our nation is making in teaching people to read.

There must be many better ways of opening and closing programmes.

Go to your radio. Listen to a few programmes. Listen to the ways in which they are opened and closed.

Did they answer the questions: "Who?", "What?", and "Why?"?

Were they interesting enough to make you want to listen to the programme?

Were you disappointed because the opening made the programme sound better than it turned out to be?

Signature Music (J18):

Look up the word SIGNATURE in the glossary. The signature or theme music should be carefully chosen and carefully used. However, it is not always necessary to use signature music. Use it only if you think it really helps the programme. Signature music should be chosen because it represents or shows the listener, the mood or the idea of the programme. The only way to decide this is to be sure you know the exact mood of the programme, as well as the information or entertainment it will give. Then you must listen to many pieces until you find one that seems to fit best.

If you have a music programme, your signature music should be the same kind as most of the selections you will use. The signature should give the listener a little taste of the kind of music that will follow.

Signature music should be interesting. It must be very good music if you are going to use it on every programme for a whole series.

If there are words to your signature tune, remember that *both* the words and the music must fit the programme. Sometimes you may use the music of the song without the words being heard. If the song is well known, the listener will remember the words even if they are not heard. For this reason the words must fit in with the mood and idea of the programme, even if the words are not heard in the theme music.

When choosing theme music always ask, "What will this make the audience think of?" If it makes your listeners think of something that fits your programme then the music can be used.

One broadcaster was doing a health programme. A listener wrote to him saying, "Did you know that in our part of the country your signature music is called "I am Ready to Die"? The broadcaster quickly found another selection.

Fitting the Words to the Music (J19):

In some very large stations, when a producer wants a signature tune, he gets a composer to write it for him, and an orchestra to play it. Very few of you will be so fortunate. For that reason, you should learn to fit the words of your opening and closing announcements to the recorded music. By doing this carefully, you can often make it sound as if the music was composed just for your words. Before you can do this, you will need to listen to your signature music many times.

Listen to see if the music is divided into phrases. Western music is divided into phrases, or places where the music pauses or changes to a new idea. A phrase in music is like a sentence in writing.

If you wish to FADE your signature so that you can speak over the top of your music, do it at the end of a phrase. Look up the word *fade* in the glossary.

Listen to several selections of your own country's music. Is it divided into phrases? Are there any pauses or changes in the music. Ask someone else, perhaps someone who understands music, to listen with you and tell you where you might be able to fade your music. It is important to find good places for fades, or they will not sound natural. As much as possible, it should seem as if the music was *composed* so that it would become quieter or louder at the place where you are fading.

Fading (J20):

You will learn the art of fading best by listening hard and often. Listen to other radio programmes to see how other producers are doing their fades. Listen to stations in your own country and to some foreign broadcasts as well. Always ask these questions: Does it sound natural? Does the music seem to fit in with the words? Does the music seem to *fade down* and *fade up* in the *right* places?

In the glossary you will find some drawings which may help you understand the ways in which fades should be handled. Notice that the music begins to fade down just a little as the announcer begins to speak. Then when he speaks, it fades quickly into the *background*. When you *fade up*, the music begins to get louder just a few short moments before the announcer finishes talking, and then goes up to full volume very quickly after the announcer finishes.

Remember that the drawings in the glossary may give us some ideas about fades, but they will not teach us how fades are really done. There are many kinds of music, and each one must be used slightly differently. There are many moods of programmes, and this too will make the fade a little different.

You need not memorise a great many different things about this. What you must do is train your ear to *hear* the little things that make the difference between a bad fade and a good one. Although your listener may not be able to explain it to you, he will feel the difference. He will enjoy a programme which is well done much more than one which is poorly done, even though he would not be able to tell you why.

Assignment Three (J21):

Find the tapes you used in Assignment Two. Listen to the opening and closing portions of the programmes. At least one of the programmes should have signature music at the beginning and end. If not, find another programme which does. Write a short paragraph explaining your answers to these questions:

What was the name of the programme? Was it a good name? Why? Could you suggest a better name?

Did the opening and closing announcements answer the questions: "Who?", "What?", and "Why?"?

Was the opening announcement interesting enough to make the listener want to continue listening? Why do you think so?

Did the signature music fit in with the rest of the programme? Was it interesting? Could you suggest better signature music? Why?

Did the words in the opening and closing announcements fit in with the signature music? Describe the way this was done and suggest ways it could have been done better.

When you have finished Assignment Three, take your paragraphs to your supervisor.

Putting a Script on Paper (J22):   PART THREE

Your last assignment in this project will be to write a music programme. You have already written several scripts as you worked through this manual. Here are some suggestions that will help you make your script easier to handle and to read.

There are different ways of putting a script on paper. Much will depend on the kind of writing you are using. Some writing, such as English, goes from left to right. Other writing, such as Arabic, goes from right to left. Some goes up and down on the page, such as Chinese. All of this will make a great difference to the way you put your script on a page.

Ask your supervisor to help you find three different kinds of scripts which were written in your language and in your country. If possible, you should have a script for a talk, one for a music programme, and another for a drama. Study these scripts carefully to see how they are done.

Here are some of the things many good producers like to have on their scripts. The first page should have:

    the name of the programme,
    the day it will be broadcast,
    the exact time of day it will be broadcast,
    the name of the writer, producer, announcer, etc., and
    the number of the programme if it is part of a series.

There may be other things which your studio also wants put on the first page. Ask your supervisor about this.

All other pages should have:

    the number of the page,
    the name of the programme, and
    the number of the programme.

Suggestions for Script Typing (J23):

Here are some ideas that many radio people found helped them in their writing:
    Use a typewriter. Writing by hand is too slow; it is hard to read; and it is hard to make carbon copies. Unless there is a very good reason why you should not learn to use a typewriter, learn immediately. If possible, use a typewriter with fairly large letters.
    Leave spaces between your lines (double space). No person can read a script with the lines close together as well as he can read a script with spaces between the lines. It may save paper to put your lines close together, but it will cost you more in poor programmes.

Radio scripts must always be typed.

Write out abbreviations (short-forms) in full, unless they are very well known to the person reading the script.

Do not begin a sentence on one page, and finish it on another. Finish each sentence on its own page, and start each new page with a new sentence.

Use soft paper. "Newsprint" is good, or any paper that is fairly heavy and soft. Do not use very thin paper like "onion skin". This will make a noise when it is held close to a microphone. A piece of paper can sound like thunder on the radio.

Use one side of the paper only. A paper turned over near a mike will sound noisy. If you want to save paper, use the other side for another script later on. Remove the paper-clips or staples before you go to the microphone. Slide the pages to one side as you read them. Do not turn them over or they will make a noise.

Never think that a script is good enough just because the person reading it does not stumble. A good announcer may not stumble or pause when reading a bad script, but he will have to work harder trying to make out *what* he is saying, instead of thinking of *how* he is saying it.

Make your script neat and easy to read. Leave plenty of space on the paper. If you have made corrections, be sure they are clear and understandable. A script carefully put on the paper, will not make a good programme. There must be good writing and good research. However, a badly-typed script that is confusing to the reader, can spoil the good work the writer has done.

There is a system used by most radio studios in countries where they use the Roman alphabet (the kind you are reading now). In this system, all of the *instructions* to the engineers, the announcers, musicians, etc., are written in capital letters LIKE THIS. Everything that is going to be *spoken* by the announcer or the actors is written in small letters 'like this'. You will find an example of such a script at *J38*.

This system may not work in your country. Arabic, for instance, does not have any capital letters. Many of the studios using Arabic underline the instructions, like this.

If there is a system already being used in your country, then find out what it is and use it if possible. It is important, however, that a person reading your script can see very easily what things should be *said* by the announcer or the actors, and what things are *instructions* for those helping to make the broadcast.

Glossary Assignment (J24):

Look up the following words in the glossary, then translate the *meaning* into your own language.

CONTINUITY	GRAMOPHONE RECORD
FADE	PRE-FADE LISTENING
FADER	SEGUE
FILL-UP	SIGNATURE
GRAMOPHONE	SNEAK
GRAMOPHONE NEEDLE	

Assignment Four (J25):

Beginning with the information you have from the research projects you have done, write and record a music programme using gramophone records. The programme should be fifteen minutes long. Before you begin, write a few sentences explaining your purpose in making the programme, the kind of listener you have in mind as you are making the programme, and the way in which the programme will help your listener.

Plan your music carefully using the suggestions in this project; then choose signature music that fits well.

You will need to know the exact length of each piece of music that you choose. If it is not written on the record, then you must use a stop-watch and get the exact length of each selection. You will also need to time each part of your script, and then add all the times together to be sure your programme is exactly fifteen minutes in length. Remember that a 15′ 00″ programme is usually 14′ 30″ or 14′ 20″ or 14′ 40″. In other words, there is usually some time allowed for station calls and other things between programmes. Your supervisor can tell you exactly how much this should be. The script at the end of the project shows one way to write in the exact time of each part of the programme, so that you can easily know if your script will "time out".

Check-list for a Music Script (J26):

When you have written your script, use the following check-list to see if it is well done.

1. Does the script fulfil the purpose of the programme?	Yes ____ No ____
2. Does the music fit the purpose of the programme?	Yes ____ No ____
3. Will the audience you were aiming for find this programme interesting and helpful?	Yes ____ No ____
4. Is all the music of high quality?	Yes ____ No ____
5. Is the music arranged in an interesting order?	Yes ____ No ____
6. Is there "variety within unity"?	Yes ____ No ____
7. Is the script interesting and lively?	Yes ____ No ____
8. Does it show a good use of your language?	Yes ____ No ____
9. Have you avoided unnecessary talking?	Yes ____ No ____

Check your script carefully several times. Remember that you should go through all the stages of writing, editing, rewriting and editing as you did in *Projects A, B,* and *D.*

When you feel that you have the best script you can write (you should be able to answer "yes" to at least seven out of the nine questions) make arrangements to record your programme. You may need to record it several times before you feel it is good enough to present to your supervisor.

Check-list for a Music Programme (J27):

Use this check-list to find out if your programme is well done.

1. Was the signature music well chosen?	Yes ____ No ____
2. Were the fades well done?	Yes ____ No ____
3. Were the fades in the right places?	Yes ____ No ____
4. Were the music cues the right length?	Yes ____ No ____
5. Did the programme seem to move naturally from one part to another?	Yes ____ No ____
6. Was the speaking part of the programme interesting and smooth?	Yes ____ No ____
7. Did the speaking help the programme?	Yes ____ No ____
8. Was the programme exactly the right length?	Yes ____ No ____

When you feel your programme is as good as you can make it (you should be able to say "yes" to at least six of the eight questions) take it to your supervisor. Do not be unhappy if he makes some suggestions and asks you to do it over again. All of the world's best radio writers and producers have learned their art of doing things over and over again until they were exactly right.

A Sample Script (J28):

BAYANIHAN
(co-operation)

ANNCR: Bayanihan!

MUSIC: SIGNATURE: BAHAY KUBO: ESTABLISH FOR 15 SECONDS, FADE
UNDER AT END OF FIRST STANZA FOR: 15″

ANNCR: The spirit of "Bayanihan" is an ancient tradition in the
Philippines. It is the spirit of co-operation. We see the
"bayanihan" at work when people are planting rice, moving
a house, in a farming co-operative, or in the music and dances
of our many islands. Here is the "bayanihan" . . . in music.   15″

MUSIC: SIGNATURE: TO FULL AND PLAY TO END OF THIRD STANZA.   15″

ANNCR: Few of our Philippine dances require as much co-operation as
the lively and popular Tinikling. The people of Leyte give us
this dance, which takes its name from the long-legged bird
called the "tikling".   14″

MUSIC: TINIKLING: RONDALLA AND CHORUS   1′ 10″

ANNCR: If a complicated dance such as the Tinikling needs a lot of
co-operation, even more "bayanihan" is needed for a couple
to live together as man and wife. The Kalinga tribesmen
realise this, and so the whole community helps. Listen to the
bamboo guitar, the gongs, sticks and drums, as a Kalinga
tribesman announces that the ceremony is about to begin and
the bride and groom begin their wedding dance.   23″

MUSIC: KALINGA WEDDING DANCE: 1′ 10″

ANNCR: The Spanish "conquistadores" never reached the Kalingas.
Perhaps for that reason their culture gives us an indication of
what the lowland Filipino was like before the four hundred
years of Spanish rule. Although we did not always like the
Spaniards, still the spirit of "bayanihan" resulted in many
customs and ideas being taken into our culture. Among the
treasures the Spanish left us is the Polka Sala.   22″

MUSIC: POLKA SALA: RONDALLA   2′ 33″

ANNCR: "Bayanihan" or co-operation may be necessary, but it isn't
always fun. In fact, this next song says it very plainly, "Planting rice is never fun." Still it sounds like fun the way these

	people sing. Here is perhaps the most popular of Philippine folk songs, Magtanim Ay Di Biro.	17″
MUSIC:	MAGTANIM AY DI BIRO: CHORUS	2′ 44″
ANNCR:	During the years, a national "bayanihan" spirit has been growing. Because of this there is more co-operation and friendship with our Muslim brothers in Mindanao and Sulu. Among the many Muslim contributions to Philippine culture is music. Here is the Sagayan from the Province of Lanao, a dance once done in preparation for war.	19″
MUSIC:	SAGAYAN: KULINTANGAN (GONGS)	1′ 05″
ANNCR:	Weddings, ballroom dances, planting rice, and war all require co-operation. So does play! The people of Panay enjoy a playful time with the dance Pukol. The dancers have great fun beating out the rhythm with their coconut shells.	12″
MUSIC:	PUKOL: RONDALLA WITH COCONUT SHELLS.	2′ 01″
ANNCR:	The spirit of "bayanihan" in music.	03″
MUSIC:	SIGNATURE: BAHAY KUBO ESTABLISH TILL END OF FIRST STANZA THEN QUICK FADE FOR:	15″
ANNCR:	Our rich heritage of Philippine folk songs is teaching us more about the spirit of "bayanihan", a concept of co-operation that is helping to build our nation. We'll be bringing you more music of the "bayanihan" next Monday evening at 7:30. My name is Juan Garcia.	16″
MUSIC:	SIGNATURE: TO FULL TILL 14′25″ MARK OF TOTAL PROGRAMME TIME: THEN UNDER AND QUICKLY OUT FOR:	ABOUT 20″
ANNCR:	This is DYSR, The Voice of Christian Brotherhood, Dumaguete City . . . 840 on your radio dial.	05″

TOTAL TIME 14′ 30″

PROJECT K

Live Talent Programmes

For Large and Small (K1):

Radio studios can be very different. Some are very large with many staff members. They make many different kinds of programmes. Others are smaller. Some have only one or two staff members and produce only one programme.

In this project we will talk about people from outside the studio who come to help, about microphones, studios, and recording techniques, and about programmes in which listeners take part. You may not be doing all of these things at your studio, but it is still very important that you learn about them.

Things you learn about one kind of programme can very often be used on another kind. Your studio may grow and begin doing such things; your duties may change in the future; or you may be able to suggest some new programme ideas at your studio. For these reasons, *Project K* is just as important as any other part of this manual, even though you may not need some of this information right now.

Outside Talent (K2):

Almost every radio station or studio asks people who are not staff members, to come in and help with some of the programmes. They may be people who write or produce programmes; they may be actors; they may be musicians. Sometimes they may receive a high wage, sometimes only a small wage, and sometimes no money at all. The studio asks them to come and help because they have a certain talent needed in the programmes.

Every studio must be able to find such people if it is going to make more than just talking or recorded-music programmes. If you plan to make dramas, you will need actors, and if you wish to have music that is not on records, you will need musicians. Even in talk programmes, there are many not on your staff who have interesting and useful things to say to your listeners.

Therefore, most studios do everything they can to find out what kinds of talent they have in their communities, and how this talent can best be used. By doing this, they are able to use the ability and the imagination of far more people than they could have on the staff of the studio.

However, a studio cannot expect a group of talented people to come in by themselves and say, "I would like to help you." There must be a plan to search for such people, to train them, and to keep them interested in the work.

Searching for Talent (K3):

One of the best ways of beginning the search for talent, is to have a meeting with the staff of the studio. Talk about the problem of finding talent. Ask questions such as the following:

> Are there groups or organisations in our listening area that would be willing to help in the kind of work we are doing with our radio broadcasts? Would these organisations help us to find the right people? How can we work with these organisations so that we can help each other?
> Do we know of people who have said they are interested in our work and would be willing to help?
> Have we received any letters from listeners who show interest and ability?

At the staff meeting you would not only try to find answers to those questions, but you would also talk about other suggestions for finding talent. Here are two such suggestions:

> Announcements are made on the programmes or between programmes telling the listener that the studio needs talent. Such announcements should tell the listener what kind of talent is needed, what kind of education or qualifications people must have, and whether or not they will be paid for their work. They must also be told how to contact the studio.
> The studio sponsors a contest to find good talent. This can be done more easily to find writers, than to find actors or musicians. People send their scripts to the studio, and the best ones are used on the air. Some studios find it is best to ask those who wish to enter the contest to write first or to come into the station. They are then given some simple instructions on how to write the kind of scripts the studio needs.

Training Talent (K4):

There are many problems in using people not on the studio staff. Although these people may have ability, they usually need training before they can really be useful. For instance, a doctor may have great skill and knowledge in medicine, but would still need training before he could write good radio scripts.

For this reason, studios often find it necessary to hold workshops or training sessions to help such people learn more about the work they are asked to do. Parts of this training manual, especially the first four projects, might be used for such workshops.

Whenever people are asked to write for your studio, they should be told before they begin that their scripts will be edited, or perhaps even re-written by a member of the studio staff. Some experienced member of the staff should also evaluate each script, and send suggestions for improvement to the writer.

Keeping People Interested (K5):

Very often volunteers will write one or two scripts, or participate in a few programmes, and then lose interest. That is why it is necessary to keep encouraging them. Here are some suggestions:

Volunteers should be told very often why their work for the studio is important, and the way in which they are helping people by their work. Their names should be mentioned on the air whenever they have helped in a programme.

The studio should let the volunteers know often that their work is appreciated.

They should receive some money for their work if this is possible. Not only will it keep them interested, but it will make it easier for the studio to suggest improvements in their work. It will also be easier to get them to turn in their scripts at a certain time or to come to the studio at the right time. When people do not receive any pay for their work, the studio will usually have problems in getting high-quality work, or in keeping up with the schedule of broadcasts.

Going to the Talent (K6):

Now that better portable tape machines are available, studios can often go out to meet the talent. They do not have to wait for the talent to come to them.

N

Many stations go to the homes or offices of important people not only to interview them, but also to record talks.

Many studios make arrangements to record concerts or festivals which take place in the community.

One station sponsored a musical programme in a different village each week and offered prizes for the best performances. The best performances were saved and put into the record library for use another time.

Many communities are rich in talent and opportunity. If a broadcaster is willing to search for this talent, he may find material for many worthwhile programmes.

Is It Worth It? (K7):

Working with volunteer talent is sometimes difficult. Some studios have found it more trouble than it is worth. Other studios have been very successful.

If there are people at your studio who have experiences with volunteer talent, talk to them to find out what advice they might have, and what kinds of experiences they have had.

Microphones, Studios and Recording Techniques (K8):

It may seem strange that we change quickly from talking about volunteer talent, to discuss the ways in which microphones and studios are used for recording. However, in most smaller studios, such knowledge is most necessary when volunteers are used. It is when musicians and actors come into the studio that we must know these things, although they are also important when just one person is talking into a single microphone.

Some of you may work in studios where there are very clever technicians, who know all about the ways in which microphones should be used in the studios to record musicians, actors, and speakers. Most of you, however, will be working in small studios where you will do this work yourself. In either case, it is very useful to know something about this. If you are to produce a programme, you should know what things are possible in a studio. You should be able to talk to your technician about the kind of sound that is being heard so that you can work together for the best results. Perhaps you may never need to touch a microphone, but you will still find it very useful to know how it works and what it can do.

The Microphone (K9):

Begin by reading the item in the glossary under MICROPHONES. Then, if possible, ask a technician or your supervisor to help you understand this portion of *Project K*.

Perhaps you have heard it said that the microphone is like a human ear. That is only partly true. There are some very important differences.

You and I each have two ears. Because of this we can tell from which direction a sound is coming. A radio cannot do this because the microphones send all the sound into one loudspeaker, and so we hear all the sound coming from one place.

When you stand on a busy street talking to a friend, you hear his conversation but you probably are not bothered too much by the sound of the cars on the road, or the other people on the street. Your mind helps you focus on the sound that you want to hear.

If you took a tape-recorder and a microphone to the same place and recorded the same conversation (holding the microphone as far away from the speaker as your ear was) you might find it almost impossible to understand the talking because of the noise.

A microphone "hears" many little noises that we do not usually notice. We may be sitting in a room that seems quiet. If we made a recording in that room we would hear many little sounds that could spoil a programme. The sounds may be someone talking in the next room, a car going by, an electric fan, or even just the bumps and scrapes of chairs and people's feet.

Microphone Presence (K10):

We said that because all the sound picked up by microphones in a studio went into one loudspeaker, we could not tell from which direction the sound was coming. However, we can tell from the loudspeaker, whether the sound is far away or close by.

Radio actors use this in their dramas to let the listener know when they are coming and going. The change in sound as they move away from the microphone, is very much like the change in sound we hear when people move away from our ears.

However, there is another difference here between the ear and the microphone. The microphone makes distances sound much greater. An actor or a singer who is 2 metres (7 feet) away from the microphone may sound as if he is 20 metres (70 feet) away from the radio listeners.

This is what is called MICROPHONE PRESENCE. It is the feeling of distance or closeness that the listener gets when he hears the sound. Look up the words *off-microphone* and *on-microphone* in the glossary.

The Studio (K11):

The way a voice or a musical instrument sounds when heard through a microphone, depends also on the studio in which it is recorded. If you take a rubber ball and throw it against the wall, it will bounce back. If the wall is hard the ball will bounce back more. If you throw the ball very fast it will bounce back harder.

A wall reflects sound, just as it reflects a rubber ball. A hard wall makes the sound bounce more than a soft wall. A loud sound is reflected more than a quiet sound.

Read the item under ACOUSTICS in the glossary. Then if possible, have a technician explain what has been done in your studios to help the acoustics. Remember that there are no two studios in the world that are *exactly* alike.

Train your ear to listen for the things which make the sound seem better. Here are some of the things to listen for:

Echo: Look up this word in the glossary. In a very large hall, or in a very "live" studio, there may be too much echo or reflected sound. It may help to move the microphone closer to the performer. A public address system may cause a lot of echo also.

Clarity: Is the sound clear? Can you hear all the parts of the sound? Often people lose clarity by having their microphones too close to the speaker or musician.

Brilliance: This means that there is just enough "echo", or that the studio is just "live" enough to make the sound seem "bright" and "interesting".

It is possible to make a good guess about the acoustics of a studio or a room by simply clapping your hands sharply. If you do this and listen carefully, you will begin to hear a difference in the length of time it takes for the "echo" to disappear after your clap. You will find that a large room has a great deal more "echo" than a small room, although very much depends on the walls, ceiling, and floor of the room. A room with many curtains will not be as "live" because the curtains will soak up the sound. A room made of concrete or metal will be very "live".

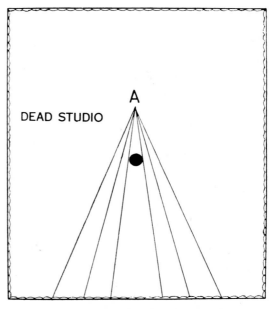

(*a*) In a "dead" studio, the sound is soaked up by the walls. Only the direct voice of the announcer (A) is heard by the microphone.

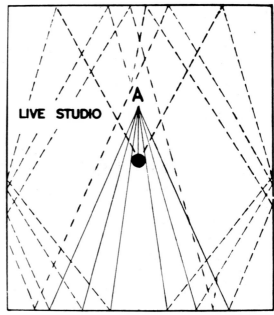

(*b*) In a "live studio, the micro-phone hears not only the direct voice of the announcer (A) but also some of the sound which has bounced from the walls of the studio.

Every broadcaster should spend some time experimenting with different microphones and different acoustic effects in his studios.

Some of the things that can affect the sound going into the microphone are:

the kind of microphone,
the direction from which the voice or sound is entering the microphone,
the distance from the microphone,
the size of the studio,
the shape of the studio, and
the kind of walls, floor and ceiling in the studio.

What we have told you will do little more than help you understand some of the problems of acoustics. As you gain experience, and if you keep your eyes and your ears open, you will learn a great deal more. Read and ask questions whenever you have the opportunity.

Microphone Balance (K12):

We have been talking about acoustics and about microphones because we must know about them in order to have good microphone balance in our programmes.

We have made some suggestions about this already. For instance, we suggested that a good way to keep members of a panel from moving about (and changing the microphone balance) is to ask them to keep their elbows on the table.

The drawing in *K13* show some arrangements of performers and microphones that have been used successfully. The same arrangements might not work in your studio, or they might work very well. That is why it is important to have a good rehearsal before the recording, so that there is plenty of time to try different arrangements. Remember that you can only judge the best arrangements of microphones and performers by listening to the loudspeaker in the control room.

Drawings of Microphone Positions (K13):

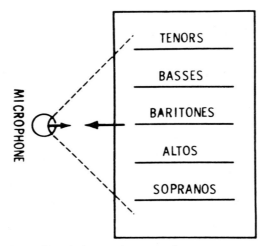

Many broadcasters have found that a choir can be recorded by having the singers form straight lines as shown in the drawing, rather than in a half circle. Experiment with many arrangements before you decide which is best.

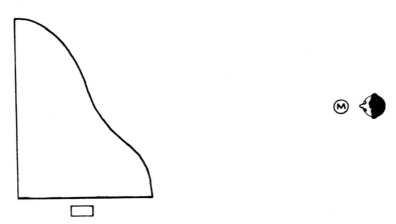

This is one way of setting up a microphone for a piano and singer. Sometimes a second microphone is placed along the curved edge of the piano.

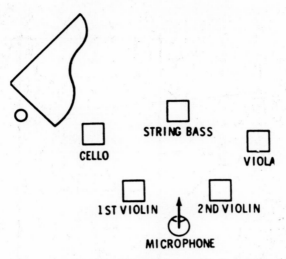

A small string orchestra may be arranged this way. There are other ways that may be more suitable for your studio.

Short-wave Broadcasts (K14):

Many of you may be preparing programmes that will be used on a *short-wave* radio station. If so, there are certain things you should watch for, because the kind of sound your listener hears is not the same as it is on a *medium-wave* broadcast. Ask a technician or your supervisor to explain the difference between short-wave and medium-wave if you do not already know.

Short-wave broadcasts almost always have some *fading*; that is, the sound gets quieter for a few moments. For that reason, it is best to use fades on your programme only when necessary. It also means that a quiet part of music may sound as if the station has grown weak and faded away.

Short-wave broadcasts suffer from *distortion*. Something happens that changes the sound so that it no longer sounds natural. Often the listener cannot understand what has been said for a few moments, because there has been distortion. For that reason it is even more important on short-wave, to be sure that a listener will not be confused because he does not hear a certain sentence. No sentence should ever be so important that the listener will lose the meaning of the programme if he does not hear it.

Short-wave broadcasts suffer from *interference*. Other stations are broadcasting on the same frequency, and so both are heard. This makes it very difficult for the listener to understand. A *cross-fade* may sound just as if one station has faded because of interference from another. It can also happen that music faded into the background may sound like interference.

When you are recording music for short-wave, remember that the highest notes and the lowest notes may not reach the listener. Music that sounds beautiful on the control-room loudspeaker may sound thin and squeaky on the listener's radio. This can even be true on medium-wave if your listener has a small transistor radio. Therefore, your music should not depend too much on very high notes or a strong bass.

If music is sung, try to have the words clear and easily understood. The words sung by a large choir will not be understood. Two or three people, or one person singing, will find it easier to make their words understood.

Assignment One (K15):

Make an experimental tape of your own speaking voice. To do this go into a studio and record samples of your voice, speaking from perhaps five or six different places in front of a microphone. As you talk into your microphone, say something like this:

> "I am about _____ centimetres (or inches) away from a _____ microphone in studio _____. I am directly in front of (or to one side of) the microphone."

Read a short item from that position. Then try another position a little farther away or a little closer. If possible try this with several different microphones in several studios. Then listen to the tape *very carefully* and write down in your notes the places where your voice sounds best with each microphone and in each studio. Listen for clarity, brilliance, and presence. Ask another staff member at your studio to listen to your tape to see if he agrees with you. Later, when you report to your supervisor, bring the tape with you so that he may listen and talk to you about the microphone positions you chose.

Assignment Two (K16):

Ask a friend who can sing to make some experiments with you. Ask him to come into your studios to try different microphone positions and different microphones. Before each test, have him speak into the microphone to say how far away he is, in what part of the studio, and what kind of microphone he is using, just as you did in Assignment One. Then he should sing a short little song. If possible, try to make some tests in a room that is not a radio studio, such as a large empty hall. Then write a report telling about the different kinds of sounds you heard on the tape. Bring both the tape and the things you wrote to your supervisor when you report.

A Word of Warning (K17):

Assignments One and Two appear to be very easy, but they are really very difficult. Unless you have had radio experience before, you will find it hard to hear the small differences in the sound. You may even think they are not important. Your listener will not be able to tell the difference either, but he will *feel* the difference. He will enjoy one recording or one announcer better than another, even though he could not tell you why. He will turn away from the bad recording and listen to the good one.

Keep working at Assignments One and Two until you feel you are beginning to make some progress. If necessary, leave them for a while but be sure to come back later on. Your ear must become aware of these slight differences in sound, or you will not be able to make good recordings.

Glossary Assignment (K18):

Look up these words in the glossary. In your own language, explain what they mean.

ACOUSTICS	MICROPHONE BALANCE
DECIBEL	MIX
DISTORTION	MONITOR
ECHO	OFF-MICROPHONE
HOWL-BACK	ON-AIR
LOUDSPEAKER	ON-MICROPHONE
MICROPHONE	OVERLOADING

When you have completed these three assignments, report to your supervisor.

Listener Participation Programmes (K19):

We were speaking in Part One of ways we may use people who are not on the studio staff. We were talking about actors, speakers, musicians, and so forth.

In Part Two, we would like to talk about the ways in which listeners can help in the programmes you make.

There are many kinds of programmes in which the listener can take part. We have already mentioned one kind in *Project I*. This was the panel programme where listeners wrote in to tell their ideas about the things the panel discussed.

In the last few years, companies making tape machines have learned to make high-quality recorders that are light and easy to use, and which can go for a long time on one battery. This means that it is possible to go out and gather material for a programme from almost anywhere.

With a machine such as this, it is possible to go out to the towns and villages, and get on tape the ideas of many kinds of people. You can then bring these tapes back to the studio and use them in place of the letters. This is far more effective, especially if the tape is well edited to remove unnecessary talk.

Taped Participation (K20):

There are almost endless numbers of programmes that can be done through the use of a portable tape-recorder. Here are just a few ideas that have been used successfully:

> People are interviewed to find out how they feel about something that has happened recently. These interviews are put together into a short programme. Usually less than two minutes are allowed for each person being interviewed.
>
> Short interviews on many subjects are used to add interest and usefulness to a music programme.
>
> A village or a town is invited to put on a public programme in the square. The performance is recorded, as well as interviews with some of the people in the village. This is edited and put together to make a half-hour radio programme. A different village is featured on each programme.

Letter Participation (K21):

In *Project H* we talked about the ways in which letters from listeners could be used to find out more about the audience. Some studios have used letters from listeners to make programmes. This can be done very successfully, if the letters are chosen carefully, and edited carefully. Here are some of the things you should remember when doing this kind of programme:

> Do not use a letter if you think the person who wrote it did not want it used on the air.
> Use only those letters which will be of interest to most of your listeners. A letter could easily be interesting to you, without being interesting to your listeners.
> Edit every letter carefully before you use it on the programme. Remove all those parts that are not important. Use only that part of the letter which makes your programmes interesting and helpful. If there are any bad mistakes in the use of the language, you should correct them, but do not change the style of the letter too much.
> If a letter is very long, tell what it is about in a few of your own words, and just read a paragraph or two from the letter itself.
> If you invite listeners to write in to a programme, be sure to say each time that only *some* of the letters will be read on the air. The listener should not expect that every letter he sends will be used on the programme, or you may soon find that you are using letters from the same people over and over again.
> When you read letters on the air, do so in a lively and interesting manner. It is usually best to copy right into your script the parts of the letters which you want to use. Your reading will be much better this way. You will not need to worry about bad handwriting, or about finding the right place in the letter.

An Edited Letter (K22):

Here is a letter from a listener, and part of a script showing the way this letter was used on a programme. Study it carefully, and notice the way only the important parts were used.

Dear Mr. Announcer,

My family and I have been listening to your programme and have always enjoyed it very much. We think it is very good. I wonder if you can solve a problem for me.

My land doesn't grow as much rice as it once did. Only about half of the seedlings grow. Why is this? Please give our greetings and best wishes to all the friends who work with you.

Yours truly,
Philippe Olomu.

ANNCR: We also have a letter today from Mr.
Philippe Olomu. Mr. Olomu has a rice
growing problem. He writes: "My land
does not grow as much rice as it once
did. Only about half the seedlings
grow. Why is this?"
Mr. Olomu, your problem sounds like the
problem many farmers are having. In
fact, we have had several letters like
yours which we have not been able to
read on the programme. All of them...etc.

There are many kinds of programmes that can be made with letters from listeners. Here are some that have been used successfully.

The Question and Answer Programme (K23):

Listeners write about their problems and questions, and these are answered on the programme. This kind of a programme can be successful only if you do not think you must have *all* the answers to *all* the questions. Often the letter does not give enough information so that you can give a good answer.

> One broadcaster received a letter which said, "My chickens are all dying. Why?" So he said on the programme, "I cannot give an answer because I would need to see the chickens first." Then he told the listener where he could find the person who might help him with this problem.

Comments from Listeners (K24):

Listeners write in to give their ideas about the subjects being discussed on the programme. As we said in *Project G*, this is sometimes done as part of a panel discussion programme. Listeners comment about people's problems, about the things that are reported in the news, about the programmes they hear on the radio, about religion, politics, and many other subjects. If you want listeners to send in letters to a certain programme about a certain topic, you must tell them so. Otherwise you will receive letters about things that have nothing to do with your programme.

Music Request Programme (K25):

Listeners write to ask that a certain piece of music be played. This is often a very popular kind of programme, and often far more requests are received than can be used. When this happens, you should tell your listeners that you can only play some of the requests. You should also tell your listeners that only a certain kind of music can be played on your programme. For instance, if you have a programme using your nation's folk music, then you would not play a piece of Western music on that programme even if you received a request for it. Remember that *you* should decide what selections you will play on your programme. The requests you receive should be a guide, not a dictator. There are many people listening who have not sent in a request. The programme is for them also. Therefore, you should be sure that the music you play can be enjoyed by all your audience, and not just by the one person who requested it.

Choosing music for a request programme.

Greetings Programme (K26):

Listeners send in their greetings to friends and relatives. Often this is to greet them on a special day such as a birthday or anniversary. People enjoy such a programme because they like to hear their own names and the names of people they know mentioned on the radio.

Message Programme (K27):

In many parts of the world, it is difficult for people to get messages to others through the mail or the telegraph. Radio stations can be a great help to people by providing a programme where messages can be sent from one person to another. These messages can be personal ones to announce a birth or a death, or about almost anything else. Sometimes groups or agencies use this kind of programme to send messages to their workers in the villages.

Be careful to edit each message carefully before it is put on the air. It might use words that should not be heard on the radio; it might contain information that should not be broadcast; it might be someone playing a joke; it might simply be too long.

In some countries, there are government regulations about greeting and message programmes. You should know what these are before considering such programmes.

Other Letter Programmes (K28):

Music is often used on these kinds of programmes because one letter after another can be very dull. Such a programme is usually far more successful if there are no more than two or three minutes of talking and then two or three minutes of suitable music. Remember that whenever you use music on a programme it should be planned carefully in the way we suggested in *Project K*.

People who do not know how to write cannot usually take part in this kind of programme. Because of this some stations or studios ask the people to come in to the studio where the messages or greetings are written down for them by a staff member. Some studios have even sent people out to the market-places or the villages to write down the things people would like to send to the radio programmes.

All of these programmes can also be done with the use of a tape machine, so that you can actually use the listener's voice on the radio. The listeners come into the studio to record their comments or messages, or someone from the studio takes a portable tape machine and goes out to the listener. This takes much more work than letters, and the editing is far more difficult but it can make a very fine programme if it is well done.

Assignment Three (K29):

Listen to some of the radio stations that can be heard in your area, and find two programmes on which letters, greetings, requests or messages from listeners are used. If you cannot find two such programmes, your supervisor may have some suggestions, or he may have some tape-recordings of such programmes. Prepare a short report on each programme answering these questions:

What kind of a programme was it? Describe the programme and tell what kinds of things were used to make up the programme.
What do you think was the purpose of the programme? In what way did it help the listener? Explain.
Were the letters or messages interesting to those listeners who did not write to the programme? Why?
Were the letters or messages read in an interesting and lively manner? Explain.
In what way could you have improved the programme? Explain.

Assignment Four (K30):

In this assignment, we would like you to make a short programme using listeners' letters. You will need to talk this over with your supervisor, since the kind of programme you do will depend on the letters you can find. After you have done this, plan to make a 15-minute programme with these letters and some music. Remember that all the things we learned about planning, research, writing, editing, etc., must be used in this assignment, as in any programme. Use the check-list as you work to be sure that you are not forgetting something important. Look back to other projects to help you remember. When you have recorded your programme, use this check-list to see if it is good enough. If you are not satisfied, then do your programme again.

o

Letter Programme Check-list (K31):

1. Were the letters carefully edited to use only those parts which were interesting and important?   Yes ____ No ____
2. Were the letters read in an interesting and lively manner?   Yes ____ No ____
3. Was the music well chosen to fit in with the mood of the programme?   Yes ____ No ____
4. Was it a good music programme, taking into consideration the things we said in *Project J*?   Yes ____ No ____
5. Was the script well written?   Yes ____ No ____
6. Would the kind of listener you chose when you planned the programme have found it interesting and useful?   Yes ____ No ____

When you can answer "yes" to each of these questions, take your programme and assignments to your supervisor.

Tokyo Broadcasting System.

This car has a transmitter so that the reporter can send her broadcast directly to the radio station.

PROJECT L

News

Many years ago when people were living in primitive tribes, perhaps living in caves, they needed information just as you and I do now. They needed everyday information about their family life, children's play, food, courtship, and so forth. They also needed a watchman. The watchman would stand on top of a hill or look from a tall tree. He would warn his people if an unfriendly tribe was coming, or he would tell them if a herd of animals was close enough to be hunted. In other words, the watchman told his people of dangers and opportunities coming from the outside world.

The work of a news reporter, whether he works on radio, TV, or the newspaper, is very much like that of the watchman. He tells his people what is happening in the places they cannot see; he tells of dangers and opportunities.

When a primitive tribesman or a modern city office-worker listens to the words of a watchman or a news reporter, he does so because he wants to be ready for any danger that he may have to face. He also wants to use any opportunities that may come.

As a country develops, the watchman (or news reporter) must look much farther than he once did. The wealthy leaders in the cities and the farmers in the villages suddenly find that they are very interested in each other. The man in the city knows that agriculture must be improved before the country can develop its industry. The man in the village learns that city people have things he wants and needs.

As the villages and cities join together to become nations, people become interested in the politics of their country, rather than just in the politics of their clan or tribe. Fifteen or twenty years ago, many nations were not too concerned with other countries in the world. Now they have joined the United Nations, and are taking part in world politics.

In other words, as a nation grows, it needs more and more information. Once the watchman needed to tell only of things happening a few kilometres away.

Now even a villager knows what happens on the other side of the world can mean danger or opportunity for himself and his country.*

Freedom of Information (L2):

The General Assembly of the United Nations agreed in 1946 that "freedom of information is a fundamental human right, and the touchstone of all the free-doms to which the United Nations is consecrated". In other words, people have a right to know what their government is doing, what other governments are doing and what problems cause trouble between nations and between groups in their own country. People must have information so that they can make up their own minds about these problems. The General Assembly also said that all the other freedoms on which the countries of the United Nations agreed, depend upon this freedom: "the freedom to know."†

   Of course, this is not the case in all nations, but an honest and hard-working broadcaster can help this freedom grow in his own country. He can do this through honest and careful news reporting.

What is News? (L3):

News is *new* information. News is *true* information. News is *important* informa-tion, important to the people who are listening to the news. News is information about things that happen. It is information about what people do, or say, or what happens to them.

News or Opinion? (L4):

There is nothing wrong with giving an opinion or your own idea on the radio. It is wrong, however, to put this opinion into a *newscast*. Opinions, personal viewpoints, interesting ideas are very important. However, it is also very important that the listener can easily tell the difference between the *facts* presented in a newscast, and the broadcaster's *opinion*. Programmes giving a viewpoint or opinion are known as broadcasts of *editorial comment*.

   Listeners often find a programme of *editorial comment* very helpful, if it is done by a person who has taken great care to study all the information. A good

* UNESCO, Paris, 1964. The ideas expressed in these paragraphs have been adopted from Schramm – op. cit., pages 38 and 42.
   † Adapted from: Courlander, Harold, *Shaping Our Times* (Oceana Publications Inc., 1960).

editorial broadcast will help the listener make wise judgements of his own. No broadcaster should try to do such a programme until he has a great deal of experience and knowledge about the subjects he is discussing.

The important thing to remember as you begin to think about news broadcasting is this. The work of a news broadcaster is to bring the *information* to the listener. The *listener* must decide what is right and what is wrong. The news reporter must present only the facts and let the listener reach his own conclusions.

Propaganda (L5):

When a broadcaster tries to use the information of a newscast to make his listener think a certain way, then his newscast becomes *propaganda*. Propaganda is information that is changed or twisted to make people agree with the broadcaster.

Most broadcasters do not try to use dishonest propaganda. Sometimes, however, they use propaganda without really understanding that this is what they are doing. For this reason, the broadcaster should be careful of such things as:

> calling people bad names,
> using big impressive words that don't really mean anything,
> choosing only those facts which fit his own viewpoint,
> claiming that his viewpoint is right because "everyone" agrees, and
> broadcasting news items at a certain time, or choosing certain items, because this will influence the listener a certain way.

We All Do It (L6):

We must realise that even the best newscast is not free of some propaganda. Your own viewpoint or the viewpoint of those people who make your studio's news policy, will always show through.

This happens, because in writing a news story, you must choose to report some facts and not to mention others. No news story can present *all* the information.

One station in Asia gets its news from the international broadcasts of Indonesia, Malaysia, Japan, Australia, the U.S.A., and Britain. Often all six stations will tell about the same event. Sometimes their stories are so different, that it is hard to know if they are talking about the same event.

This problem can be seen most clearly when two nations are having a quarrel or are fighting with each other. Each will report the same event differently. If you ever have an opportunity to compare newspapers or listen to radio broadcasts from two nations who are having a quarrel, you will see this very clearly.

Dangers in Selecting News (L7):

Even those who put a newscast together are selecting certain news stories, and leaving others out. They spend more time on one item than they do on another.

Every news reporter, and every news editor must choose his material. He cannot report everything. How then can a news broadcaster be honest and truthful to his listeners if he cannot tell everything?

The most important thing is your honesty as a news broadcaster and your desire to let the listener decide what is right and what is wrong. You should always try your best to give your listener the important facts in the news, even reporting those things with which you do not agree or which you do not like. Then you will be a reporter, and not a propagandist. Remember, however, that an honest news broadcaster is always looking at himself and his news programmes to find those many subtle ways in which opinion takes the place of reporting.

Accuracy (L8):

One of the problems a news reporter must constantly face is that of getting correct information. Very bad things have happened, because a news broadcaster said something that was not true. A good news reporter spends a great deal of time checking to be sure his information is right. He knows that once the wrong information goes out over the air, there is no way to get it back. Even if he explains his mistake on a later programme, it will not help very much. Many of those who heard the first broadcast will not hear the second.

> One broadcaster wrote a news item about an accident in which he said a certain man had died. The broadcaster had been given this information by someone who had seen the accident. If the reporter had checked, he would have learned that this was not true. The wife of the man he said was killed, suffered a heart attack when she heard the news on the radio, and she died in the hospital.

Newsworthiness (L9): *

How do we know when some information is important or interesting enough to be used on your programme? There is no way we can answer this question

* Adapted from: Van Horne, Marion, "Write the Vision" (National Council of Churches, 1952).

exactly, because each broadcaster must decide what is best for his own country. However, there are eight reasons why many broadcasters feel a news item should be used on a news programme. The length of the news item may also depend on one or more of these eight reasons. The more newsworthy the story, the longer it will be.

Importance: We must ask the questions: How *many* people will be affected by the event about which this news item tells? How *much* will they be affected? For how long?

Nearness: An event often becomes more important when it happens near home. People know they will usually be affected more by things that happen near them, than by things that happen far away. People are also much more interested in things that happen to their friends, their family, and their neighbours. However, these days when we can travel so quickly from one part of the world to another, people are becoming more interested in what is happening in other places. They know that something which happens in South America, for instance, can easily affect people living in the Middle East. Nearness is not nearly as important for a newscaster as it was in the days before international radio and jet aeroplanes.

Timeliness: The more recently something has happened, the more interesting it is for people. That is why every good news reporter tries to get things on the air as quickly as possible. However, he is less concerned about timeliness, than he is about being sure all his information is correct.

Prominence: New information about well-known people is news. Many people die every day, but their deaths are not reported on the radio. If the Prime Minister of a country dies, then almost every radio station in the world will tell about it. The more a person is known to the listeners, the more interesting they will find his viewpoints and his activities.

Unusualness: Things that are different or unusual are almost always interesting to the listener. The good news broadcaster is always looking for something unusual about which he can tell his listeners. There is a very old saying about news:

"If a dog bites a man, that is *not* news.
If a man bites a dog, that *is* news."

Human Interest: We have said before in this manual that "people are interested in people". They are interested in themselves and in people who are like them. That is why your listeners will have a real interest in news stories that tell of anything unusual or important happening to another person.

About Everyone's Problems: Some subjects are of interest to everybody. Things such as food, health, houses, sex, education, work, politics, religion, war, hunger, and suffering concern us all. News items about such things are almost always interesting, and often very important.

Conflict and Suspense: Conflict could be described as disagreement or problems between people, groups of people or between nations. This kind of conflict is always interesting. Suspense in a news story makes people wonder what will happen next. You will learn more about conflict and suspense when we talk about dramas, because this is what most good stories are made of.

Where to Find News (L10):

We have said that "nearness" usually makes a story important. That is why the radio reporter begins in his own city and nation when he is looking for news. This is done in the same way that a reporter for a newspaper looks for his news. A radio reporter writes his story differently than a newspaperman, but he finds his information in the same way.

The first thing you must do if you are to become a good news reporter, is to become familiar with your own country. You should have a good knowledge of the history, geography, economics, and culture of your nation. Then you must read your newspapers and magazines regularly, so you always know what is happening.

The way in which the news is gathered is different from country to country. Here are some of the ways in which reporters have found their news.

Asking Questions (L11):

A reporter may spend most of his day going from place to place asking questions of important people. He might visit the office of the government, the police, the hospitals, the churches and other community organisations. He would not only gather information, but he would also try to get the help and friendship of these people, so that when something important happens, they would let him know.

The Telephone (L12):

A telephone can save a reporter many steps. By using it, he can contact people very quickly to find out if certain information is true or not. He will be most successful in using the telephone, however, if he has first gained the friendship of these people by visiting them personally. Many stations have a way of recording the voice on the telephone on to a tape. This can be useful in two ways. The reporter can listen to the tape later, and be sure he understood exactly what was said. Some stations use such recordings as part of their news programmes. In *Project M* we will tell you how these recordings can be used. Remember, however, that you must always be sure the person you are recording *knows* that he is being recorded, and that his voice may be heard on the air. People have become very angry when they heard their voices on the radio saying something they did not know had been recorded. Also be sure that the sound of the recording is clear. Telephone recordings are often very poor quality.

Newspapers (L13):

In some places, radio stations have asked newspapers for permission to use their items on the air. Remember, however, that newspaper news is written in a different style than radio news, and therefore the items must often be rewritten or at least edited. In most places, it is not necessary to have the permission of the newspaper if you are simply going to use the *information*, or the *facts* (not the words) from the newspaper.

News Releases (L14):

Many governments, organisations, and agencies send out what is known as a "news release". This is an item they hope you will use on the air, because they would like your listeners to know about certain information. There are several things to remember about news releases:

> They are often written from a certain point of view; that is, they may try to make the listener believe something, rather than try to inform him.
> They are almost always too long for a radio broadcast.
> They may have a "release time"; that is, the organisation or person who sent it may not want it broadcast until a certain hour or day. He has sent the news to you so that you can prepare your broadcast ahead of time. Therefore, you should never put it on the air until the time that is shown.

News Services (L15):

Many organisations send radio stations a group of news items once a week, once a month, or perhaps even once a day. Some of these news services are free, while others cost money. Most of these news services are run by organisations or groups of organisations, and so the things we said about news releases are often true of news services.

Wire Services (L16):

These are companies that gather news from all parts of the world, and send it out on a special kind of radio signal. The radio station then must rent a teletype machine and pay to use the news. Most of this news is "world news" rather than "local news". Even these wire services write their news from a certain viewpoint, usually the view of their home country. There are five big world news agencies: Reuters (British), Agence France Presse (French), Tass (Soviet), and Associated Press and United Press International (American). Here is an example of news from a wire service.

```
          REUTERS FIRST NEWSCAST FOR AFRICA.

             TUESDAY, FEBRUARY 21ST, 1967.

          - - - - - - - - - - - - -

     KINSHASA: PRESIDENT JOSEPH MOBUTU SAID HERE YESTERDAY THAT
THE TWO-MONTH DISPUTE BETWEEN HIS GOVERNMENT AND THE
BRUSSELS-BASED UNION MINIERE DU HAU KATANGA HAS COST
THE CONGO NEARLY THREE BILLION BELGIAN FRANCS
(ABOUT 21 MILLION STERLING).
     COPPER EXPORTS - A VITAL SECTOR OF THE CONGO'S
ECONOMY - WERE SUSPENDED LAST DECEMBER BECAUSE
UNION MINIERE HAD REFUSED TO TRANSFER ITS HEADQUARTERS
TO THE CONGO. LATER THE GOVERNMENT SET UP ITS OWN COMPANY
IN PLACE OF UNION MINIERE.
```

Other Radio Stations (L17):

Sometimes, if there are several radio stations in a country, newsmen may record newscasts from other stations and use the information for their own broadcasts. Sometimes they can actually use part or all of the recording they have made on the air. If they use only the information, not the actual words from the other station, then it may not be necessary to ask for permission. However, if you use the same words, or use a recording of another station's newscast, then you must always ask permission. Some international radio stations carry news which is spoken very slowly so that newsmen in other countries can copy it down. If you write to these stations, they will usually give you the times and frequencies of such broadcasts.

Gathering news is very interesting and exciting work! A good reporter can rightly feel that he is making a contribution to the development of his nation. He is helping to keep people informed, and this is very important. Only informed people can make wise choices about their nation and their government. That is why a good reporter will work hard and do his best so that he may have a part in the exciting adventure of nation building!

Assignment One (L18):

Listen to two newscasts that are heard in your country, but *which come from two other nations.* If possible, have these newscasts recorded, so that you may listen to each one several times. Answer each of the questions in the list found after Assignment Two. Think about each answer carefully before you write it down.

Assignment Two (L19):

Listen to two newscasts which are *made in your own country.* If possible choose two different radio stations. Try to have them recorded on tape, and then answer the following questions:

Questions for Assignments One and Two:

Did the news reporter speak from a certain point of view? What point of view? How did you know this was so?
Do you think the newscaster was honestly trying to give correct information? Why do you think so?
Were there places where the news reporter was giving his opinion rather

than the facts? Make a list of these places. Why do you think they were opinions, not facts?

Listen carefully to the first three items in each newscast. Were they newsworthy? Tell the reasons why each of the three first items were or were not newsworthy.

Report to your supervisor after you have finished Assignments One and Two.

Making a News Broadcast (L20):   PART TWO

In Part One, we talked about news, what it is, and where it could be found. There are still four important things you must know about news broadcasting. These are writing, editing, compiling and announcing.

Writing (L21):

It is the work of a news writer to tell exactly what happened. He never tells why *he* thinks something happens, nor does he tell his listeners what *he* thinks about the people he writes about. He does all he can to stay with the facts.

A news report must not only be correct, however. It must also be easily understood and interesting. It must be good writing. For this reason, you may want to read *Projects A, C* and *D* again, to help you remember some of the things that are needed for good writing.

News on radio is usually written differently from news in a newspaper. It is almost always much shorter. Some radio news items may only be one or two sentences long, and only when a story is very important is it longer than one or two minutes. For this reason, a radio news writer cannot waste his words. He must be sure that he gives as much of the important information as he can in the short time he has. At the same time, the reporter must not put facts or ideas so close together that the listener cannot understand. To do these two things, he must choose his words and phrases carefully.

The Important First Sentence (L22):

The first sentence in a radio news item is almost always different from that in a newspaper item. A newspaper writer will usually try to give all the important facts in the first sentence. In radio, the purpose of the first sentence is to give the listener an *idea* of what the item is about, and to make him interested in the story.

A news item from "Voice of Ethiopia,"
Addis Ababa, November 16, 1966.

World Journalists
Meet in Delhi

"The world is changing much faster than we are able to change ourselves and what is really required is a change in human nature and in society", observed Dr. S. Radhakrishnan, President of India, opening the 15th General Assembly of the International Press Institute in New Delhi yesterday.

The Indian President appealed to the representatives of the World Press to help "achieve the central aim of social equality and world unity and peace". He said "the world has become one. Whether we like it or not, east and west have come together and they can never again part".

The same item re-written for a radio broadcast.

"The world is changing much faster than we are
able to change ourselves." This was stated by
Dr. S. Radhakrishnan, President of India, in
New Delhi yesterday. He was addressing the
opening of the 15th General Assembly of the
International Press Institute.

"What is really required," the Indian President
said, "is a change in human nature and society."
Dr. Radhakrishnan appealed to the world press to
help achieve what he called, "the central aim of
social equality and world unity and peace." The
world has become one," he said, "Whether we like
it or not, east and west have come together, and
they can never again part."

Look at those two news items, and notice these differences:

The first paragraph of the newspaper item has only one sentence. The radio news item has three.

The radio item is written in the *spoken style* of English. Most people seem to use their language differently when they are writing than when they are speaking. Things written for radio must always be done in the spoken style, since the script will be spoken on the air.

The item written for radio gives the listener a better chance to understand the information. It does not put the facts too close together. A radio listener cannot go back and read something a second time the way a newspaper reader can. If he does not understand the first time, he will never understand, unless he hears this news repeated at a later time.

The first sentence of the radio story is only thirteen words long. There are fifty-one words in the newspaper sentence. The first sentence of a radio news item should always be as short as possible. One very successful news chief said that no first sentence should ever be more than twelve words in length. You will have to decide if such a rule would fit your language. Perhaps you can make a better rule.

Before you begin to write a news story, decide what part of the information is the most newsworthy. Look at the other facts, and remove any that do not have something to do with the main part of your news item. Sometimes you may find that the facts really should be used in two stories instead of one. In other words, be sure that each news item is about *one* thing only.

Five "W's" and an "H" (L23):

Be sure you have all the information you need. One way to check this is to use what are called the "Five W's and an H".

What happened?
Why did it happen?
When did it happen?
How did it happen?
Where did it happen?
Who was involved?

If you remember to ask yourself these questions, you will probably get most of the important information. Often your news story will answer all of those "Five W's and an H", but there will also be times when some of this information is not important. In that case, leave it out.

When you have all your information together, and you have chosen the most important part of your story, then work out your first sentence.

Now write the rest of the item in short clear sentences. Use simple words, and tell the story in a way that flows easily and naturally. If you have trouble knowing how to write the item, then ask yourself this question, "If I were going to tell this to my friend, and if I were very excited because of this news, how would I tell him?" The way you would tell your friend might give you some ideas about how to tell the story on the radio.

After you have written the story the first time, edit it carefully. Read it out loud as you do. Look for places where there are unneeded words. If you had trouble reading any part of your item smoothly, then you may have some words that are hard to say. If so, change them. In some cases, you may need to re-arrange the words to make them flow more easily.

Other Suggestions (L24):

Here are a few things to remember when writing your news story:

> Always check the names of people and places to be sure they are correct. Do this also with any word that you are not sure of. If it is a word that is hard to pronounce, find out what is correct. Write the word in your script in such a way that you (or the person who is reading your item) can easily *say* it right. Ask your supervisor about the best way of doing this in your own language. The important thing in radio is not so much to spell it correctly, but to say it correctly. That is why in a radio script, you might see something like this:

> ANNCR: He had been a colonel (*ker*-nal) in the army before he joined the government.

> Be careful with titles (such as Doctor, Honourable, Major, etc.), especially of high-ranking persons. Use titles whenever it is polite to do so, but leave them off if they are unnecessary. Many titles and long names often add confusion to the news item. Be familiar with the customs of your own country.

Kyung-Do, Kim, HLKY, Korea

Important events in the life of a nation should be reported on radio news.

Use round numbers. For instance, the listener would probably not re-member if you told him: "There were fifty-one thousand three hundred and forty-eight people at the rally yesterday." It would be much better to say: "There were more than fifty thousand people at the rally yesterday." Too many numbers are confusing.

Do not use words your listener will not understand. Never use a word or a phrase just to show your listener that you understand big words.

Editing a News Story (L25):

The news reporter very often finds that he must edit news items written by someone else. These stories may have come from a news release, from a news service or newspaper, or they may have been written by another person on the staff. Every news reporter will, of course, also edit the stories he has written himself.

There are many reasons why editing is necessary. Here are some of them:

> to make the item shorter,
> to correct mistakes,
> to change words and phrases so that the listener will be able to understand more easily,
> to make the story fit the style of news reporting used by the studio, or to improve the style in any other way, and
> to add new information.

Most good news reporters find they must edit almost all the news that comes into the studio from an organisation or a news service. The things to watch for when editing someone else's writing are the same things you would look for when writing and editing your own news stories. Here is an example of the way in which a news item has been edited.

The Iloilo City Council

~~16 people~~ gathered ~~in the office~~ of the Mayor
~~of Iloilo City~~ this morning, to discuss the city's new
water system ~~for the city.~~ The Honorable Mayor
Juan Garcia told the city ~~council~~ ~~fathers~~ of the
difficulties the city had been having with it's
water supply, and suggested that ~~the amount of~~ almost 388 thousand pesos be spent to put in
~~₱ 387,986.00 be expended to install~~ a new system.
Alderman Pedro Roble suggested however, that an
engineer be asked to study the situation before
the council could decide. The Council did ~~No decision was~~
not reach a decision but will meet to
~~reached, but the council did decide to meet and~~ talk about
~~discuss~~ the matter again next Wednesday.

Compiling a Newscast (L26):

A newscast is planned differently from other radio programmes. Most radio
programmes have an outline made first, and then the programme is written
afterwards. A news reporter often writes his news items one by one, and then
makes his plan for the newscast later on, sometimes just a short time before he
is ready to go on the air. This is because new items are always coming in, and the
plan of a newscast must change every time another important story is received.
To compile a newscast, take all the news items that you feel might be included,
and lay them out on a large table. Decide which item is the most newsworthy,
and place it at the beginning of your newscast. The rest of the stories should then
be put one after another so that each follows as naturally as possible after the
one before. If you have two or three very important items, have them follow
each other at the beginning of your newscast.

An item may follow another because it is about the same or a similar subject.
For instance, if you had a story about an irrigation project in Egypt and a lack
of water in India, you could put the two items together. This would probably
mean that you would need to change the first line of one of the stories so that
you could move smoothly from one to the other.

If there is no connection between the subject-matter of the stories, then the stories are often arranged according to the place from which they came. For instance, if you were a news reporter in Lima, Peru, you might arrange your news items like this:

> the city of Lima,
> other parts of Peru,
> other countries in South America,
> North America,
> Asia,
> Africa and the Middle East, and
> Europe.

The arrangement of the news follows the idea that news stories are put next to each other because there is a relationship between them. If there is no relationship in the subjects of the news stories, then we can find the relationship in the place from which the news came.

Many news editors like to add a humorous item at the end of their newscast. Such an item has no importance, except that it makes the listener smile or laugh a little. This is good, especially if the rest of the news has been about sad things. It must still be a news item, however. It must be a report on something that really happened.

There are many ways of arranging a news broadcast. Perhaps you will be able to suggest a better way than the ones we have mentioned here. The important thing to remember is that the listener should feel that the news moved easily and naturally from one item to another.

Voicing the News (L27):

Everything that was said about speaking in *Projects A* and *D* is important for news announcing. Now we would like to say a few more things about speaking on the radio. These things are not only important for news announcing, but for most kinds of radio speaking. The best kind of practice for reading a script is to read it out loud several times, before you actually go into the studio. This is far more helpful than simply reading it over quietly. When reading out loud you become familiar with the sounds used in that script. If there are words that give you trouble, or names with which you are not familiar, reading your scripts out loud will help you find these.

Never read a word on the air unless you know what it means. Never read a script on the air unless you understand what it is saying. If you do not understand, this will show in your voice, and the listener will feel this. The listener will soon lose interest if he feels the speaker on the radio does not understand his script.

As in all radio speaking, the news announcer must be easily understood and interesting. He should be able to use all of the tones and colours that make the voice interesting. He must find a speed of speaking that is slow enough so that all can understand, yet fast enough so that your speech does not sound dull.

Assignment Three (L28):

From one of the newspapers printed in your nation, choose three news items which you consider to be important. Rewrite these items in radio style, and according to the suggestions we have made in this project. Shorten the newspaper stories so that none of your rewritten articles is more than a minute and a half long. When you are finished rewriting each item, use the check-list which follows Assignment Five to find out if your rewriting has been done well enough. Rewrite your items as often as necessary to be sure they are good enough. Remember that although the newspaper item may have been written by one of the best writers in your nation, it would still need to be rewritten to fit the radio medium.

Assignment Four (L29):

Below you will find some information for a news story. From this information write a radio news item. If you wish, you may add some more information to what is given, or you may change names and other things to fit your own area.

Kinji Ito, twenty years old,
blind since birth,
teacher, Komatsunagi Elementary School, Tokyo,
on the beach at the seaside yesterday afternoon,
shouts of people on the beach told him a child was drowning,
the child was a ten-year-old girl: Midori Iguchi, daughter of Mr. and Mrs. Takeya Iguchi,
guided by cries, Mr. Ito swam to little Midori's assistance,
people on the shore shouted at Mr. Ito to tell him which way to go,

just as the girl was going under the water, Mr. Ito reached her,
the girl was given some medicine by a doctor, then taken home to her
parents.

When you have written this news story, use the check-list which follows Assignment Five to find out if it is done well enough. Rewrite your story as often as necessary.

Assignment Five (L30):

Ask your supervisor to help you choose an event about which you can write a news story. It may be a conference, a meeting, or something important that is happening in your community. Perhaps an organisation in your community is doing some interesting work that would make a good news story. Take a note-book and a pencil and find out all the information you need. Then come back and write your news story. You may find, as you begin to write, that there is other information you need. If so, you may need to go back and get it, or per-haps a phone call will do. Use the check-list to find out if your story is good enough.

Check-list for News Items (L31):

1. Does the first sentence give the listener an idea of
   what the story is about?   Yes ____ No ____
2. Is the first sentence short?   Yes ____ No ____
3. Does the news item give the listener a chance to
   understand the information?   Yes ____ No ____
4. Is the story written in the spoken style of your
   language?   Yes ____ No ____
5. Does the story include all the important information?   Yes ____ No ____
6. Does the story leave out any information that is not
   important?   Yes ____ No ____
7. Does the story begin with the most important part,
   and then tell the other things in a natural order?   Yes ____ No ____
8. Is the story told in short clear sentences?   Yes ____ No ____
9. Have all unneeded words been removed?   Yes ____ No ____
10. Does the news item use only words the listener can
    easily understand?   Yes ____ No ____

11. Does the item give only the facts, without any of
    your own viewpoints or opinions?   Yes ⎯⎯ No ⎯⎯

You should be able to say "yes" to at least nine of these questions before
you give Assignments Three, Four and Five to your supervisor.

When you have completed these assignments, arrange the five items into a
short news programme. Write opening and closing announcements, and record
the programme for your supervisor.

Assignment Six (L32):

If you have a news department in your studio, ask for ten or fifteen items from a
recent news broadcast. If not, select ten or fifteen items from a recent newspaper.
Using only one sentence (or not more than two lines on a piece of paper) tell
what was the most important idea in each story. For instance, the news item in
Assignment Four could be summarised like this: "Drowning girl saved by
blind man."

After you have done this, arrange the items in the order you feel they would
be used on a news programme.

Check-list for News Broadcasts (L33):

1. Is the first item the most newsworthy for your
   listener?   Yes ⎯⎯ No ⎯⎯
2. Have the items been arranged so that they follow one
   another according to the subject or according to the
   places from which they came?   Yes ⎯⎯ No ⎯⎯
3. Is the most important idea in the news story found in
   each of the one-sentence summaries?   Yes ⎯⎯ No ⎯⎯

When you have finished Assignments Three to Six, take them to your
supervisor.

PROJECT M

Documentary and News-reel

In the last project we told you about news broadcasting. Most news programmes are made up of items read by one announcer. This is the simplest and often the best way to present the news.

There are, however, other things that can be done to make a newscast more interesting. There are also other kinds of news programmes, such as the radio news-reel. Then there are programmes that are like the news broadcast in many ways, the radio documentary and magazine programmes. The radio news-reel, documentary and magazine programmes are the subjects of this project.

We would like to remind you again that the things you learn and the ideas you develop while doing one kind of programme, can also be used on other programmes. It will help if you keep checking back on your other projects, so you will remember the things that were said before.

Pictures in Radio News (M2):

You have heard news broadcasts where one announcer read all of the items. If the items are well written, and if the announcer speaks well, such a news broadcast can be very effective. However, radio news can use "pictures" to make the items more interesting, just as a newspaper will use photographs. In radio, these are "pictures in sound". Just as the photographs in a newspaper can often tell you things that cannot be put into words, so the "pictures" in radio can communicate certain things the announcer would not be able to say.

For instance, you may write a news item like this:

NEWS ANNCR: The Prime Minister of our country today called on all young
people to help solve the food shortage. He told the National
Youth Rally that better food production is "something worth

fighting for". "Let the youth of our nation stand up," the Prime Minister said, "and build a better world for their children! I know that . . . etc."

On the other hand, the listener would feel some of the fire in the Prime Minister's speech if he could hear his voice. Something of the Prime Minister's personality would also be communicated by his manner of speaking. The same news story would communicate more if it was written like this:

NEWS ANNCR: The Prime Minister of our country has called upon all young people to help solve the food shortage. Speaking to a National Youth Rally, the Prime Minister said:

TAPE: (EXCERPT FROM SPEECH BY PRIME MINISTER: DURATION 30 SECONDS.) IN-CUE: "Let the youth of our nation stand up and build a better world for their children . . . END CUE: This is something worth fighting for! It is something worth working for!"

Taping Speeches (M3):

Many news reporters try to tape-record important speeches, even though they do not intend to broadcast the whole talk. They are then able to select a few sentences which give the most important part of the speech, and use it in their news broadcast.

Be sure, however, that you select a portion that is important and gives a true impression of what the person was trying to say. It is very easy to take a sentence or two out of the speech which will give a completely wrong idea.

If you are not certain what the most important part of the speech was, it is sometimes possible to ask the speaker afterwards, or even to telephone him later. It is much better to do this, than to give a false impression to your listener.

If you have taken a portable tape-recorder along, you might ask the speaker after he has finished his talk, to record a short summary of his speech. This can be done even when you are quite sure what part of the speech was most important, but you were not able to record it.

You might say to the speaker, "I wasn't able to record all your speech for the radio, but I'm wondering if you could repeat what you said about such and such . . ." Of course, even this will probably need to be shortened before it can be used in a news broadcast.

Another warning! If you are recording someone's speech, be sure you ask permission first. There are times when a speaker wishes to say things only to the people in the room with him. It is not enough to think, "Well, he could see the microphone. He must have known it was recorded." The speaker might easily think it was a microphone for a public-address system.

Interviews (M4):

We told you in *Project F* that short interviews can be used as part of a news item. Turn to *F7* and read again the section called "News Interview".

Sometimes an interview (or some other programme) prepared by your studio, or carried on your station, may be important enough for a news item. In that case, it is very helpful to take a little portion out of that programme for your news story. Of course, mention the name of the programme and the time it is on the air.

On-the-spot Reports (M5):

A very effective way to make a news item, is to have the report made right from the place where things are happening. This is particularly true when there are background sounds that help communicate some of the feeling or the excitement of the event.

Whenever possible, a news reporter should carry a portable tape machine with him. If he can record his news story at the scene of the accident, in the hall where the convention is being held, or from the office of the official who has just made a statement, his report will be much more interesting and exciting for the listener.

Sometimes a reporter may telephone his news item to the station. If this can be recorded, and if the recording is clear, it too can be used on the newscast.

Even if none of these things can be done, many stations ask their reporters to record their own news stories after they have been written. This is not as exciting as on-the-spot reports, but it does help a news broadcast simply because more than one voice is heard.

Such items, whether they are recorded on-the-spot, from the telephone, or are spoken by another reporter, usually need an introduction something like this:

NEWS ANNCR: The All Africa Cultural Research Society has just completed what it calls its most successful project. Abiodan Aloba reports from the Society's headquarters in Addis Ababa.

TAPE: ALOBA: 49 SECONDS.
                   IN-CUE: The study of African origins has been the subject . . .
                   END CUE: This is Abiodan Aloba reporting from Addis Ababa.

Sound and Music (M6):

Sounds and music are not often heard on a news broadcast, but there are times
when they can be used very well. A report on the building of a new dam might
begin with the sound of big machines working, or the story of a national
festival might include people singing a song usually heard at that event.

However, too much of this sort of thing can easily distract a listener away from
the report itself. When using sound or music as part of a news report, be sure the
recording is authentic; in other words, take a tape machine and get the *real*
sound. Never take something from a sound-effects library or a gramophone
record to use on a newscast. In news, use only the "real thing".

The Radio News-reel (M7):

The radio news-reel is usually not too different from an ordinary news broadcast. The two are not the same, however.

A *news broadcast* uses portions of speeches, on-the-spot broadcasts, and
special reports *when they are available*. The news must be presented as
quickly as possible, and usually in not too much detail unless it is a very
important event.

A *news-reel* on the other hand, uses on-the-spot broadcasts and special
reports *almost entirely*. The news is often presented in more detail, with more
of the colour or atmosphere of the events included. It is not nearly as important to get things on to a news-reel quickly, as it is with an ordinary
newscast. Remember, of course, that if the material gets too old, people lose
interest.

A news-reel, then, is really a special kind of newscast. There is usually more
time to spend on a news-reel, and there is usually more material to choose from.
This is because stations often present many news broadcasts, but only a few news-
reels. Still, all the care of searching for materials, choosing the right items,
writing, editing, compiling, and so forth, must go into a news-reel, just as they
go into any news broadcast.

Assignment One (M8):

Do *one* of these two assignments:

A. If you are working at a radio station where this is possible, ask someone in your news department to suggest a news event on which you could report. The report (between one and three minutes long) should be made with the use of a tape-recorder, and should be made outside of the studio where you work.
B. If "A" is not possible, prepare and record a news item about the studio in which you are working. The news item might be about:

> the important work being done by your studio,
> future plans of your studio,
> a new radio programme your studio is planning, or
> any other subject you might find worth while.

Tape an interview with one of the senior people (perhaps your supervisor) at your studio. The interview should be at least three minutes long. From the interview, select from thirty to forty-five seconds to use in a news story. Then write a news item that is between one minute and one minute and thirty seconds long.

Check-list for Recorded News Report (M9):

1. Is the news story well written and presented?   Yes _____ No _____
   (Use check-list *L31* in *Project L* to find this out. Those questions should be used to judge the taped interview as well as the written portion of the story.)
2. Did your story move smoothly from the written part
   to the taped interview?   Yes _____ No _____
3. Was the taped interview well edited?   Yes _____ No _____

When you can answer "yes" to all three questions, record the whole news item on tape, and bring it along with your script to your supervisor.

Magazine Programme (M10):   PART TWO

A very useful kind of radio broadcast is called a "magazine" programme. The word "magazine" comes from the Arabic word "makhzan" which means "storehouse", a place where you keep a variety of things. Magazine has also come to mean a kind of publication which contains a variety of articles by many different writers.

A radio magazine programme is one in which you can put many different kinds of materials. It might contain short talks about various things, perhaps a poem, a story, or even a song.

This does not mean that you can put anything you wish into a magazine programme. It must still be carefully planned, and the materials must be chosen according to that plan. If you are working on a series of magazine pro-grammes, it will be important for you to spend a great deal of time looking for materials before you begin. Put these materials (or a little note which tells you where the materials can be found) into file folders or envelopes, which are marked according to the many subjects you might be able to use on your pro-gramme. If you continue to do this day by day, as you read books, newspapers and magazines, listen to gramophone records and tapes, and hear people talking, you will soon have a large collection of material that will make your work much easier.

Credits (M11):

As you collect your material, be sure you write down where the item was found. If it comes from a magazine, book, or newspaper, write down the name of the author, the publication, the date it was published and its name and publisher. It is necessary to get a letter of permission from the publisher before you use the items on the radio. On your programme you must always give the "credit"; that is, the name of the author and the publication.

Sometimes a publisher will give you permission to use all of the articles out of a magazine or newspaper, provided you always give credit. This is very helpful, because it means you do not need to ask permission for each item you use.

Finding Materials (M12):

Of course, the items for a magazine programme can come from many places. Among the many ideas you might use are:

interviews with interesting people. (There are many such people in every community, and they can provide one of the best kinds of materials for this sort of broadcast. If you read *Project E* and *F* again you will find some suggestions.)

parts of recorded speeches. (Sometimes it is possible to take a story or a few paragraphs from a talk that has been recorded, and include it in a magazine programme.)

articles written by staff members and volunteers who help the studio,

selections from magazines and newspapers,

poems,

music recorded specially for the programme or from gramophone records,

short stories,

short dramas, and

paragraphs from a good book.

Planning a Magazine Programme (M13):

As with all radio programmes, you must begin with your listener. You must have a clear idea (which you can only get from research) as to what your listener needs, what he finds interesting, and how things can be made interesting for him. A magazine programme can only use those things which will communicate with the kind of listener for whom you are aiming.

A magazine, just like a music programme, must follow the principle of "variety within unity". Read all of *Project J* again to help you remember the things we said about music programmes. The ideas in that project are useful in most broadcasts, especially the magazine programmes.

There must be a theme or an idea that is followed in all the items used in a magazine programme. This does not mean that all the items must be about the same subject. It does mean that there must be a real connection between them, so that the programme is not just a group of unrelated articles thrown together, but a whole programme with both unity and variety.

After you have selected the idea or theme of your programme, spend some time making a list of all the various items that might be included. It is always good if you can list more things than you will use. From this list select the two or three items that you feel would be the "highlights", that is the most exciting and interesting parts of your programme. Do not choose all the items at this point, but only those which are the most important.

Magazine Outline (M14):

Keeping these items in mind, make an outline for your programme. Just as in a music programme, you should begin with something that will catch the attention of the listener. Next find the closing article, one that will make people want to listen again to your next programme. Then fill in the rest of your plan, being sure that you have unity and variety. This must be true, not only of the subjects, but also of the way the material is presented.

As you make your outline and fit in the items you have chosen, also decide how long each article should be. Remember the problem of "attention span" which we talked about in *Project D*. Never make your items any longer than necessary, but do not cut them so much that there is nothing important left.

Editing Materials (M15):

If you have a problem in editing any item, it often helps to read the whole thing carefully first. Then put the article to one side and write out what you feel is the most important idea. After this, write down any ideas or information that must be included if the main idea is to be understood. Read your item again to be sure you have not left out anything; then use the notes you have written down as a guide to your editing.

Always type any items from magazines, books and newspapers right into your script. Do not read them from the book or magazine. Not only is the writing usually too small, but also you may be confused by your own editing. Next you must plan and write your CONTINUITY (look for this word in the glossary). Be sure you write in a style that fits the programme and the materials you are using. The continuity should help to move the listener easily from one item to the next, and should also explain things when necessary.

Music Bridges (M16):

MUSIC BRIDGES may be used to link together the items in such a broadcast (look for this term in the glossary). Remember, however, that music must always have a real purpose in the programme. It should not be used just to fill in time, or because you heard another magazine programme that used music. In fact, it is better to use too few music bridges than too many. Signature music and the bridges must fit the style and the idea of the programme. You will learn more about the use of music bridges in drama *Projects N* and *O*.

One of the ways to make your broadcast a little more interesting is to use several announcers. This should be remembered in any programme. A change in voice helps catch the attention of the listener and adds variety to the broadcast.

Timing (M17):

You will need to keep a careful check on the time you allow for each item and for your continuity. Find out the total length of your items before you write the continuity, so that you can adjust your writing to fit the time you have left. Of course, you may need to cut or add to the articles in order to make sure your programme is exactly the right length.

The openings and closings of magazine programmes can take many different forms. There are so many ways that this can be done, that it is best for you to begin a list of possible ways. Do a lot of radio listening and write any new ideas in a notebook.

We do not mean that you should copy other broadcasters. In fact, you should always try to make the programmes come from *your* background and *your* personality. In other words, be original, not just in the openings and closings, but in your whole programme. Listen to the radio in order to feed your mind with new ideas. Your mind can take these ideas and from them develop something new and better.

Documentary Programmes (M18):

A documentary programme might be in the form of a talk, or it might be a very complicated programme with drama, music, sound effects, and many other things.

The word *documentary* tells us what the programme does. It does not tell us how the programme is made. To *document* means to prove or to teach. It means gathering together information and evidence to teach your listener, or to convince him that something is true. Before you begin to make documentaries, you should have had a good deal of experience in other kinds of radio programmes. However, you can begin to train your mind for such programmes by listening to your radio and by reading widely.

Kinds of Documentaries (M19):

Here are some kinds of documentary programmes:

Historical documentary. This programme tells about something that happened in the past, and shows how it happened.

Cultural documentary. It tells about some aspect of the life of people. Any aspect of culture may be presented in such a programme, from a study of music to the reasons why wars are fought.

Biographical documentary. It tells the story of someone's life.

Scientific documentary. This tells about things that are happening in the world of science. This may deal with medicine, agriculture, archaeology, etc.

News documentary. This takes an important and recent event and presents it in much more detail than could be done on an ordinary news broadcast.

There are, of course, other kinds of documentary broadcasts. The important thing to remember is that a documentary tries to present things as they actually are, or were. In this way, it is like a newscast, although in a documentary there may be a little more room for the writer to present his own interpretation. Still the main purpose is to present the information to the audience, and then let the listener decide what is right and wrong.

This does not mean that you could not write a biographical drama, for instance, and use your imagination in showing what the person was like. You may put many things into the drama that may not really have happened, and some very fine work can result.

Be Fair with the Listener (M20):

The important thing to remember is that the broadcaster must be fair and honest with his listener. He must somehow let the listener know how much of his programme is based on known facts, how much comes from his imagination, and how much is his opinion.

This is especially important when you are making programmes for listeners who may not have had very much education. An educated listener can often decide for himself what should be believed. The uneducated listener may not have enough information to allow him to decide. The broadcaster should be much more careful with the uneducated listener, than with the educated person.

Q

Documentary Formats (M21):

Documentary programmes can deal with many subjects. They can also use many methods, or formats. A documentary can be done through the use of:

> interviews with people who have something important to say about the subject,
> talks (short or long) by people who have important information,
> continuity written about the subject, and read by one or more announcers,
> dramas (short or long) written about the subject, and
> old recordings that have to do with the subject.

A documentary can be written using several of these methods, or it might use only one. Much depends on the subject and the materials.

It is important that a documentary be done only after you have spent a good deal of time in research. You should find out all you can about any subject before you begin writing.

The Morgue (M22):

Many stations have what is often called a "morgue". Usually a morgue is a place where dead people are kept until they are buried. In a radio station it is the place where old tapes, gramophone records, and scripts are stored. These are kept because of the great value they have for historical documentaries.

> One station was able to do a wonderful series of programmes on the twentieth anniversary of the nation's independence. This was because the staff had kept recordings of important speeches and events all during those twenty years.

There are three things to watch for when putting materials in a morgue:

> Save only those items which have real value. If you save too many things, your morgue will soon grow too large and you will have no more room.
> Keep a careful record of all the items in your morgue so that you can find them later.
> Be careful to keep dust, mould, heat and humidity away from your morgue, otherwise it may be destroyed. Look in the glossary under GRAMOPHONE RECORDS and TAPES for some suggestions that will help.

Glossary Assignment (M23):

Look up the following terms in the glossary. Describe what the word or phrase *means* in your own language.

BRIDGE

CALL LETTERS

INTERVAL SIGNAL

NETWORK

PRE–RECORD

PROGRAMME AS BROADCAST

PROGRAMME AS RECORDED

PROGRAMME JUNCTION

STAND–BY PROGRAMME

STATION IDENTIFICATION

Assignment Two (M24):

Select a popular magazine that is read in your country. If possible, find one that is printed in your own country. Make a list of all the main items (not the advertising) that are found in the magazine, and describe each item very briefly (about one or two lines). Answer the following questions about the magazine:

How many different *kinds* of items did you find in the magazine? Describe each kind in a line or two.

Was the magazine trying to reach only one kind of reader or many kinds? Tell what kinds, and why you think this was so.

Was there "variety within unity" in the magazine? Why do you think so?

Would any of the magazine articles be useful for a radio programme? What would need to be done to these items before they could be used?

In what ways is a printed magazine different from a radio magazine programme?

Assignment Three (M25):

Prepare a 10-minute magazine programme. Talk to your supervisor about the subject of your programme and the materials that you might use. Then follow the suggestions in this project. Here is a check-list to help you find out if your programme is of good quality.

Check-list for a Magazine Programme (M26):

1. Does the programme meet the needs of your listener? Yes ____ No ____
2. Does the programme follow the principle of "variety within unity"?   Yes ____ No ____

3. Do all the items in the programme follow the main theme or idea?   Yes ___ No ___

4. Will the first article catch the attention of your listener?   Yes ___ No ___

5. Will the last item make the listener wish to tune in again to this programme?   Yes ___ No ___

6. Are the items short enough to fit into the "attention span" of your listener?   Yes ___ No ___

7. Is each item well edited so that it will be suitable for the radio medium?   Yes ___ No ___

8. Do the opening and closing parts of the programme fit in with the mood and the idea of the rest of the programme?   Yes ___ No ___

9. Is the programme exactly the right length?   Yes ___ No ___

Although it may take some time to finish this assignment, keep working at it until you are certain it is satisfactory. Remember that writing, rewriting and re-recording are necessary even for experienced broadcasters. When you can answer "yes" to eight of the questions, take Assignments Two and Three (along with the Glossary Assignment) to your supervisor.

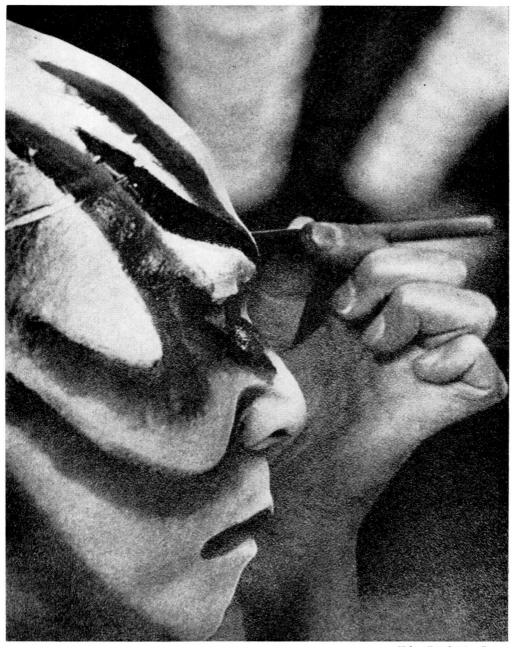

A Japanese actor puts on his make-up.

PROJECT N

Drama: Section One

How Drama Began (N1):

Before the dawn of history, when men were first beginning to communicate with each other, drama began. We don't know how it began, but we can imagine. Perhaps it happened in this way.

> A hunter was returning to his family with a large animal he had just killed. It had been an exciting hunt. The man tried to tell his family how he had tracked and killed the animal. Because he had only a few words, and he couldn't find the right ones to describe what had happened, the hunter said, "I'll show you what happened." Then step by step he went through all the movements and actions of the hunt. That may have been the world's first drama.

The important words in that little story are, "I'll show you." When our words fail us, we communicate our feelings, our thoughts, our desires through action. Children do this very easily and naturally. They watch their parents working, and then play or pretend that they are doing the same things. Parents are often amused to see their children pretending, because the parents see themselves interpreted through the actions of their children.

What the children play is not exactly the same as what the parents did. The children do what they *think* the parents are doing. They interpret. And this is another very important part of drama. A drama is not just telling facts. A drama says:

"This is the way we think it was," or "This is how we feel about it."
The best drama is an interpretation of a part of man's life.

Drama Around the World (N2):

There is no place in the world that does not have some kind of drama. Sometimes it is a very simple form of drama, such as an old man showing what he means with his hands as he tells a story. Sometimes it is drama without words, and this is called a dance or a pantomime. Sometimes actors in the drama sing their parts, and this is called an opera.

In many parts of the world there are long histories of very great drama.

The ancient Egyptians had developed some fine dance-dramas. The Turks were famous for their shadow puppets. Shadow puppets can be seen in Java, Indonesia, where their use is a highly-developed art.

The people of India are justly proud of the long history of great Hindu drama. Perhaps that is why India is one of the world's leaders in making moving pictures.

Chinese theatre is more than four thousand years old. Its highest development came during the Ming dynasty from the fourteenth to the seventeenth century. Chinese opera is seen and heard on stage, radio and television in many parts of China today.

Japan also has an old and highly-developed theatre. The ancient No plays are still being performed, along with the more poular Kabuki.

Western drama developed out of the Greek theatre which is almost three thousand years old. Greek and Western theatre have had their influence all over the world.

Most of these drama forms have been used by people as an expression of their religious faith. In fact, most drama (along with music) grew out of the need to say something more about faith than words alone could say. Much of the greatest drama today is still religious drama.

When we talk of drama in this manual, we will have to be talking about the Western form. We do this, not because it is the best, or because you should use it in your area. We do it because:

> Western drama is more widely understood in the world than any other form of drama.
> Western drama has a highly-developed style for radio.

We hope this study of Western radio drama will help you search your own culture for ways in which you can use your national drama on your radio programmes.

What is Radio Drama? (N3):

Radio drama uses sounds to tell a story. The sounds may be voices of people or noises of animals. They may be sounds made by the things people use: axes, pots and pans, automobiles, shoes, bicycles, and a host of others. These sounds can be as soft as the breath of a young girl, or as loud as thunder. They can be words whispered or shouted. The sounds can be music that is quiet and sleepy, or sharp and exciting.

Sounds on radio can become louder or quieter. A running horse may be heard from far away. It comes closer and closer, and then disappears again as if it had passed by. Or a voice comes closer gradually, as it does when a person walks up to you.

Sound on radio can do many things, but the art of a radio drama is much greater than simply thinking of new ways to use sounds. The sounds must tell a good story, and every sound must help this story grow and live.

How to Tell a Story (N4):

When I first began working in radio, I went to see a producer about a drama script I hoped to write. I was full of enthusiasm.

"I've got a wonderful idea," I said. "I want to put an old man and a young boy together, with violin music in the background . . ."

"What's the story about?" the producer asked.

"Wait," I said. "In my script there'll also be this fellow with a very wicked voice, and each time he speaks you'll hear drums in the background."

"What's the story?" repeated the producer.

"I'll work on that after I find out if you want to use the script," I said.

But the producer didn't want the script. He was looking for a story. He knew that no matter how wonderful the sound effects and music and everything else may be, a radio drama is a failure unless it has a good worthwhile story to tell. The story must always come first. Sounds are used to tell the story.

That is one reason why the first part of this project will deal with the writing of a short story. Many radio writers put their dramas into the form of a short story before they make it into a drama. Most of them agree that you will not be able to write a good drama until you can write a good short story.

Another reason is that short stories can be very useful as radio material. Many excellent programmes have been made using short stories. Some of these have been written especially for radio, while others have been adapted.

Dramas are often too expensive and too difficult for a small studio to produce. A short story is just as difficult to write but much easier to produce. It can be almost as effective as a drama. Sometimes it is even more effective, especially if it is well told.

Here is an example of a short story written by an Angolan. Study it carefully.

"Threshold to Colour Bar" (N5):*

I recall walking home one day from school at the mission. I could have taken a short cut. For no other reason except, perhaps, that I was in no hurry, I decided upon going the long way. I had to pass the general store which, like all other general stores, belonged to a white man, Senhor Ribeiro, was his name, And there, seated on the front porch with a sandwich in her hands, was the white man's daughter.

She was about my own age, eight or nine years old. Her black hair was parted in two long braids that fell over her chest. Her eyes were big like the eggs of a turtle-dove. They were a colour I had never seen before, somewhere between the mango, not quite ripe yet, and the twilight sky of a grey day. Her face was round, and it shone like the moon.

The girl was sobbing slightly as she bit her sandwich. Obviously she had been crying, and someone had tried to quiet her by keeping her mouth busy.

I looked at her and thought I was seeing an angel from a reproduction of a scene from the Nativity, which I had so many times admired hanging on a wall in my teacher's home at the mission. I wanted to speak to the girl but found no words. Instead I fell on my knees and sat on my heels facing her, unable to take my eyes away from her. Then I smiled at her, and she smiled back. She asked my name and told me hers was Linda. She offered me a bite of her bread. I started stretching out my hand but withdrew it and said "No, thanks."

Then from inside the house came her mother's voice, calling her in.

"No!" Linda refused.

"You're coming right into the house like I'm telling you!"

The next minute Senhora Ribeiro came out, grabbed Linda's arm, and to me, her eyes flashing with rage I could not then understand, she yelled:

"And you, boy, get out of here! You hear me? I'll have no goddam black messing around with my daughter."

I did not move. I just squatted there, so grave, so serious like a man, my lips compressed, my eyes lowered lest they disclose my anger or showed my tears.

That was my threshold into this thing called race prejudice. And I will never forget it.   (Angola)

* From: M. Van Horne, *Write the Vision* (National Council of Churches, 1952).

What is a Story? (N6):

We could spend a lot of time trying to tell you exactly what a story is, and in the end we would not agree because there are so many kinds of stories. Here is one description of a story that may help.

> Writing a story is making a world in your imagination and in the imagination of your listener. There are people in this imaginary world. The way they live and the things they do are very interesting to your audience. The actions and lives of these people move from one happening to the next, always leading to a conclusion or the end of the story.

The imaginary world we have created can be called the "setting", or the place where things happen. The people in this world are called "characters", and the things they do are called the "plot".

Sometimes setting is most important in a story; sometimes it is the characters; sometimes it is the plot. All three are always there, but usually one becomes more important than the others.

The listener to your radio programme doesn't think of all this, of course. In fact, if it is a good story which he finds very interesting, he will simply enjoy it. He will have no idea why, because he was too absorbed in the story to stop and wonder about it.

However, if you are going to write and produce good radio stories and dramas, then *you* must certainly know why. People who are just beginning to write often think they have found a wonderful idea for a story. They find it a thrilling and interesting idea. That is good.

The hard part is to take a good idea and work out all the details of the character, plot, and setting, to make sure they will work into an interesting story. This is the place where writers fail most often.

Something Happens (N7):

A story is not a story unless something happens. It is because the listener is expecting something to happen that he keeps listening. This *action* must lead to a climax, the place where all the parts of the story come together. The action and the way in which it leads to the climax is the *plot* of the story. When the story ends, things are different. The characters may be richer or poorer, they may be better or worse, happier or unhappy, but they are never the same as at the beginning. Look at the story "Threshold to Colour Bar" and try to find the way in which the plot leads to the climax.

What makes the difference between a good plot and a bad one? The answer is usually in the *conflict* or tension found in the plot. There are many kinds of conflict, but they can be described as opposing forces or opposing wills. The conflict may be between:

one person and another,
one person and many people.
a person and an idea (such as one man fighting for freedom in a nation where most people don't really care),
two different ideas (one political or religious viewpoint against another), or
a person and something inside himself (such as a man trying not to be a coward).

Developing Conflict (N8):

The first thing to do when you are beginning to write a story or a drama is to think carefully about the conflict in your plot. Sometimes there may be many conflicts in one plot.

Here, for instance, is a question that could make a very good story. What if a young woman, who was going to be married the next day, suddenly found out that there was insanity in her family which might be passed on through her to her children. If she had not made this discovery, she would probably have been happily married and there would not have been a story.

But after the discovery there is a problem, or rather several problems. Is she likely to become insane herself? Should she go ahead with her marriage? Should she keep the discovery secret? Should she tell the man whom she is going to marry and let him decide? If so, what will he decide? Is it fair to make him decide this? Should the girl decide herself and spare the man his decision? How will the man feel about it?

These questions tell us about some of the problems facing the girl and about some of the ways she can act. They do not tell us about the conflict. Before we can know what the conflict is, we must know what kind of a girl we have in our story. Her character will determine how she acts. Depending on her character, the conflict may be between the girl and her conscience; or, if she tells the young man, it may be between the two of them if they disagree. If they agree, the conflict may be between the two of them and their families or their neighbours.

So you see, a simple idea must be studied and analysed before it can develop into a good story. It must be analysed in relation to the characters of our story and the setting in which it takes place. All must be woven together tightly like a good piece of cloth with many different kinds of thread.

Secondary Conflicts (N9):

While every good story has one or two main conflicts, many stories also have smaller conflicts, or secondary conflicts. A full-sized novel may have many secondary conflicts. A short radio story or drama usually has only one main conflict. Longer radio dramas might have one or two secondary conflicts. The shorter the programme, the simpler the plot must be.

A secondary conflict must always be tied to the main one. In the story of the girl and her family's insanity, there might be many kinds of secondary conflicts, or *sub-plots*, as they are sometimes called. Perhaps the girl's father doesn't like the man. Perhaps there is something in the man's background which he is trying to keep from the girl.

It is important to remember, when working out the plot for a story, that the listener must be completely clear in his understanding of the problem at all times. He must know what *is* happening, but he must not know what is *going* to happen. Never make your plots so difficult that your audience has trouble understanding. It is better to be too simple than too difficult.

Remember also that the kind of audience you have will determine how difficult your dramas can be. An educated listener will be able to appreciate a complicated drama more easily than will someone without an education.

Plot Example (N10):

A broadcaster in Ethiopia made this outline for a drama. Study it to see how it goes from one incident to another and finally reaches a climax.

> A young man has been married according to the tradition of his people; his wife was chosen for him. She is a pleasant but simple and uneducated girl. After his marriage his family suddenly finds it possible to send him to college to complete his education. He returns home with the impression that marriage with an educated girl would be much better for him. He begins to dislike and despise his wife. With these thoughts there follow in quick succession thoughts of getting rid of her and marrying one of the college girls. A friend to whom he tells his feelings agrees with him and

assures him it is the right thing for him to do. The young man's mind is made up and he is ready to reveal his intentions to his wife and family. But before he can do so, he accidentally meets someone who takes the opportunity, after learning the young man's intentions, to show him the true meaning of marriage – that it is a fellowship and union for life. He is further shown that this new life formed by their union in marriage will begin when he accepts the problem of their different education and begins to overcome it by sharing his new-found knowledge with his wife.*

Movement (N11):

As a drama or a story goes along, the listener learns about the problems faced by the characters. As the characters face each incident or each happening in the story, the possible outcome of the story changes. This is called the *movement* of the plot.

Here is an example of a plot that has no movement:

> Jawan decided to leave his village and go to the city. He finds the city very big and bewildering. However, he works hard and manages to get through school. He then finds a good position with the government and becomes a successful man. When he returns to his village, all his people greet him as an important person.

Although things happen in this story, nothing occurs that changes the possible outcome of the story. It is simply one event after another. There is little that is interesting for the listener because he is never in doubt about what will happen.

The Character Outline (N12):

The best writers of dramas and stories usually make a careful step-by-step outline of their plot before they begin to write. Many also find it useful to write several paragraphs describing each of the characters in their story. They realise that a writer cannot really work out the plot until he has a very clear idea of the characters.

The first step then, is to outline your characters. Write a few paragraphs telling who they are, how they are related to each other, how they feel about each other, how they feel about the problem they face, what kind of work they do, their education, social standing, and many other things. Even describe the way

* RVOG, Addis Ababa, Ethiopia.

they look, so that you have a clear picture in your own mind. Do this for each major character. Then in one paragraph (not more than twenty-five words) write down a description of the conflict. This description should be very clear. Give it to a friend to read, then ask him to explain it back to you. If your friend has trouble understanding the conflict, then make it more simple. If you cannot summarise your conflict in less than twenty-five words, then it is probably too difficult for a short radio programme.

The Plot Outline (N13):

Now you can begin your outline. You have described your characters and their problem. Now you must tell what happens to them.

The Beginning and the End (N14):

Begin by finding the best place to start the story. How you do this will depend on the kind of story or drama you are going to write. However, a good rule (until you gain more experience) is to find a place in your story where your major conflict will be quickly understood by your listener. Think of various possible places to begin the story, and choose the one you feel is best.

Next, outline the climax and the end of the story. A good climax is a place where your listener can say, "Yes, that's the way it had to be." The conflict is finished. The problems are solved, or at least we can see that they will be solved. Sometimes the climax comes when a problem becomes clear.

The end of the story should come very quickly after the climax. After the main conflict is finished, explain only those things which are completely necessary, then stop.

In the story, "Threshold to Colour Bar" (N5), the climax comes on the line, "And you, boy, get out of here." There are only two short paragraphs after the climax. If the author had said anything more, he would have spoiled his story. If he had tried to add a paragraph about the evils of race prejudice he would have spoiled the story. The author could not have said anything more powerful than what he had already said in his story: "It hurts to be hated." He said that, and he stopped. That was all he needed to say.

We could draw a picture of the way a story rises from the beginning of the action to the climax, and then ends very quickly right afterwards. The picture would look like this.

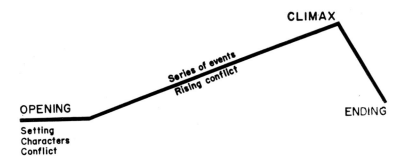

CLIMAX

Series of events
Rising conflict

OPENING   ENDING

Setting
Characters
Conflict

The Middle (N15):

Now comes the most difficult part – the middle. Often writers think that this is just a matter of tying the beginning and the end together. Others think that if many things happen, it will be a good story.

However, each event or happening in the story must move the plot a little closer to the climax. Also, each event must change the strength of the opposing forces, so that for a while it seems one side will win, and then it seems that the other side will win. Every event must have an effect on the way the story ends. The listener should be kept in doubt as to what will happen.

We can compare a good story to a race.
Six men are ready to start. The people watching are interested to find out who will win. The men start with equal speed, each one beside the other. No one runs faster; not one drops behind. One man is shorter than the others and for a while the people watching wonder if he will keep up. He does, and the six men finished the race shoulder to shoulder, although the short man ran just a little ahead and won the race.
That is a very dull story. Here is a better story.
Six men are ready to start. The starting gun sounds and number 3 takes the lead immediately. The short fellow, number 5 has a bad start and is far behind. Number 4 runs faster and begins to get closer to the leader, number 3. Number 3 drops back to second place, then to third. The short fellow, number 5 is running faster now. He passes number 3, then number 6, and now he has passed number 2. At the same time, the first leader has gained speed again and is catching up. The short fellow has passed everyone, but number 3 is running fast and is catching up. Now both of them are running

side by side. They are near the finish line. In a final burst of speed the short fellow races ahead and wins the race.

The beginning and end of both stories were the same. However, we can easily see which story will keep the listeners interested. In the second story we did not know until the very end who was going to win. At first we thought it would be number 3, then we thought it would be number 4, but it really turned out to be number 5.

Of course, we must remember that there are many kinds of stories, many kinds of dramas, and many kinds of plots. We have talked about only one kind. If you can learn to do this type of story well, you will have gone a long way towards understanding other kinds as well.

Become familiar with many kinds of stories and dramas, especially those of your own country. When you read, study the stories to find how they were put together. Ask yourself, "What is the conflict? What is the plot? Who are the characters? Why is this story interesting?"

If you do this whenever you read a story or hear a drama, you will find your own writing improves because of your greater understanding.

Assignment One (N16):

Read "Threshold to Colour Bar" several times. Write a paragraph or two describing:

> the conflict,
> the setting,
> the plot (make an outline of the plot such as the author might have used), and
> the characters (use your imagination to add things that are not in the story).

Assignment Two (N17):

Write a short story in your own language. Make the story suitable to be told on the radio, and one that will be of interest and value to most of your listeners. The story should be from two to five minutes long. When you have written the story, use this check-list to find out if your story is of good quality. Do not be surprised if you must write your story several times over before it is good enough.

Check-list for a Short Story (N18):

1. Does the story begin at a place where the audience will understand the conflict quickly?   Yes ____ No ____
2. Does the story move from one event to another, each time bringing us closer to the climax?   Yes ____ No ____
3. Does the story keep the listener wondering, until the very end, how things will turn out?   Yes ____ No ____
4. Does the story end very quickly after the climax?   Yes ____ No ____
5. Are your words clear, interesting, and simple?   Yes ____ No ____

When you have finished writing your story, record it and listen to yourself and your reading. Record it again if you are not satisfied. When you feel you have a good story on tape (you should be able to say "yes" to all the questions) take it to your supervisor, along with your character outlines, your plot outline, and your final script. Also bring your work from Assignment One.

Writing for Radio (N19):   PART TWO

Several times in this manual, we have said that radio must use the spoken style of language. We will say it again, because it is so very important.

Newspaper and magazine writers look over their work to judge how well it *reads*. The radio writer must look over his work to see how well it *sounds*. Most of us have been taught in school to write for the printed page. However, in radio nobody, except the studio staff, ever sees the page on which a script is written. The listener certainly doesn't see it.

One of the important differences between the written style and the spoken style is this. The eye can understand a much longer sentence than the ear. Furthermore, a person reading can always go back and read a sentence again if he doesn't understand. The radio listener cannot do this. That is why the radio writer must be very careful to make his sentences short, clear, and easily understood.

This does not mean that radio writing must be dull and uninteresting. Keeping your writing clear and simple is one of the best ways to be sure that it is not dull.

Narration (N20):

There are the two kinds of speaking in a radio drama. The *narrator* or announcer may introduce the story, or may even take part in the telling of the story all the way along. Sometimes a narrator may be one of the characters in the drama.

R

There are some people who will warn a young writer against using a narrator in a drama. A narrator, however, is like almost everything else a writer uses. Used well, and in the right places, a narrator can be very useful.

The person who wrote "The Contrary Wife" (N35) used a narrator very well. There are others, however, who use a narrator only because they do not want to spend the time writing the dialogue carefully.

Use a narrator when you feel it will really make your drama better. Do not use one just to make the drama a little easier to write.

Dialogue (N21):

The other kind of speaking is called *dialogue*. This is the conversation between two or more people in the play. Every writer must understand the use of dialogue, because it is the most important part of a drama. Through the use of dialogue, the writer must let the listener know what is happening, where it is happening, why it is happening, and to what kind of people it is happening.

Real conversation between people doesn't do all these things. Radio dialogue must, however, and at the same time it must seem to be just like ordinary conversation. For instance, in ordinary conversation, if you wanted your brother to open the door, you might just say, "Open it!" Since you and your brother are standing beside the door, there is no more that needs to be said. However, in a radio drama, you would need to let your audience know *what* was to be opened and *who* was to open it. The radio audience would not be able to see your brother or the door. Therefore, the same idea in a radio play would be:

"Open the door, Lader."

How do People Talk (N22):

Have you ever listened to people talking to each other? Have you listened to the *way* they talk? You will find it a great help in your radio writing if you really make a point of listening to ordinary conversation: in your home, on the bus, in the studio, and on the street corner. Listen to the way people put their words and their sentences together. Listen to the way they express themselves.

When people are talking to each other, they don't usually speak in complete sentences. They begin to say something, then they stop and say something else. Sometimes they start to say a sentence one way, and then finish by saying it another way. When you are writing for radio, it is this kind of talking that you are trying to imitate. Remember, though, that you must try more to create the *feeling* that people are talking naturally. If your radio dialogue is exactly like an ordinary conversation, your listeners would find it very boring because it would not move along from one event to another quickly enough. Ordinary conversation has too many wasted words.

In an ordinary conversation, people usually speak only a few sentences or a few words at a time before somebody else begins to talk. When they get excited, or when they are arguing, they often interrupt each other.

Radio dialogue imitates this kind of conversation for two reasons. First, it is more like real life. Secondly, the radio listener's attention span is very short. Only a very skilful writer and a very talented actor can keep an audience interested for even a one-minute speech in a radio drama. A radio drama is different from a stage play or a movie where the actor can keep the audience interested with his movements. In a radio play the dialogue must move quickly from one character to another, or the listener may forget that the other people in the drama are there. Remember, the listener cannot see the other characters, and must be constantly reminded of who is there.

If it is necessary to have one person give a long speech, then be sure the speech is broken up by remarks or interruptions from the other characters in your play.

Characters Speak in Their Own Style (N23):

Everybody has his own personality. You have a personality, and I have a personality. Each of the characters in a radio script must have personality, the little things that make each person different from all others.

In real life, our personality is shown in many ways: in the way we dress, the way we walk, the way we look, the way we act, and in the way we speak. In a radio drama, the personality of each character can be shown only through his speech. The listener cannot see what he looks like. He can only hear. From what he hears, the listener forms a picture in his own mind of what he thinks each character is like.

The radio writer must help the listener form this picture in his mind. However, he must be sure that the picture in the listener's mind fits the kind of character the writer is trying to show in his drama.

To do this, the writer must do a great deal of listening to conversations around him. He must be aware of the little differences between one kind of person and another. Personality, age, education, the work he does, his home town, and many other features will show in the way he speaks.

Of course, the actor must also be able to interpret the different kinds of personalities. He must do as much listening as the writer. However, the writer must write the dialogue in such a way that the actor can easily interpret the kind of personality the writer intended.

Putting Personality into Dialogue (N24):

You can do this by having the character use certain kinds of words, or by repeating certain phrases. You may create a character who speaks very easily, or one who has a very hard time finding the right words. If the character is educated, he would use words different from those used by the character who is not educated.

Be careful not to overdo this, however. It is very easy to make a character seem ridiculous by making his personality seem unnaturally strong. There are certain plays (such as some comedies) where this can be done, but as a rule you should not overdo a character unless you want him to appear silly.

When you have found a certain style of speaking for one of your characters, be sure to keep that style through out the whole play. Your audience will be confused if someone talks like a politician during the first part of the drama, but speaks like a shopkeeper at the end.

The writer must be sure that there are personality differences between the characters in his drama. That is why so many good writers spend a lot of time describing the personalities of their characters before they begin to write. If you do this (as we suggested in *N12*) you will find it much easier to put personality into your characters. One of the most common problems found in radio dramas is that all the characters speak and act the same way.

Accents and Dialects (N25):

It is often easiest to give personality to people by having them use a certain accent or dialect. However, accents and dialects are far more difficult to write than most people realise, and there are some real dangers.

Before you write an accent or a dialect into a script, be sure you have an actor who can speak this way extremely well. There are few things that will offend people more than hearing a poor interpretation of their accent. However, if you have an actor from one part of your country who speaks with a certain accent, then use him if it fits into your drama. Do not make fun of people by using accents.

In some countries, radio stations have prepared dramas using several languages or dialects at once. These are prepared for listeners who have some knowledge of more than one language.

In some cases, switching from one language to another can be an excellent way to teach a new language through radio drama.

> One successful series was about a young girl who had married a foreigner. She brought the man to live in her village. The young man and his new in-laws had many very humorous misunderstandings. Everyone enjoyed the programme, and many listeners learned quite a bit of language.

How Many People? (N26):

Because radio listeners find too many characters in a drama confusing, it is usually best to have only a few major characters in each drama. The shorter the drama, the fewer major characters there should be.

By major characters, we mean those which have a big part to play in the action, characters the listener would be able to remember by name.

The drama, "The Contrary Wife" (N35) has three major characters: the narrator, Sium and his wife. The "voices" at the end of the play are not major characters. In some dramas you might have a great many more of these small or minor characters. The listener doesn't need to remember who they are. He is only aware of what they do for the moment, and then he can forget them because the drama moves on.

Some drama writers feel there should be no more than six major characters in any radio drama that is half an hour or longer. A 15-minute drama should have even fewer. Other writers might disagree. Still it is wise to remember that the more people there are, the more difficult it is for the listener to keep them separated in his mind.

There should seldom be more than three or four people in any one part or scene of a drama. There is a good reason for this. The radio listener has a very short memory. If he does not hear a character speak for a while, he soon forgets him. Therefore, all those who are taking part in that scene must have something to say quite frequently. It is very hard to have more than three or four people taking part in the same conversation.

Who is in the Scene? (N27):

Because of the listener's short memory, it is necessary to keep reminding him who is talking. Use names as much as you can without being unnatural. This is especially important as each scene begins. The characters should call each other by their names.

In a stage play or at the cinema, the characters can be seen. Often they are introduced to the audience by the titles at the beginning of the programme, or by a printed list of actors and the parts they play. This cannot be done on radio. The audience doesn't know who is there unless the writer uses the dialogue to tell them.

If for some reason, there is a character in the scene who doesn't have anything to say, then the other characters must be constantly reminding the listener that he is there.

For instance, if Jhinabhoi and Jasvanti are talking, and Sundar is asleep in the same room, the conversation might be something like this:

JHINABHOI:　I've got to talk to you, Jasvanti.

JASVANTI:　　All right Jhinabhoi. But please let's not quarrel. I don't want to wake up Sundar. She was so tired . . . she just threw herself down over there . . . and she fell fast asleep.

JHINABHOI:　I don't want to wake Sundar either; in fact she's what I want to talk about.

The listener has learned the names of the two people speaking, and also that there is a third person sleeping in the room. The listener will not be surprised when Sundar wakes a little later and begins to speak.

Dialogue Tells Where (N28):

Whenever a listener hears dialogue in a drama, he will imagine that the conversation is going on in a certain place. Even if there is nothing in the dialogue that tells him where it is happening, he will imagine a place. That is why it is important to help the listener imagine the right place; otherwise, the listener may think the conversation is taking place in a home, and then later realise it is really in an office or in a restaurant. His attention will be taken away from the action in the play, because he is wondering where the drama is taking place.

You can help the listener know the location of the scene in the same way as you let him know who is there, by putting the information into the dialogue. You do not need to give a complete description of the place. Just a hint or two is enough.

This can be done with a narrator who may say, "A few days later, Jasvanti was talking to Sundar on the grounds of their school." However, it is always better to let the characters set the scene themselves. One way is to use the last line of the scene that goes before to tell the listener where the next scene is going to take place. For instance:

SUNDAR: Listen Jasvanti, I have to go to my class. I'll meet you in one hour on the school grounds. (FADING.) You and I have to talk about . . . (OUT.)
(3-SECOND PAUSE.)
JASVANTI: (FADING IN QUICKLY.) (CALLING.) I'm over here Sundar . . . over here by the door to the school.
SUNDAR: (COMING ON MIKE.) Oh hello, Jasvanti . . . etc.

Or, you can let the listener know through the dialogue in another way. Suppose Jasvanti and Sundar were talking in their school dormitory.

JASVANTI: Goodness, I wish they would give us better rooms at this school. Look at this place! Crowded and so small.
SUNDAR: I know. May I sit on your bed?
JASVANTI: Of course. Did you know that Jhinabhoi plans to go back home?

Give Eyes to the Listener (N29):

All through the radio play, the listener imagines he sees people moving around, just as they do in real life. They come into the room or they leave the room. They sit down, stand up, walk around. They open a package, eat their supper, or do any number of things. The actors who portray these characters do not move around. They move just enough to go off microphone or on microphone. However, it is through the actors' voices and through the dialogue in the script that the feeling of action is given to the listener.

Sometimes a sound effect goes with an action, but even then the listener must usually be told something about it.

What is wrong with this scene?

JASVANTI: Well, I guess it's settled then.
SUNDAR: Well maybe it is, but I still don't feel happy.
JHINABHOI: Neither do I.
SOUND: DOOR OPENS AND CLOSES.

We don't know which one of the three people left. For all we know, somebody else may have come in. To have any meaning, the scene would need to be like this:

JASVANTI: Well, I guess it's settled then.
SUNDAR: Well, maybe it is, but I'm still not happy. Anyway, I have to go. (MOVING OFF MIKE.) Good-bye Jasvanti . . . 'Bye Jhinabhoi.
SOUND: DOOR OPENS.
JASVANTI: 'Bye Sundar!
JHINABHOI: 'Bye.
SOUND: DOOR CLOSES.

Now we have no doubt as to who went and who stayed.

Even little things must be clear to the listener. Here's another scene that would be confusing.

SUNDAR: Here's something for you.
JASVANTI: Why Sundar . . . for me?
SUNDAR: Sure!
JASVANTI: Well, you really shouldn't have . . . but I like it. Thank you so much.

What did Sundar give Jasvanti? The listener doesn't know. Written another way, however, the listener can almost taste the sweets.

SUNDAR: Here's something for you.
JASVANTI: Why Sundar . . . for me?
SUNDAR: It's nothing much. Open it!
JASVANTI: How wonderful! (SLIGHT EFFORT AND RUSTLE OF PAPER.) There! Mmmmmm. Candies! They look wonderful! Here, have one.

It takes some time for a writer to develop the skill to be able to write his dialogue so that the listener feels it is completely natural, at the same time never leaving any doubt about *what* is happening, *where* it is happening, *who* it is happening to, and *why* it is happening.

Much More to Learn (N30):

There are still many things that must be said about dramas. In the next project, you will find more ideas about writing radio plays, and about producing these plays. Nothing will help you as much, however, as listening to a great many radio dramas and making notes on all that you hear. Listen critically. Listen and try to discover the way things are done and why they are done. Decide in your own mind what things are good and what things are not so good. Then write! Write as many dramas as you have time for. Criticise your own dramas, and ask others to criticise them for you. Do not be afraid to make mistakes. Only by making mistakes and then discovering them will you learn to write well.

Assignment Three (N31):

Write a short paragraph to answer each of the following questions about the sample drama, "The Contrary Wife", which follows Assignment Five. Remember that although it is a good drama, it is not perfect. There are things wrong with it, and you should try to find out what they are.

> Does each of the characters have his (or her) own manner of speaking? What are the differences?
>
> Are there too many people in each scene, or too few? Why do you think so?
>
> Will the listener have difficulty knowing who is in each scene? Explain.
>
> Will the listener have difficulty knowing where each scene takes place? Explain.
>
> Will this drama be interesting and useful to listeners in your area? Explain.

Assignment Four (N32):

Listen to at least two dramas on the radio or from tapes which your supervisor gives you. If possible, these should be in your own language and written for listeners in your area. Write a short paragraph answering each of the questions in Assignment Three.

Assignment Five (N33):

Write a short drama, about five or ten minutes long, about life in your own country. It should be about a subject that is interesting and useful to your listeners. Follow all the steps for planning and writing as suggested in this project. Be prepared to write and rewrite your drama at least three or four times before it is satisfactory. The following check-list will help you decide when your drama is satisfactory.

Check-list for Drama Script (N34):

1. Do you feel your drama has a good exciting story?　Yes ＿＿ No ＿＿
2. Is something happening at all times in your drama?　Yes ＿＿ No ＿＿
3. Do the things that happen help to bring the story closer to its climax?　Yes ＿＿ No ＿＿
4. Will the listener become easily aware of the conflict in the story?　Yes ＿＿ No ＿＿
5. Is the drama written in the spoken style of your language?　Yes ＿＿ No ＿＿
6. Does each of the characters have a personality that shows in the way he speaks?　Yes ＿＿ No ＿＿
7. Does each scene have only a few characters so that the listener does not become confused with too many people?　Yes ＿＿ No ＿＿
8. Will the listener know which characters are in the scene?　Yes ＿＿ No ＿＿
9. Does the dialogue tell where each scene is taking place?　Yes ＿＿ No ＿＿
10. Is a narrator used only when there is a very good reason?　Yes ＿＿ No ＿＿

When you are certain that your drama is of high quality (you should be able to answer "yes" to eight of the ten questions in the check-list) then take your character outlines, your plot outline, and your script to your supervisor.

Sample Drama Script (N35):

THE CONTRARY WIFE　　　　　　　　　　　BROADCAST DAY ＿＿＿
AN ETHIOPIAN FOLK TALE★　　　　　　　　TIME OF BROADCAST ＿＿＿
　　　　　　　　　　　　　　　　　　　　　WRITER ＿＿＿

CAST:	NARRATOR
	SIUM
	HIS WIFE
	TWO VOICES
SOUND:	RIVER AFTER HEAVY RAIN.
MUSIC:	HUMOROUS INSTRUMENTAL FOLK-SONG.

★ RVOG, Addis Ababa, Ethiopia.

1. MUSIC:	ESTABLISH FOR A FEW SECONDS TILL APPROPRIATE FADE, THEN INTO B.G. FOR:
2. NARRATOR:	This is a story for wives. And especially wives who sometimes find themselves behaving in a very contrary way towards their husbands. And therefore, it is a story for husbands too, perhaps. There was once a man whose name was Sium. Sium had a wife who contantly made him miserable. She was so stubborn that she always did things by opposites. (MUSIC FADES OUT.) For instance, the daily conversation between Sium and his wife often went something like this . . .
3. SIUM:	I think we should build a new house, a round stone house.
4. WIFE:	No! We should build a square clay house.
5. SIUM:	But a round stone house would be . . .
6. WIFE:	(INTERRUPTING.) No! We will build a square clay house!
7. SIUM:	(SIGHING.) Yes, Dear.
8. NARRATOR:	So the new house that Sium built was square and made of baked clay. Another time the conversation might go like this . . .
9. SIUM:	The water at the river is stale. When you go for water, better go to the spring.
10. WIFE:	No. The water at the spring is no good, the river is best.
11. NARRATOR:	Or, again another time . . .
12. SIUM:	I am thirsty. Give me some coffee.
13. WIFE:	It isn't coffee, but pancakes you need.
14. NARRATOR:	So she would give him pancakes when he asked for coffee, roasted durra when he asked for meat, and stew when he asked for roasted durra. When Sium asked his wife to buy a basket, she would come home with a pot. And when he said to buy spices, she would decide what they really needed was salt.
15. SIUM:	It is time to go across the plain to visit your family.
16. WIFE:	No! We will go over the hill to visit your father and mother!
17. NARRATOR:	So life was very miserable for the poor man, until, as any wise man should do who has a contrary wife, he began to learn how he could get what he wanted.

18. SIUM:	(CLOSE TO MIKE. VOICING THOUGHTS.) Hmmmm . . . it is always exactly opposite to what *I say*. Therefore, the best thing I can do is to suggest the very opposite to what *I want*! Yes! That's what I'll do. When I want tea, I'll ask for pancakes. When I want pancakes, I'll ask for tea. When the river water is bad to drink, I'll tell my wife to fill her jars there . . . and she'll always go to the spring instead! If I want to see *my* parents, I'll suggest we go to *her* parents. When I want music, I'll demand quiet! Ahhh, what a clever plan! Why didn't I think of this before. I'll try it at once. Right now I'd like to have some pancakes! (LOUD.) I'm thirsty. give me some tea!
19. WIFE:	No. You don't need tea. Rather, you need pancakes.
20. SIUM:	(CLOSE.) That's fine. Now I know how to get the things I want.
21. NARRATOR:	Sium's new idea proved to be very useful.
22. SIUM:	(CLOSE.) The water from the river is too bad to drink. (LOUD.) I think you should fill your jars at the river, Wife, the water is really good!
23. WIFE:	It's no good! I'll go to the well.
24. NARRATOR:	Or, another time . . .
25. SIUM:	(LOUD.) Shouldn't we go to see your parents?
26. WIFE:	No. We'll go to *your* parents.
27. SIUM:	(CLOSE.) That's what I wanted.
28. NARRATOR:	Or, another time . . .
29. SIUM:	(CLOSE.) Our guests should really be entertained with some music. (LOUD.) Let's just sit here and have it *very* quiet.
30. WIFE:	No! I'm going to call the musicians. It's music we need!
31. CONTROL:	MUSIC: ESTABLISH AND FADE INTO B.G.
32. NARRATOR:	So this is the way things were with Sium for a long time, and the people of the village were very sorry for him. No one knew, certainly not his wife, that he was secretly getting his way all the time. (MUSIC GRADUALLY CROSS-FADES INTO B.G. TO SOUND OF RUSHING WATER.) One day they went into the city. As they returned to the village, a heavy rain came. It rained very hard. When Sium and his wife came to the river they found a rushing torrent. The swirling water

carried small trees and bushes along, and overflowed its banks.

33.	SIUM:	(OVER SOUND.) The crossing is dangerous!
34.	WIFE:	It is not dangerous!
35.	SIUM:	Perhaps we should wait until the water goes down.
36.	WIFE:	Nonsense!
37.	SIUM:	Well, then I'll go first and feel the way with my feet . . . (SLIGHTLY OFF-MIKE) brrr . . . the water is cold. It is swift and almost carries me along! . . . There! I'm almost across! You may start – but be careful! Don't put your foot where the water is foaming – there is a deep hole there!
38.	WIFE:	I will put my foot where I like. And if I like to step where the water is foaming, then that's exactly what I shall do . . . (SUDDEN GASP, GURGLE, SPLUTTERING.)
39.	SIUM:	(CALLING.) Help! Come help me! Help, someone! My wife is drowning! Bring a rope! Help! Help!
40.	VOICES:	EXCITED MURMURS, GROWING LOUDER.
41.	SIUM:	(CALLING.) Come and help me find my wife!
42.	FIRST VOICE:	(OFF-MIKE.) Where is she? Where is she?
43.	SIUM:	She disappeared under the water. I did not see which way she went!
44.	SECOND VOICE:	(SLIGHTLY OFF-MIKE.) Where is she?
45.	SIUM:	I am quite sure, since she is always so contrary, that she floated upstream!
46.	NARRATOR:	So they all ran upstream and searched for her, but she wasn't to be found. And finally, as it was getting dark, they went back to the village without her.
47.	CONTROL:	MUSIC FADE IN QUIETLY BEHIND SIUM.
48.	SIUM:	(SADLY.) That is how it is, my friends. You see the lengths to which some people will go to have their own way!
49.	CONTROL:	MUSIC FULL TO TIME.

PROJECT O

Drama: Section Two

Drama Productions (O1): PART ONE

In *Project N* we gave you some suggestions on how to write a drama for radio. In this project we will discuss some of the ways in which a drama is produced for radio. However, as you work through this project, you will also learn more about writing dramas. The writer must know how music, sound effects, and other things are used, if he is to put them into a script. Even if you intend to write only dramas, you should study this project carefully.

The Three Tools (O2):

When you make a radio drama, you have three tools with which to work:

    speech,
    sound effects, and
    music.

You may use these tools one at a time, sometimes two together, sometimes all three. The secret of a good drama production lies in using these to paint an exciting and interesting picture in the imagination of the listener. Like any other tools, the usefulness of speech, sound effects and music depend on the workman who uses them.

In radio, speech usually does most of the work, but sometimes sound alone, or music alone can create the action or the movement in a drama.

Volume (O3):

Whenever you are using two or more of these tools in a drama, the one that has full-volume will have the attention of the listener. Here is an example. If you have the voice of a speaker talking to a crowd, as well as the sound of the crowd, the person in the control room will decide which will be important for the listener.

If the sound of the crowd is at full-volume, and the sound of the speaker is at half-volume, the listener will think the speaker is trying unsuccessfully to address an unruly crowd.

If the sound of the speaker is at full-volume, and the sound of the crowd is at half-volume, the listener will think the speaker is being successful in gaining the attention of an unruly crowd.

In each case the sound effects and the speaker are the same. The difference is in the volume.

Volume is like the spotlight in a stage drama. In a stage drama, the actor standing in the brightest light will have the attention of the audience. In radio, the sound having the most volume will have the attention of the listener.

Sound Effects (O4):

Every sound effect used on radio helps the listener to imagine some activity – something that is happening. Perhaps this is why sound is so exciting. Drama producers often have good fun thinking of new ways to use sounds, and experimenting with new ways to make sound effects. It is very useful to do this sort of thing, since you may discover many interesting ideas and methods. You may try anything you wish when you are experimenting, and you need not be afraid of a bad result.

When you are actually producing a drama for the radio, however, remember this very important rule.

Every sound, just like every word and every bit of music, *must serve a purpose*. It must only be there when it really helps the programme. When it does not help the effect of the whole programme, it should not be used.

Sounds used on radio can be divided into two kinds.

Sounds which the listener can easily recognise. He will not need to be told what the sound is, because he will know as soon as he hears it. Here are some of these sounds:

  horses' hooves,
  angry crowd,
  rattle of dishes, and
  wind howling.

There are, of course, many others that can be recognised easily.

Sounds which the listener will not be able to identify without help from the writer. *Most* sounds are like this. Unless there is a hint from the writer, the listener will have no idea what the sound is.

Using Sound Effects (O5):

You may already know that you can make the sound of fire by crackling a piece of cellophane near a microphone. However, the same piece of cellophane could also be used to make the sound of rain falling. What makes this sound seem to be fire at one time, and rain at another? Let us suppose we have a drama that goes like this:

> Two men are talking together on a street corner. All of a sudden their conversation is stopped by the sound of a fire truck going by. In the distance we hear the shouts of frightened people. The two men talk about the fire down the street and decide to rush to the scene. As they get closer, we hear the sound of the crowd at the fire gradually getting closer. Along with the crowd we now hear the crackling of the cellophane.

By this time, the listener has no doubt that he hears the sound of the fire. Imagination is a wonderful thing. If we are given a few suggestions, we can paint a complete picture of a fire from just a few sound effects and a few hints in the dialogue. The imagination of the listener will also put in many little details that are only suggested in the drama.

Let the Listener Know (O6):

In most cases when you are using a sound effect, you must somehow let your listener know what the sound is. Sounds such as the following almost always must be identified in the dialogue:

rain,
fire,
waterfall,
river,
noises in a factory,
thunder,
automobiles, and
aeroplanes.

It is usually best to let the listener know what the sound is before it is heard. When this is done, there is no danger that the listener will get the wrong idea. An example:

FRANCISCO: Maria . . . where is that coffee! Hurry up!

MARIA: (OFF-MICROPHONE.) It's coming . . . just wait a minute! (MOVING ON-MICROPHONE.) I wish you wouldn't always be in such a hurry. (CLINK OF CUP AND SPOON.) Here.

FRANCISCO: Well, I wish you wouldn't always be so slow!

Sometimes, of course, the sound must be identified just after it has begun. In fact, you may wish to make the listener puzzle a moment before you let him know what it is. This may be dangerous, because he can easily come to the wrong conclusion. He may think he hears the sound of a factory when it is really a waterfall you want him to hear. If that happens, the listener may miss part of the drama while he is wondering what happened.

Usually sounds are identified through the dialogue or the narration, but sometimes they can be identified by another sound. The noise of an automobile could be mistaken for the sound of any machine, but if the horn sounds, the listener will immediately know what it is.

When identifying the characters in a scene, the place where the scene takes place, or a sound effect, try to be natural. Here, for instance, is the wrong way:

SOUND: MOTOR-CYCLE IN THE DISTANCE COMING CLOSER.

PEDRO: Oh, here comes my good friend Juan riding his new motor-cycle. I can hear the sound of it.

It would be much better to do it this way:

SOUND: MOTOR-CYCLE IN THE DISTANCE COMING CLOSER.

PEDRO: (CALLING.) Juan! Juan come over here!

SOUND: MOTOR-CYCLE COMES CLOSER AND STOPS.

JUAN: Hello Pedro . . . how do you like my new motor-cycle?

Of course, if you were going to use a sound like that, there would have to be a very good reason why it should come into the drama. A motor-cycle might be used to show that Juan had plenty of money, or that Pedro was jealous of Juan. If there is no good reason for the sound, the attention of the listener will be taken away from an important part of the drama.

S

Choosing Sounds (O7):

Next time you are in a room with three or four people in it, close your eyes for a moment. Listen for *all* the sounds. Think how noisy a radio drama would be if you put in *all* the sounds you heard. The shuffling of feet, the noise of children playing, the bump and scrape of a chair, the rattle of dishes – these are sounds that are all there in real life. To include them all in a drama would simply make it noisy and confusing for the listener. Use only those sounds which are important to the drama.

For instance, you might use the sound of footsteps if you wanted to give the impression of a lonely man walking down a street all by himself late at night. The sound of someone running down a pathway, or the creak on the stairs late at night might be very useful in your drama. However, the footsteps of someone walking about in his own house as he talks are not very interesting. They would not add anything to the drama.

In the same way, it is not always necessary to use the sound of a door opening and closing each time someone comes in or leaves. There may be dramas where you would wish to make the listener very much aware of the doors, but usually an actor moving off microphone is enough to tell the listener that he is leaving.

Radio drama should not try to be just like real life. It does not try to give *all* the sounds, or *all* the words, or *all* the ideas. Radio tries to *suggest* things, and leaves the listener to fill in the details with his own imagination.

Background Effects (O8):

Before we continue, look in the glossary for the term EFFECTS. Also look up the word BACKGROUND.

Sounds not only tell of action, they can also help tell the listener where the scene is taking place. A scene set in a restaurant may have people talking in the background (usually written "B.G." in scripts). The sounds of birds or cattle may tell the listener that the scene is in the country.

Background sounds can be very effective if used very carefully. In a very short scene, background can be used during the whole time. However, the listener will very soon become tired of the sound. That is why, when you have a longer scene it is usually best to "show" the listener the scene by having the sound quite noticeable for a few seconds, and then fading it more and more into the background so that soon it can hardly be heard at all. Sometimes you might want to fade it out altogether. Then towards the end of the scene, you would sneak the sound in again very gradually. Background sounds can also be very useful for moving from one scene to another. We will talk about that some more later.

Making Sound Effects (O9):

Most sound effects can be found on gramophone records. If you are planning to produce many dramas, and if your studio has enough money, such a collection of sound-effects records can be very useful. There are many collections that can be bought or rented. Most large radio networks would be able to tell you where they can be found.

Most studios, however, will have only a few records of sound effects. In this case, it is best to buy sound effects that you cannot make in your own studio. Of course, every studio should begin building its own library of sound effects recorded in its own listening area. A careful list should be kept of the sounds, along with a description of each. This is important, because local sounds have a local flavour. The traffic in Hong Kong, for instance, sounds different from the traffic in Bogota, Columbia. There are also sounds of animals, activities, events, and people that can only be recorded in your listening area.

Many sounds can be made in your own studio. Some ideas and suggestions for sound effects can be found in Appendix X.

Music in Radio Drama (O10):

Music is not as necessary to radio drama as the other two tools: sound effects and speech. In fact, there are many dramas that are produced without any music at all. In other dramas, of course, music can have very great value.

Music can do strange and wonderful things in a drama. It can give the right mood for a scene almost instantly, or wipe out one mood and give the listener another just as quickly. It can add tension to your drama, making it amusing, or even frightening.

Music can help the listener make pictures in his mind. It can help the listener add colour and emotion to the scene he has built in his imagination. Because of this power, music can be useful:

as part of the opening of the programme (it can set the right mood for the programme),

as a bridge or a transition between the scenes (it can help the listener keep the mood of the drama, or change the mood), as the closing of the programme (it can help bring the drama to a satisfying conclusion) or

as background (music can give a drama greater emotion and sometimes add meaning to narration or a scene).

Background Music (O11):

When used in the opening, the closing, or as a bridge, the music gets the whole attention of the listener, even if only for very short periods. However, music used in the background should be almost unnoticed by the listener. It should fit in so well with what is being said, that it almost seems to be part of the speaker's voice.

Background music is used more often behind narration than it is behind dialogue. Sometimes the music background will help to set the narration off from the dialogue and to make the drama seem clearer to the listener.

Background music should seldom be used behind dialogue. In fact, there would be only a very few scenes of very high emotion or feeling where music would help. Often music behind the dialogue simply takes the attention of the listener away from the drama.

There is one exception, however. Sometimes the writer may put in several very short scenes. These can sometimes be tied together very nicely when the same piece of music is used for the bridges between the scenes, and then fades into the background during the scenes themselves. This can be very effective, but should only be used once in a while.

Choosing the Right Music (O12):

No one doubts that music communicates. It is much harder to say just *what* it communicates, because music communicates moods and feelings. These are very hard to describe in words. Feelings, moods, emotions that we cannot put into words are usually more powerful than those we can talk about. That is why music is such a powerful force in the hands of the broadcaster.

Music can turn an ordinary drama into something excellent. It can also destroy a very good drama. That is why it is important that you choose each piece of music for your drama with this question in your mind:

"What kind of feeling will this bring to my listener?"

Of course, it will be very hard to be sure of an answer, but if you learn all you can about your listener, through research and through personal contact, you will be able to make a very good guess.

The name of the music may not give you any help in deciding what kind of mood it will communicate to your listener. Read the first few pages of *Project J* again, to remind you of some of the things we said about this.

People in every country respond best to their own kind of music. It is more meaningful to them because it has become a part of them. Whenever possible, you should try to use only the music of your own nation in your dramas. Your dramas will communicate much better if you do.

In some places, foreign music is used in dramas because it is easier to find, or because the national music is not suitable for dramas. You will have to decide for yourself what kind of music to use, but do remember that the more familiar the music, the better it communicates.

What Kind of Music? (O13):

There are two ways we can go about finding the right kind of music for a drama.

We can look for a song or a tune that will remind the listener of a certain place or a certain kind of thing. For instance, if your drama takes place in a village, you may decide to use a folk-melody that will remind listeners of a small village. A drama about harvesting rice may use a song that is usually sung when this is done.

We can look for *symbolic* music, music that makes people feel a certain way. In this case it is the *feeling* which the music communicates that is important. It should not make the listener *think* of anything particular.

Use Only One Kind of Music (O14):

Never mix two different kinds of music in one drama. If you begin with a folk-melody played on a flute, then you must stay with this kind of music for the whole drama. You will spoil your programme very quickly if you first use a flute, then an orchestra; or even worse, if you use your own national music for part of the drama and then change to music from another part of the world.

Opening the Drama (O15):

We have said quite often that you should have in mind exactly the kind of person you are aiming for in your broadcasts. However, we must also say, that it is not only the broadcaster who selects his audience. It is even more true that the audience selects its broadcast. This most often happens in the first few minutes of your programme, and that is why the openings are so important.

We can use the three tools of radio in order to get the attention of the listener, and to make him want to listen to the programme.

Sound effects can be used quickly to suggest a scene or some kind of activity. For instance, the shout of a boatman on a river will quickly bring a picture to the listener's mind, as will the sound of traffic in a city.

Music is used when it is most important to get the listener into a certain mood, or to remind him of something.

Speech is best to give information to the listener that will get his attention immediately.

Opening with Speech, Music and Sound (O16):

Of course, openings of radio programmes may make use of two or three of those tools, sometimes together, or one after the other. Often the writer will divide the information which should be in the opening into two or more parts. He may surround each part with music to suggest a mood, or sound effects to suggest action. Here is an example:

MUSIC: QUICK SURGE OF HAPPY BUT DIGNIFIED MUSIC: INTO B.G. AT 8 SECONDS
        FOR:

ANNCR: Here's Health!

SOUND: BABY CRYING: HOLD FOR 3 SECONDS THEN FADE INTO B.G.

ANNCR: The lusty cry of a strong baby is a sign of good health. (CRYING CROSS FADES TO MUSIC IN B.G.) Health is something we all search for. Here's Health to you! Today our story is about a baby, a bottle, and a bug . . . etc.

We could draw a picture of this opening, like this:

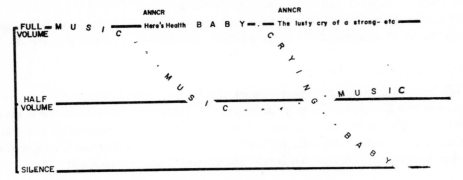

Opening with Music and Speech (O17):

Of course, it isn't necessary to use all three tools, or to have a complicated introduction. Some of the best openings are very simple. Here is an example:

MUSIC: SITAR MUSIC: CONTINUE FOR 15 SECONDS, FADE SLIGHTLY INTO B.G. FOR:
RAHUL: I spend much time playing my sitar now . . . now that I can no longer go back to my village. I play my sitar, and I wonder what happened . . . and why.
MUSIC: UP TO FULL FOR 10 SECONDS, THEN INTO B.G. FOR:
ANNCR: "The Sitar", a drama for radio about a small Indian village, and how everything changed one dark night in October.
MUSIC: UP TO FULL FOR 20 SECONDS, ENDING AT CONCLUSION OF MUSIC.
RAHUL: October is a month of . . . etc.

Opening with Sound and Speech (O18):

Sometimes the opening can be very quick, using only very simple sounds, or no effects at all.

SOUND: CLOCK TICKING FOR 5 SECONDS THEN INTO B.G. FOR:
ANNCR: We have only thirty minutes to cover ten thousand years.
SOUND: UP FOR 10 SECONDS, THEN STOP SUDDENLY:
VOICE: Haaaaa! Move along there you flea-bitten donkeys . . . etc.

As you can see, there are numberless ways to open a radio programme. If you listen to many dramas and make notes, you will find many good ideas. If you allow your own imagination to work, and if you experiment with new methods, you will discover even better ideas.

The important things to remember when making the openings of a programme are discussed in *J17*. Read that portion again to be sure you remember.

Scene Changes (O19):

In a stage drama, when we wish to show the audience that the action has changed to a different place, we change the things on the stage. If the action has been taking place in a home, and the next scene must be in a park, we remove the furniture and put some trees and bushes on the stage.

Of course, we cannot do that in a radio drama. The only way we can tell the listener that a change has taken place is through sound.

We change a scene for two reasons:

because the action in the story has moved to a different place, or
because the action has moved to a different time, perhaps two days or three years later.

The scene may be changed for both those reasons at the same time. These scene changes may be shown to the listener in several ways. Through:

a pause,
a narrator,
a sound effect,
music, or
combinations of narrator, sound effects and music.

The Pause (O20):

The simplest and often the best way to move from one person to another is simply by having the voice fade down, then two or three seconds of silence (not more), followed by the first voice in the next scene fading up. A fade should be done with the volume control, not with the actors moving away from the microphone.

VATSALA: Yes, I agree. But still I must go and speak to my husband about it; (START FADE.) I'll come to your house tomorrow, and we can talk about it . . . (FADE OUT.) (PAUSE.)

VIJAYA: (FADE IN.) Ah . . . there you are . . . I was wondering when you'd get here. Come in, come in.

When you are using a pause to change a scene, be sure that the words being faded up or down are not too important. The listener may miss them, especially on short-wave radio. Many broadcasters feel that pauses and fades should not be used on short-wave radio at all.

The Narrator (O21):

This is one of the easiest ways to shift scenes. Because it is easy, it is often used too much.

VATSALA: Yes, I agree. But I still must go and talk to my husband about it. (START FADE.) I'll come to your house . . . (FADE OUT.)

NARRATOR: Vatsala did come the next day. And she had exciting news. Vijaya was waiting for her.

VIJAYA: (QUICK FADE IN.) Ah . . . there you are . . . I was wondering when you'd get here. Come in, come in.

Notice that the speeches are still faded out and faded in, but that the fades are much shorter than when using a pause. This is because the narrator can come in quickly and take over the attention of the listener.

Scene Changes with Sound Effects (O22):

This kind of a scene change is usually more difficult. It can only be done when the sound effect has a real part to play in the movement of the drama.

BEBEY: Now you know what to do just as soon as you get off that aeroplane . . . do you hear me?

BOULAHIA: (FADING.) Yes . . . yes, sir . . . I hear you. (CROSS FADE TO:)

SOUND: AEROPLANE ENGINES IDLING: UP FOR 5 SECONDS, THEN FADE DOWN SLIGHTLY INTO B.G. FOR:

VOICE: Tickets, sir?

BOULAHIA: Here you are.

VOICE: Thank you. Seat number 26, please.

We could draw a picture of this opening, in this way.

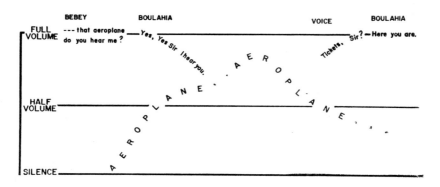

Music (O23):

Music scene changes, or *bridges* as they are often called, have a big advantage, as well as a big disadvantage.

> Music bridges can be done in any style or mood desired. The music can end the scene quickly, or slowly; the music can seem to laugh or cry; it can create the mood of happiness or sadness or fear.
>
> Music scene changes that really fit the drama are difficult to find on recordings. It is also difficult for a small studio to find musicians who can make the right kind of music. However, good music bridges can usually be found if you are willing to spend plenty of time listening to recorded music in the search for them. Better still, your music bridges will be most successful if you can find local musicians to make them from your own national music.

Here is a scene change using music.

DOCTOR: Yes . . . yes there is still *some* hope . . . but not very much. I shall stay here with you. (MUSIC BEGINS IN B.G.) I will do all I can to help you. (FADING.) There is nothing more I can do for your husband.

MUSIC: FEAR AND TRAGEDY. UP FOR 15 SECONDS, CROSS FADE INTO B.G. AND OUT:

CU: (SCREAMING.) Papa! Papa!

TAW: Please don't Cu! Please! (MUSIC OUT.)

CU: But the telegram says he is dead . . . etc.

Music for a scene change, as well as mood music for a drama, must be very carefully chosen. A music bridge can be used most effectively when there is a a lot of emotion in a drama. When the drama is about the actions of people, rather than their feelings, it is often better to use other types of scene changes.

Combinations (O24):

As your skill in writing and producing radio dramas increases, there may be times when you will use several of these scene changing methods at one time. Do not attempt the combination, however, until you have had plenty of experience with each kind of change. To find out how these combinations are done, you will need to listen to many dramas on the radio, and make notes on all that you hear.

Closing the Radio Drama (O25):

When the story in your drama is finished, you should conclude the programme as quickly as possible. Be sure not to forget the "credits"; that is, the names of the writer, producer, actors, technical people, etc. Keep the list of names as short as possible since the listener is not usually very interested. However, giving names on the air will often encourage those who took part to help you again next time.

Radio Tricks (O26):

There are very many tricks that can be used in a radio drama. It would be impossible to tell you about them here since there is not enough space. In any case, these should be used only by an experienced and skilful director. Until you have gained this experience and skill, stay away from the trick effects. They cannot make a poor drama a good one, but they can certainly turn a good drama into a poor one.

Assignment One (O27):

Listen to at least three radio dramas. If possible, choose them from radio stations in your own country. If not, then listen to three foreign dramas. Try to find three different kinds of dramas if you can. As you listen, describe in a few sentences each scene change, each piece of mood music, and the opening and closing of each programme. Describe each scene change used, and the way in which it is fitted into the drama. Also write a sentence or two telling whether you think each scene change was good or bad, and why you think so.

Assignment Two (O28):

With a tape-recorder, go around your home, your studio, and your community, recording fifteen or twenty sounds that are heard very frequently and a few that are not heard frequently. At a gathering of your studio staff, or perhaps during a party or social gathering, play each sound. Have people try to guess the name of the sound. Make notes on what happened, and then write a paragraph or two describing this experiment. The purpose of this assignment is to show how misleading sounds recorded on a tape can be. However, you will also find this assignment is good fun, and that it makes a good amusement at a party.

Glossary Assignment (O29):

Look up the following words in the glossary. Describe what the word or phrase *means* in your own language.

CROWD NOISE	MONTAGE
EFFECTS	MOOD MUSIC
FILTER	

Assignment Three (O30):

There are several examples of parts of scripts in this project. Translate these into your own language and then produce them. Of course, you should change the music to a kind that fits your listeners, and you may need to change some of the sound effects and dialogue also. However, do not change the sound effect until you have tried to go out with a tape-recorder to find it in your neighbourhood. The script portions to be produced are found at *O6, O16, O17, O22, O23.*

Assignment Four (O31):

Check over the drama script you wrote in the last project. Now that you have learned more about sound effects, music, scene changes, etc., you should want to change many parts of your script. Study your script carefully to see what changes you can make. It will probably be necessary for you to rewrite your script.

When you have completed all of these assignments, take them to your supervisor.

The Drama Director (O32):   PART TWO

Recording a radio drama is the job of a team. Unless the team works together, with each person doing his job well and helping others to do their jobs well, the result will be a poorly-produced drama.

A team works best when it has a good strong leader. The leader of a team making a drama must be able to get good results from his team. Sometimes he may do this with praise, other times with encouragement, and sometimes with scolding. In other words, he must know exactly what he wants the people in his drama team to do, and he must know how to make them do it. In radio, such a team leader is usually called a director.

Any person who is hoping to direct dramas must have a searching mind. He must always be listening and looking for different ways of getting an actor to say a line in just a certain way, or of finding a new way to put more meaning into the drama.

If you hope to become a director or a writer of dramas, you must learn a good deal about them. The things you find in this book will only be an introduction. Your best training will come as you write, act, do sound effects, and produce drama after drama after drama. This manual is only the beginning.

Using Amateur Actors (O33):

In the large cities of the world, there usually is a group of professional actors; that is, actors who earn their living completely by acting. If your studio or station can find enough money, it is usually best to work with such professionals.

Most of those using this manual, however, will not be able to do this. Either there will be no professional actors available, or there may not be enough money to pay them. Nevertheless, a studio can develop excellent dramas through using amateur actors, people who receive little or no money for their actions.

Most directors agree that it is best to pay the actors, even if it is only a small amount. It is always easier to ask them to work harder if they are receiving some money, and they will also take criticism much more easily.

Developing an Acting Group (O34):

If your studio hopes to do quite a few dramas, then you may need to make plans to begin a training programme for actors. You will, of course, need to work out a plan that is best for your own area. Here is one system that succeeded:

The actors were divided into three kinds: newcomers, minor actors, and major actors.

Newcomers were given weekly lessons in acting and speaking. Most of the lesson time was spent practising with scripts, listening to recorded dramas, and watching recording sessions with major actors. Major actors were often asked to come in and help the newcomers. Very small roles were given to newcomers who seemed to be making progress. When newcomers had been successful in a number of very small parts, they became minor actors. Newcomers received no pay.

Minor actors were given medium-sized roles in the dramas. They also helped with sound effects and other things. Minor actors were also expected to spend a good deal of time listening to dramas, and they received acting lessons every two weeks. When the director felt they had gained enough experience, they would become major actors. Minor actors would receive a small amount of money for their work.

Major actors could be given any role in any drama, but usually worked on the big parts. Major actors also would spend a lot of time teaching newcomers and minor actors, and would sometimes also direct dramas. Major actors received the highest wage for their work.

It is good to have some way of making sure that actors come on time when they have agreed to do so. The studio using the method above, had a rule that if an actor was more than ten minutes late for three rehearsals, or if he missed two complete rehearsals or one performance, he would drop down one rank.

Choosing the Right Actor (O35):

Speech is the most important tool of the radio dramatist. This is why the director must always choose exactly the right actor for each part. It is a difficult thing to do.

When choosing actors we must not think that because someone is a good speaker, or a good announcer, or a good stage actor, that he will make a good radio actor. The radio drama is something quite different, and needs its own particular style of speaking. Choosing actors for a drama is usually called *casting*, while the actors are known as the *cast*.

Be careful not to cast people by their looks. A big, fat man may sound small and thin on the radio. It is best to hear the actor speak through the microphone into the control room. Do not look at the actor as you listen to him. Close your eyes and say to yourself, "What does that voice sound like? What kind of a personality does this voice have?" It makes no difference at all what the actor looks like.

Here are some other suggestions for *casting* a drama:

The real age of the actor should be as close to the age of the character in the drama as possible. There are some very excellent actors who can play roles of different ages, but most actors will not be able to do this.

Try to have variety in the voices of your cast. The listener must be able to tell one voice from another. If, for instance, there are three women in your play, and they all have about the same kind of voice, the listener won't be able to tell them apart. Instead you should choose actors whose voices have different qualities.

Most of your cast should have medium or low voices. Very high voices can be annoying to the listener, although there are times when such a voice is exactly what is needed.

Choose actors who can take suggestions and directions easily. The person who does not do what the director asks will not be a good member of the team. Even if he is a good actor himself, he may spoil the performance of the other actors.

Talent Card File (O36):

Many directors have found it very helpful to keep a card file listing the various actors in the community. This card tells the director very quickly how much experience any actor has had, what roles he has played, how well he has played them, and other information that might be useful. Such a file can save the director a lot of time, because he does not find it necessary to have a casting; that is, a meeting when the actors read the play and the director picks out the person for each role.

Such a card file can also be very useful to others in the studio who may be looking for an actor to do another kind of programme. Actors can sometimes do a good job of announcing certain kinds of programmes.

Such a card file can be kept concerning all of the people in the community who help the studio in one way or another. Musicians, speakers and writers can also be listed in this way. Be careful, however, to keep this card file locked in a safe place. To be really useful, it should contain information that should not be known to the actors. For instance, a card might say, "This man is very hard to get along with and quarrels with the other performers." It is important for a director to know this, but it would not be good if the performer saw the card. Here is one such card.

NAME: Mr. Kyung Do-Park   AGE: 23 SEX: M
ADDRESS: 127 Chongro 3 ka   Phone 39-145
Voice: Low baritone, well controlled.
Roles done best: Businessman, Professional
Experience: Some stage, T.V., sings well
Dramas done: Jan/60 Minor, March/60 Minor
Feb/61 Major, April 61/ Minor

Remarks: Tries hard but has some trouble
reading. Always on time. Worth developing

Rehearsals (O37):

Actors are sometimes impatient and want to record their drama before they are really ready. They may think that if they do not stumble over their lines, they are ready. This is far from the case.

The director must work carefully with his cast, and should insist on at least seven or eight rehearsals with amateur actors. Even professional actors in the big radio stations always have at least three or four rehearsals.

Here are the steps through which many directors take professional casts. When you are using amateur actors, you should probably do each of these steps at least twice.

Table Rehearsal: During this time the director explains the drama to the actors. He tells them something about each character, and how the various parts of the drama are to be done. The director should encourage the cast to ask questions and to offer suggestions about the characters. The director should accept such suggestions when they are good, but should also have the courage to use his own ideas if the suggestions are not good.

The director may read the script out loud to the cast, stopping to explain things as he goes along. Then the cast should read the script through out loud, several times with the director stopping them often to explain more about the lines or the characters. Each actor should have a pencil, with which to make notes and marks on his script.

The actors should then be asked to take the script home with them and spend some time studying it, to be sure they can read all their lines without a mistake.

First Microphone Rehearsal: There are five things that must be done during this practice:

> The actors must continue to improve their interpretation of the character they are playing.
>
> All the *business* is put into the drama. Business means any action which the script calls for the cast or the sound-man to do. If the script calls for someone to get out of a chair, fight with another character, come in and out of the room, or anything else, these things are practised.
>
> All the *sound perspective* is worked out. There may be some lines where the actor is very far from the microphone in order to give the feeling of distance; or, he may be very close to the microphone to give the feeling of being very near to the listener. The actor should make a note on his script to remind him of the *exact* distance from the microphone for each line.
>
> The *microphone balance* is worked out. We talked about this in *F17.*
>
> *Sound effects* are practised. Some of these may be live; some may be recorded; but they should all be practised to be sure they fit into the script. Remember that the problems of sound perspective and sound balance must be considered when using sound effects, just as they are when using voices. For instance, if an actor is saying "Good-bye" and he is quite far off microphone, it would sound strange to have a door open and close very close to the microphone.

Cue rehearsal: During this rehearsal all the music is worked into the script. At the same time, the sound effects are given another rehearsal, and the actors try to give an even better interpretation of their roles.

Dress Rehearsal: During the other rehearsals, the director has been making notes on his script. Every time he hears something that isn't quite as good as he feels it should be, he makes a note of it. During dress rehearsal he goes over all these trouble spots. Then the entire drama is practised without any stopping, just as if it were being recorded.

Recording a Drama (O38):

Dramas are seldom done "live" on radio any longer. The tape-recorder makes it much easier to produce a drama, since it is possible to stop the tape and start again if something goes very wrong. It is also possible to add things later after the actors have finished, and it is possible to edit the tape to cut out mistakes.

Recording a drama gives us one big problem, however. When a programme is going on the air "live" the performers seem to work much harder and do much better because they know there must be no mistakes. When a programme is taped, however, actors and announcers often relax too much. The programme, whether it is a drama or any other kind, can very easily lose the life and the sparkle which are so important.

When programmes are taped, the director or producer must do all he can to give his performers the feeling of excitement that should be part of a radio production. Of course, newcomers who are just beginning in radio, will almost always be too nervous and excited. The director must help them to gain control of themselves. But the performer or actor who has made many programmes may be much too calm, and so may give a dull performance. He must be encouraged to bring more liveliness and energy into his work.

For this reason many directors, even if they are recording, will refuse to stop the tape if somebody makes a small mistake. They have found that if they do stop whenever somebody does something wrong, they have one mistake after the other. The actors don't try as hard. Of course, if it is a very long drama, the director may divide it into several parts and give the actors a rest in between.

Communication Through Drama (O39):

It is important as you begin working on radio dramas, to understand a little more about the ways in which drama communicates. The drama communicates to the listener in two ways: through *information* and through *empathy*.

Information (O40):

This is the easier of the two kinds of communication. If your information is believable, if it is interesting, and if it is given in such a way that it falls within the field of experience of your listener, then you will probably communicate.

Even so, it still requires a good knowledge of the listener, a good understanding of the information to be communicated, and the ability to present the material in an artistic manner. This is the kind of communication we have been discussing in the other projects of this manual.

Empathy (O41):

When a listener has become so interested in a drama that he feels as if he has almost lived through the experiences of one of the characters, this is known as *empathy*. Empathy is the ability to share or to live the experiences of another. If a listener hears a drama about a man whose wife has died, and then feels he has almost lived through the tragedy himself, the play has gained the empathy of the listener.

Because of this power of the listener to enter into the experiences shown in a drama, much can be communicated that goes deeper than information. What we as people believe and do, and the kinds of personalities we have, is very much related to our emotions or feelings.

People often feel with their hearts, more than they think with their minds. Mankind's greatest moments have been possible because of love, which is an emotion. Mankind's greatest tragedies have happened because of hate, which is an emotion.

It is very difficult to say exactly what it is that will make people *empathise* with the characters in a drama. We do know, however, that the world's greatest drama writers have been able to do this because they understood their own people and their own culture very well.

How to Gain Empathy (O42):

We also know that people in a drama must seem real to the listener. That does not mean that the character in the drama must act and speak exactly as a real person does. The listener should have the feeling, however, that such a person could be alive, or has been alive.

If the character is such that the listener will say to himself, "He reminds me of Saw Taw in the next village", or, "I almost have the feeling I know that person", then you have an even better chance of gaining the listener's empathy.

If your listener says to himself, "That person has the same kinds of problems as I do, and he feels just as I do about them," then your chances of gaining your listener's empathy are excellent.

This kind of communication needs all the technique and knowledge that is necessary to communicate information. In fact, it needs more understanding, more skill, and much more practice.

We mentioned earlier in *Project I* that if we wanted to bring change in one area of a person's life, we had to know how this change would affect the rest of his life. We also learned that very strong habits and customs sometimes made changes very difficult. Good radio dramas can help this situation, but not only by giving more information.

A radio drama will say, "Here is the way one family felt about such a problem." Understanding other people's feelings always helps us to understand our own. As the listener experiences the feelings of the people in the radio drama, he will be able to understand his own feelings, and sometimes make the changes more easily.

Drama in all Programmes (O43):

What we have said about communication through drama can be true of a great many programmes. Whenever a radio programme tells any kind of story, especially if it is about people, it is beginning to be a little like a radio drama. A good story told skilfully can gain as much listener empathy as a complicated drama. A good speaker may capture the imagination so that he and the listener are almost thinking their thoughts together. This is also empathy, and it is far more powerful than information.

What to Communicate (O44):

There is very little value in being an excellent communicator, if you have nothing important or valuable to communicate. It is like having a powerful radio station without any programmes to broadcast.

A radio programmer must not only know how to make programmes. He must also know *what* he wants to say. He must know his subject very well, and must constantly read and listen to be sure he is keeping up with new discoveries and new thoughts whether they be agriculture, medicine, religion, or politics.

Why Communicate (O45):

There is an even more important thing the radio communicator must know. He must know why he is communicating.

Why should the listener know these things?
Why should he act in this way?
Is it really for his benefit?
Might the listener be better off if he didn't know this?
Am I being really honest with myself and with my listener?
Am I really serving the best interests of my country and my people?

These are very important questions, and the honest communicator will constantly struggle with them. He will always try to answer them, knowing that next year or next month he may be a little wiser, and his answers may change with his growing wisdom.

Assignment Five (O46):

From one of the radio stations that can be heard in your area, choose a drama that you think is of high quality. If possible, tape record the drama from the radio. If this is not possible, ask your supervisor for a drama on tape. Listen to this drama very carefully (several times if you have it on tape), then write several paragraphs answering each of these two questions:

In what ways, and through which characters, do you think the drama gained empathy from the listeners?
Does the writer of the drama have some worthwhile things to say? If so, tell what these are and how he says them. Also tell *why* they are worth while. If there is nothing worth while in the drama, describe the way in which you might rewrite the drama to give it some value.

Give a full explanation for each answer, and tell *why* you think this way.

Assignment Six (O47):

Produce the drama you wrote for *Project N*. Before you begin, however, talk to your supervisor about which people to use as actors, where to find sound effects, music, and so forth. It may be necessary for you to record the drama several times before you feel it is good enough. Use the check-list O49 to find out if your work is of high quality.

Assignment Seven (O48):

Produce the drama "The Contrary Wife" just as you did the drama in Assignment Six. Once again it may be necessary to record it several times.

Check-list for Drama Production (O49):

1. Do each of the sound effects serve some purpose?	Yes ____	No ____
2. Will the listener easily be able to identify each sound effect?	Yes ____	No ____
3. If you have used any background sounds, do they serve the purpose of the drama, rather than taking the attention of the listener away from the drama?	Yes ____	No ____
4. Does the music fit in with the mood of the drama?	Yes ____	No ____
5. Is music used only when it really helps the mood and purpose of the drama?	Yes ____	No ____
6. Does the opening of the programme catch the attention of the listener quickly?	Yes ____	No ____
7. Are the scene changes easy for the listener to understand?	Yes ____	No ____
8. Does the voice of each actor fit in with the kind of character he is playing?	Yes ____	No ____
9. Does the drama communicate something of value to the listener?	Yes ____	No ____

You should be able to say "yes" to eight of the nine questions in the check-list before you take your work to your supervisor. Bring your tape recordings of the drama, the scripts, and the paragraphs you wrote in Assignment Five.

Assignment Eight (O50):

Make a list of five different subjects which you feel your listeners should know about. Be sure they are important things that will be of real value. Then beside each subject, write four short paragraphs. In each paragraph describe a different way you could make an effective programme about that subject. This list should go into your idea file, after you have talked about it with your supervisor.

Assignment Nine (O51):

In most of the projects you have been asked to describe in your own language, the meaning of the words in the glossary. Now that you have finished the manual, you will also have most of the words in the glossary translated. Put all these translations together into a neat booklet. You will find this helpful later when you need to look up new words, and it will be useful to other people in your studio who may want to understand certain radio terms.

Take your work from Assignments Eight and Nine to your supervisor.

One Final Word (O52):

Now you have begun! You have finished this manual, and this means you have begun to learn radio. This manual did nothing more than open the door to the exciting world of radio. You must now explore this world. There is much more to learn.

If you stop now, you will have achieved almost nothing. However, if you keep your eyes and your ears always open, if you read new things constantly, if you keep on criticising your own work and studying the work of others, then you will grow. You will become an expert broadcaster. You will be able to do great things to help your fellow man.

APPENDIX W

A Glossary of Radio Words

Sometimes the British and Americans use different words for the same thing. This glossary gives both. The explanation is given under the British term, however.

How to Use This Glossary:

All the words are listed according to the English alphabet. When you see any word written in LARGE or CAPITAL letters it means that you will find the word explained in the glossary also. Be sure to find it and read the explanation if you do not already know what the word means.

ACOUSTICS: The study of sound. The way in which a sound bounces from one wall of a studio to another, is called *acoustics*. When the sound bounces around a studio because the wall surfaces are hard, it seems as if you are in a large, empty room or hall. This is called a *"live"* acoustic. When the walls have been covered with a soft or uneven surface to soak up the sound, and you don't hear any "echo", it is called a *"dead"* acoustic. Listen for the *acoustics* in your studio when RECORDING music or drama.

ACTUALITY: A programme done at the *"actual"* scene of the event. A description of a parade going by, or a programme presented from the town square during a festival would be an *actuality* broadcast. It is also called a REMOTE BROADCAST or OUTSIDE BROADCAST.

ADAPTATION: To change something (such as a script or a programme) to fit another situation or another audience (see *C13*).

AD-LIB: *Unscripted comments* by an announcer or a speaker. To speak without reading from a script.

AUDITION: To listen to a RECORD, TAPE, or musician before deciding to use the material in a programme (also see PRE-FADE LISTENING).

AMPLIFIER: Makes the sound *louder*.

BACKGROUND: Sounds which are not as loud as the speaker or the music, but which help to create a mood or feeling. A programme about a factory would have machine noises in the *background,* or a programme about the church might have religious music in the *background.* If you are reading a poem or telling a story, the right kind of *background* music could make the programme more effective (see MOOD MUSIC). *Background noise* can sometimes spoil a programme. For instance, if you are RECORDING a talk, and the carpenter is hammering on the studio wall, this is *background noise,* but it certainly would bother the listener (see CROWD NOISE).

BALANCE (see MICROPHONE BALANCE).

BAND (or CUT): The separate selections on a GRAMOPHONE RECORD. For instance, if there were two items on one side of a RECORD, separated by a small blank space, the first would be *band* one, and the second would be *band* two. LONG PLAYING RECORDS can have anywhere from one, to more than twenty-five *bands* on each side. In a script, the music on a RECORD is usually referred to in this way:

LP 234 SIDE ONE, BAND 3.

Sometimes the words CUT or CUE are used in place of *band.* CUE is used more often to speak of the items on a MAGNETIC TAPE (see CUE).

BLASTING: A very *unpleasant change* in the sound that happens if a person moves too close to a MICROPHONE and speaks directly into it.

BRIDGE (or MUSIC BRIDGE): By placing a short piece of well-chosen music between two parts of a programme, it will serve as a *link* or a *bridge* between them. In a drama, it may be a good way of helping the listener to imagine that he has moved from one place to another, or from one time to another. For a more complete explanation (see *O23*).

CALL LETTERS: Letters of the alphabet given by a government to a radio station as a name, or identification. The station uses these *call letters* as part of its STATION IDENTIFICATION.

COMMUNICATION: The means by which information, an idea, or a feeling goes from one person to another. For a more complete explanation (see *I1*).

COMPÈRE (or for a lady, COMMÈRE): A French word meaning an *announcer* or MASTER OF CEREMONIES (or M.C.) on a light music or quiz programme. A *compère* is not the same as a NARRATOR.

CONTINUITY: This is the *plan* used to be sure that the many parts of a programme move smoothly from one part to the next. *Continuity* is also the script which has been written for the programme, or it may mean the announcements which are used in between the various parts of a programme. The person who reads this material is called a *Continuity Announcer*. The person who writes it is called a *Continuity Writer* (see FORMAT).

CONTINUITY ROOM (American: MASTER CONTROL): A CONTROL ROOM where the technician at the radio station switches from one programme to another. The technician in the *Continuity Room* also sees to it that all the programmes are going out over the air in the proper manner.

CONTINUITY STUDIO (American: TALK STUDIO, TALK BOOTH or ANNOUNCE BOOTH): A small *studio* from which an announcer can make any announcement needed by the CONTINUITY ROOM.

CONTROL DESK (American: CONTROL BOARD, GROUP FADER or MIXER): A place where the sounds from the MICROPHONES, the TAPE-RECORDERS, and the GRAMOPHONES come together. Here the technician sets the VOLUME of each sound to the proper LEVEL and mixes them together. This sound then goes into the machine where the programme is being RECORDED, or out to the transmitter.

CONTROL ROOM: The *room* where the CONTROL DESK is located.

CROWD NOISE: The sound of many voices, giving the feeling that there are many people present. The listener should not be able to understand any of the words that the crowd is saying, unless the words have a meaning for your programme. The *crowd noise* should be angry, sad, loud, or quiet, depending on the mood you desire. Five people in your studio can make enough *crowd noise* to sound like fifteen, and ten people can sound like fifty. For more than fifty people you should have as many people in your studio as possible. Place the group at least $1\frac{1}{2}$ metres (4 or 5 feet) away from the MICROPHONE and tell them to talk or shout or laugh or applaud depending on the kind of *crowd noise* you need. Listen in the CONTROL ROOM to the sound, to be sure it is exactly right (see BACKGROUND).

CUE: A *signal* to show the beginning or the end. When you point your finger at a speaker to tell him to begin his talk, you are using a *hand cue*. If a light goes on in the studio to show the start of a programme, that is called a *light cue*. If you have placed the last words of a talk on a paper, so that the technician will know when you are finished, this is called a *word cue*. If your script shows that something is to begin at a certain time, that is a *time cue*. A *cue* can also be a place marked on the TAPE or a RECORD to indicate where to begin. When you set a TAPE-RECORDER or GRAMOPHONE to begin at a certain place,

the Americans call that *cueing*. The English would say you have *set up* the
TAPE or RECORD (also see BAND).

CUE: The length of time between one part of a programme and another. When
the producer says *"pick up your cues"*, he means to leave less time between
one RECORD and another, or between one actor and another in a drama.
Long cues make a programme seem slow. *Short cues* or *fast cues* make it seem
lively.

CUT (see BAND).

DEAD (see ACOUSTICS).

DECIBEL: A unit used to measure the VOLUME of sound, just as an inch or a
centimetre is a unit for measuring length. The short way of writing *decibel*
is *"db"* (also see PEAK PROGRAMME METER).

DISC (see GRAMOPHONE RECORD).

DISTORTION: A *change* in the sound of music or a voice that makes the sound
unnatural or unpleasant. This is usually caused by equipment that is not
working well.

DUBBING: Taking sound from one RECORDING and putting it on another. When
you RECORD music from a GRAMOPHONE RECORD on to a TAPE-RECORDING,
you are *dubbing*. A TAPE that has been RECORDED from another TAPE is
sometimes called a *dub*. To *dub* is to RE-RECORD.

ECHO: When the sound of your voice or your music bounces back from the
walls, and it sounds as if you are in a very large room, that is known as *echo*.
Some studios have a special room containing only a LOUDSPEAKER and a
MICROPHONE to add the *echo* to your sound. This is an *echo room* or *echo
chamber*. An *echo* can also be made by using a TAPE machine, although this
kind of *echo* doesn't sound as natural as the one made in an *echo room*.

EDITING: Checking a script for any mistakes, removing any words or sentences
that are not needed and adding words and phrases that make it sound
better. This is known as *script editing*.
Tape editing is done by cutting out any parts of a RECORDING which you do
not want in your programme. The parts wanted are then SPLICED together.
Tape editing can also be done by RECORDING (DUBBING) the good parts of one
TAPE on to another.

EFFECTS: These are sounds which are added to a programme to make it seem
more real and natural or more interesting. *Effects* should only be used when
they really help the main message of the programme. *Spot effects* are sounds
made in the studio at the same time as the rest of the programme. *Recorded*

W1. An African broadcaster DUBBING the sound from one tape on to another.

effects are those that come from a TAPE or RECORD. An *effects microphone* is one placed in the studio especially to RECORD *spot effects*. A list of *sound effects* and how to make them is found in Appendix X.

ERASE: To remove the sound from a TAPE-RECORDING. This can be done by running the TAPE through the machine with the RECORD switch "on", or by using a special *bulk eraser*. A *bulk eraser* is really a large magnet. To use it, turn the switch on, then move it slowly towards the TAPE which is held in the other hand. Move it slowly in a circle over one side of the TAPE reel, then over the other. Move the *eraser* slowly away as far from the TAPE as your hand can reach before you turn it off.

Do not have any other TAPES or TAPE machines near by. The *eraser* may take some of the sound from the TAPES or cause damage to the TAPE machine. Remove your watch, since the *eraser* can damage this also.

FADE: Making the VOLUME of the sound become slowly louder or softer. In a *fade* the sound changes slowly. In a CUT the sound stops quickly or starts quickly.

Fade in: To have the sound *come in* slowly.

Fade out: To have the sound become *softer* until it is all gone.

Fade up: To have the sound get slowly *louder*.

Fade down: To have the sound become *softer*.

Cross-fade: The VOLUME of one sound is turned down, while the VOLUME of another sound is turned up. For instance, in Drawing W2, sound "A" is being *faded out*, while sound "B" is being *faded in*.

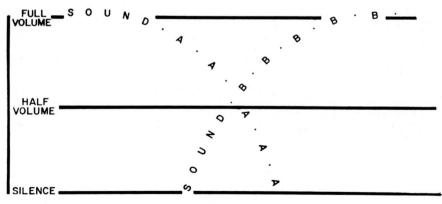

W2.

It is difficult to *cross-fade* music because the two kinds of music may sound unpleasant together. A *cross-fade* of music should be done quickly, as in Drawing W3. It is better not to do this at all, unless there is no other way.

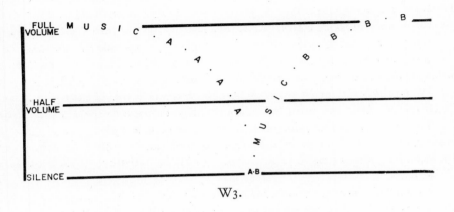

W3.

To *cross-fade* people's voices, it is usually best to *fade* the first voice all the way out before *fading* in the second voice (see Drawing W4).

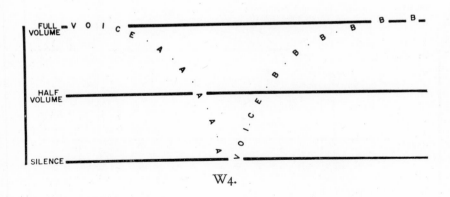

W4.

There are many kinds of *fades* and *cross-fades*. The best way to learn about them is to listen carefully to many good radio dramas.

FADER (or POT): The knobs on the CONTROL panel which the technician uses to FADE the music or the voice.

FAST FORWARD: To run a TAPE machine forward more quickly than usual, in order to get to a part of the TAPE that is further along on the reel. When this is done, the TAPE should also be removed from the HEADS (see RE-WIND).

FEEDBACK (see HOWL-BACK).

FILL-UP (American FILL): Music or announcements used to *fill-up* the extra time which sometimes occurs when a programme is too short or a programme is not available.

FILTER: Used to remove part of the sound from a RECORDING or a MICROPHONE. When a *filter* is used on a MICROPHONE it removes the lowest part of the sound, so that your voice will sound as if you are speaking on a telephone. This is called a *filter microphone* or *distort microphone*. Some *filters* can also remove the high or the middle parts of the sound.

FORMAT: The *plan* or *outline* of a programme. If you decide to have a musical introduction, then some lively music, followed by a talk and some more music, you would be deciding on the *format*. Dramas, talks, PANEL DIS-CUSSIONS, are all different *formats* (see CONTINUITY).

GAIN: The difference in the VOLUME of sound between the time that it enters an AMPLIFIER, and that when it leaves the AMPLIFIER. Usually when a technician speaks of *"controlling the gain"* or *"riding the gain"*, he means that he is controlling the VOLUME of the sound by turning one of the FADERS or POTS.

GROUP FADER (see CONTROL DESK).

GRAMOPHONE (PHONOGRAPH or RECORD PLAYER): A machine which changes the vibrations from a RECORD or DISC into sound. The way in which the NEEDLE of the *gramophone* vibrates as it slides along the groove of the RECORD, determines the kind of sound you hear.

GRAMOPHONE NEEDLE: This is the tiny sharp point that rests on the GRAMOPHONE RECORD. It is made of a very hard stone, such as sapphire, ruby, or diamond. It can be damaged very easily. The most common *needle* today is made for the 33⅓ and 45 r.p.m. RECORDS. It is called a *micro-groove needle*. If you are to play a 78 r.p.m. RECORD, you will need a larger *needle*. Most GRAMOPHONES have both kinds. Be sure you use the right one, or you will damage the RECORD.

GRAMOPHONE RECORD (or DISC, PLATTER): The round flat piece of plastic with tiny grooves in it. There are four kinds of *records*. When you put them on to the *turn-table* of the GRAMOPHONE, they go around at 16, 33, 45 or 78 times each minute, or revolutions per minute. (r.p.m.)

16 r.p.m. *records* are very seldom used by radio stations. They are used in some places because you can put a lot of sound on to one *record*.

33⅓ r.p.m. *records* are used most often in a studio. They are also called *Long Playing Records* (or *L.P.'s*). Most 33⅓ r.p.m. *records* are 30 centimetres (12 inches) wide but there are some that are only 25 centimetres (10 inches) wide.

45 r.p.m. *records* are most commonly used for popular music. Some of these *records* are marked "Extended Play", (or E.P.) which means that they contain about twice as much sound as the ordinary 45 r.p.m. *records*.

78 r.p.m. *records* were once very common. Now they are made in only a few places. Most of the 78 r.p.m. *records* that you may see will be old ones; so listen to them carefully before using them. They may be badly damaged. 78 r.p.m. *records* can also be either 25 centimetres (10 inches) or 30 centimetres (12 inches) wide.

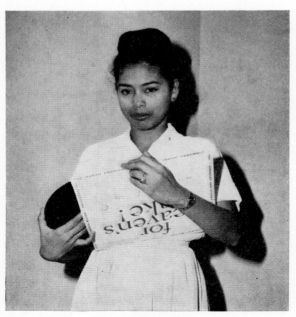

W5.

How to Care for Gramophone Records:

Gramophone records should be carefully handled at all times. There are several important things to remember when you are using *records*.

> Never touch the grooves of the *record* with your fingers. Learn to take the *record* out of its cover by placing your fingers only on the outside edge, and on the label in the centre. The smallest amount of oil from your fingers will damage the surface no matter how clean your hand appears to be (see Photograph W5).
> Wipe the dust from the *record* before playing it. Use the special kind of cloth or brush that *record* companies sell, or else a soft cloth that doesn't leave lint on the *record*.
> Always keep your *records* in a cool, dry place (air-conditioned if you are in the tropics). Keep dust away from the *records*, and store them straight up and down on a shelf. Don't lay them down for more than a few minutes, and don't lean them against anything. *Records* bend easily, especially in the heat.
> If your *records* become dirty, you can wash them off by using clean, warm (not hot) water, and a mild detergent (not soap). After washing them with a soft cloth, rinse the *records* well in clear water, and allow them to dry in a clean place.
> When playing *records* on the GRAMOPHONE, place the NEEDLE down very carefully. If you drop the NEEDLE even a little, or slide it over the *record*, it will cause damage that can never be repaired.

HEAD : The parts of the TAPE machine that put the sound on the TAPE, "hear" the sound from the TAPE, or ERASE it. On most machines used by radio stations there are three *heads*:

> The first *head* which the TAPE moves over, is usually the *erase head*. If the machine is RECORDING, this *head* removes the sound that was on there before.
> The second one is usually the *recording head*. If your machine is RECORDING, it puts the new sound on to the TAPE.
> The last *head* which the TAPE moves over, is usually the *playback head*. This takes the sound from the TAPE and puts it through the AMPLIFIER so that you may hear it.

On some cheaper TAPE machines, the *erase head* and the *recording head* are put together into one. The *heads* of a TAPE machine must be kept clean if they are to work properly. It is best to ask a technician to show you how this is done. However, if there is no technician, use a soft clean cloth, and if possible some carbon tetrachloride (which you can buy at a chemist's or drugstore) and wipe the *heads* gently. This should be done after every three or four TAPES are used (also see TAPE).

HEAD-PHONES (or EAR-PHONES, HEAD-SET, "CANS"): Small LOUDSPEAKERS held together by a clip. These are worn directly over the ears.

HIGH-FIDELITY (or HI-FI): Sound of the very best quality.

HOWL-BACK (American FEED-BACK): The high whistling *sound* often heard in a public address system. It is caused by the *sound* from the MICROPHONE going through the LOUDSPEAKER, then back into the MICROPHONE again. The *sound* goes round and round getting louder all the time.

IDEA FILE: A place where *ideas, suggestions* and *material* for programmes are placed. Each new suggestion for a programme, as well as newspaper clippings, magazine articles or notes written at a meeting, are all put into the *idea file*. Broadcasters can look in the *file* to find materials for their programmes whenever they need to. *Idea files* are usually kept in neat folders, each one with a title or label, so that items can be put in the right place and easily found.

INTERNAL BALANCE (see MICROPHONE BALANCE).

INTERVAL SIGNAL (WAITING MUSIC or SIGNATURE TUNE): A group of sounds or musical notes which a radio station uses between programmes so that listeners can tell which station they are hearing (also see STATION IDENTIFI-CATION and PROGRAMME JUNCTION).

LEADER: A piece of *plastic tape* usually attached (SPLICED) to the beginning and the end of RECORDING TAPE. There are several reasons for using *leader tape*:

> It keeps the beginning of the RECORDING TAPE from being broken off. It helps you to see exactly where the programme begins and ends. Sometimes *leader* is used in the middle of a RECORDING TAPE to mark the places where different things begin. Different colours are used by some studios to tell what kind of a programme is on the TAPE, or sometimes where the programme comes from.

LEVEL (see VOLUME).

LIVE: A *live* programme is one that is heard on the air at the same time as it is being performed. It is not RECORDED first and then put on the air at a later time. A *live insert* is a part of a programme that is performed at the time the programme goes on the air. The rest of the programme may have been RECORDED earlier. A *live* MICROPHONE is one that is turned on, so what is spoken into it can be heard in the CONTROL ROOM. *Live circuit* or *live wire* means that there is electricity moving through it (see ACOUSTIC).

LOG (or PROGRAMME LOG): A *list* of all the programmes that go over the air, any mistakes that are made by a radio station, any trouble that happened, and often many other things. It is the law in most countries that radio stations keep a *log*.

LOUDSPEAKER (or SPEAKER): The MICROPHONE turns the sound of a voice or music into electrical vibrations. The *loudspeaker* then turns these electrical vibrations back into the kind of sound our ears can hear.

MAGNETIC TAPE (see TAPE).

MASTER CONTROL (see CONTINUITY ROOM).

MASTER OF CEREMONIES (M.C.): The *person* who introduces the various speakers or performers in a programme (see COMPÈRE).

MICROPHONE (or MIKE): Takes the sound of a voice or music and turns it into electrical vibrations which may be sent out over the air or put into a RECORDING. A LOUDSPEAKER turns the electrical vibrations back into sound your ears can hear.

There are many kinds of *microphones*, but we can talk about them in two ways: the way they are used, and the way they hear the sound.

These are some of the ways *microphones* are used:

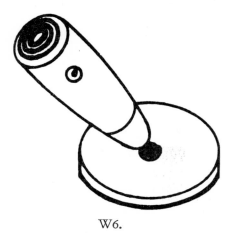

W6.

Desk Microphone: is placed on a small stand so it can be used on a table (see W6).

Boom Microphone: is put on a large stand (*boom*) so that it can hang down between the speakers or musicians.

Floor Microphone: is put on a stand that rests on the floor (see W7).

W7.

Lapel Microphone: is attached to your clothing so that it cannot be seen very easily. Sometimes it hangs from a string around your neck. Also called a *neck microphone*.

Lip Microphone: is used when you are working in a very noisy place. You can hold this *mike* so close that it actually touches your lips. It is also called a *"close-talking"* microphone.

Microphones hear the sound in different ways. They are not the same as your ears. They hear some sounds better than your ears and some sounds not as well.

Talk to a technician, and ask him to explain the different ways *microphones* are made and how they hear sounds.

The way in which a *microphone* hears the sound is what we call its *pickup*. There are many kinds of *pickup patterns*, but here are the three you will use most often:

> *Non-direction or Omni-directional:* If you used this kind of *microphone*, it would not matter what side you spoke into. It can hear just as well for all sides (see Drawing W8).

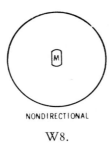

NONDIRECTIONAL

W8.

> *Bi-directional or Figure "8":* Using this kind of *microphone*, you would discover that it would hear your voice best from the front and the back, but not too well from the sides (see Drawing W9).

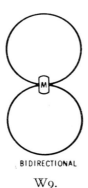

BIDIRECTIONAL

W9.

Unidirectional or Cardiod: This *microphone* would hear your voice best from only the front. If you spoke into the back or the sides of this *mike* (or into the sides of the *Bi-directional mike*) it would hear some of your voice, but this would be the part of your voice bouncing from the wall of your studio and then into the *microphone.* It would not sound as clear as when you are speaking into the best side (LIVE SIDE) of the *microphone* (see Drawing W10).

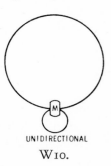

UNIDIRECTIONAL

W10.

How to care for a microphone. *Microphones* are very easy to break. Handle them very carefully. If you wish to test a *mike* to see if it is working, *never* blow into it. Say a few words into it in your normal voice, or tap it gently with your fingers.

If you are going to use a *microphone* outside where the wind is blowing, cover it with a handkerchief or a light cloth. This will prevent the wind from making too much noise on your programme.

To keep the dust out of microphones make a plastic or canvas bag to cover them when they are not being used.

Microphone technique (Mike technique) is the knowledge of how to use *microphones* so that your voice will sound best on the air. Most people find that their voices sound best when they are between 25 to 35 centimetres (10 to 14 inches) from the *microphone.* However, the kind of studio you are in, the kind of *microphone,* and your voice all make a difference. The best way is to try many different methods, listening carefully to a TAPE-RECORD-ING of each one, so that you will know which one is best for you. To do this you must train your ears very carefully. Whenever you listen to the radio, learn to listen for all the small differences in the sound which the average listener would never notice.

MICROPHONE BALANCE: *Microphone balance* means that your musicians or actors have each been placed the best distance from the MICROPHONE, so that the sound you hear is natural and pleasing. To have a good *balance*, a singer may need to be closer to the MICROPHONE than the piano. One actor in a drama may need to be closer to the MICROPHONE than another. You can only get good *balance* by trying many different distances for each person and by listening carefully through a LOUDSPEAKER.

MIX: To take the sounds from several places, such as from the MICROPHONE, the TAPE-RECORDER and the GRAMOPHONE, and put them together in one programme. This is usually done through a CONTROL DESK, sometimes called a *mixer*.

MODERATOR: The *leader* of a PANEL DISCUSSION. For a more complete description see *G3*.

MONITOR: To listen to the sound coming from a LOUDSPEAKER to be sure it is of good quality. Sometimes, a person who has the job of listening to the test quality of the sound is called a *monitor*. Also sometimes, the LOUDSPEAKER used for this purpose is called a *monitor*.

MONTAGE: A *group of sounds* or voices one following after the other, used in a drama to give a certain mood or feeling. For instance, to give the feeling of a person travelling a long distance on a train journey, your script might look like this:

SOUND:	NOISE OF TRAIN IN RAILWAY STATION.
CONDUCTOR:	(A LITTLE OFF-MIKE.) All aboard . . . all aboard for Manila.
SOUND:	TRAIN STARTS UP, GATHERS SPEED. CROSS-FADE TO MUSIC.
MUSIC:	UP FOR 5 SECONDS, CROSS-FADE AGAIN TO TRAIN.
SOUND:	TRAIN AT FULL SPEED.
CONDUCTOR:	(OFF-MIKE.) Manila . . . Manila.
SOUND:	TRAIN SLOWS DOWN TO STOP.

Or the following example of another kind of *montage*:

MUSIC:	UP FOR 5 SECONDS, DOWN QUICKLY FOR:
JUANITA:	Did you ask him Pepito? Did you ask him?
PEPITO:	I tried. He would not listen . . .
JUANITA:	Then you must ask again tomorrow.
MUSIC:	UP FOR 5 SECONDS, DOWN QUICKLY FOR:
JUANITA:	What did he say, Pepito?

PEPITO:	Nothing . . . he did not say anything, Juanita.
JUANITA:	Then tomorrow you must go again!
MUSIC:	UP FOR 5 SECONDS, DOWN QUICKLY FOR:
JUANITA:	Well? Tell me . . .
PEPITO:	I'm sorry, Juanita . . . he said no . . . he said no . . . he will not do it . . .
JUANITA:	Then *we* must do it Pepito . . . we must.
MUSIC:	UP FOR 10 SECONDS, DOWN AND OUT FOR: . . . etc.

MOOD MUSIC: Music that helps the listener feel a certain way. It puts the listener in the right *mood*. *Mood music* is sometimes used as part of a drama. When it is played quietly in the BACKGROUND, it can help the listener become interested in the drama. Sometimes *mood music* is played along with the reading of poems or stories. Different kinds of music mean different things to people. Music that may make the people of one country feel happy may make people from another country feel very sad. You must understand your listeners before you can choose good *mood music* (see BACKGROUND).

MUSIC BRIDGE (see BRIDGE).

NARRATOR: The *announcer* or *story-teller* in a drama. Sometimes the *narrator* ties the parts of the story together. Sometimes the *narrator* is one of the actors who tells part of the story, and acts one of the roles as well. For an example of the way a *narrator* is used, see the script in *N35*. A *narrator* is different from a COMPÈRE or a MASTER OF CEREMONIES.

NETWORK: Several radio stations working together, and often carrying the same programmes.

O.B. (see OUTSIDE BROADCAST).

OFF-MICROPHONE (OFF-MIKE or OUT OF BEAM): To speak into a MICROPHONE from greater than the usual distance, to make the listener think the speaker is far away. In a drama, the actors will sometimes speak from an *off-mike* position. They may want the listener to feel they are on the other side of a room, in which case they would need to be about one and a half metres (7 or 8 feet) away from the MIKE. If they wanted the listener to feel they were very far away, they might go as far as 3 to 4 metres (10 to 15 feet) away. You can sound as if you are *off-mike* simply by speaking into the DEAD SIDE of a MICROPHONE (see MICROPHONE).

ON-AIR: This means that the programme is going out over the radio station's transmitters. Sometimes a RECORDING studio will have a sign that says *on-air.* When the technician turns on the MICROPHONE, this sign lights up outside the door and inside the studio, to warn people not to open the studio door or to make any noise if they are inside.

ON-MICROPHONE (or ON-MIKE): This means that you are speaking or singing at a distance from the MICROPHONE, which will give the listener the feeling that you are only about one metre (3 feet) away from him. You should be *on-mike* for most of the talking you will do (see MICROPHONE).

Coming on-mike means that the actor begins talking when he is in the OFF-MIKE position, and moves gradually closer to the MIKE. This gives the listener the feeling that he is coming nearer. *Going off-mike* is just the opposite.

OUTSIDE BROADCAST (or O.B.) (American REMOTE BROADCAST): Any programme that is made somewhere away from the studio. Usually it refers to a *broadcast* about something that is already in progress, such as a convention or a sports event (see ACTUALITY).

OVERLOADING: Putting too much VOLUME into a TAPE machine or a radio transmitter. This may change the sound so that it becomes unpleasant, or it may even cause damage (see BLASTING, DECIBEL and DISTORTION).

PANEL DISCUSSION (ROUND-TABLE): A *programme* in which several people talk about a certain idea or a problem. There are usually three or four people in such a *programme*, plus a MODERATOR. For a more complete description, see G1.

PEAK PROGRAMME METER (P.P.M.) and V.U. METER (VOLUME UNIT METER): These measure the amount of sound that is going into a CONTROL DESK or a TAPE-RECORDER. By using them, the technician can make the sound louder or softer, and so avoid poor use of the equipment and an unpleasant sound (see DISTORTION and OVERLOADING).

POTENTIOMETER (or POT) (see FADER).

PRE-FADE LISTENING (American AUDITION): Listening to part of a programme or RECORDING before it is actually used. While you are giving a talk from the studio, the technician may listen to a part of the RECORDING he will use next, to be sure it is the right one. He will do this by using his *pre-fade* MONITOR (also see AUDITION).

PRE-RECORD: To make a RECORDING of a programme which will be put on the radio at a later time.

PROGRAMME AS BROADCAST (or P. as B.): An *information sheet* with some of the most important facts about the programme that has been put on the radio.

PROGRAMME AS RECORDED (or P. as R.): An *information sheet* with some of the most important facts about a programme that has been RECORDED.

PROGRAMME JUNCTION (or SWITCHING TIME): A short period between two programmes which gives enough time for technicians to switch from one transmitter to another, or sometimes to switch from one NETWORK to another (also see STATION BREAK and INTERVAL SIGNAL).

REBROADCAST: To make a RECORDING from a programme broadcast from one transmitter, and then to *rebroadcast* that programme over another transmitter. Also, to repeat a programme that has been broadcast before (see DUBBING).

RECORD (see GRAMOPHONE RECORD).

RECORD (RECORDING): To take the sound of music or speech and put it on to a TAPE or a GRAMOPHONE RECORD. There are many types of *recordings*: *Disc recordings*, *Film recordings*, *Magnetic recordings* and *Tape recordings*.

REMOTE BROADCAST (see OUTSIDE BROADCAST).

RE-RECORD (see DUBBING).

RE-WIND: To run a TAPE machine backwards, so that the TAPE goes back on to the reel from which it came. On many machines, the TAPE must be taken away from the HEADS, before it is *re-wound*. This is to stop the TAPE from wearing down the HEADS when it is going so fast (also see FAST FORWARD).

ROUND-TABLE (see PANEL DISCUSSION).

SCRIPT: The *papers* where all the words that the speakers will use, and all the instructions necessary for the technician are written. For instructions on how to type and use a *script* (see *J22* and *23*).

SET UP (see CUE).

SEGUE: To go directly from one music RECORDING to another, without any talking in between.

SIGNATURE (or THEME MUSIC): A piece of music used at the beginning and end of a programme. The purpose of a *musical signature* is to help the listener know what kind of programme it is going to be, and to develop the right kind of MOOD for listening. Usually, the *signature music* should be very short. *Signature music* can easily become very tiresome if it is used too often.

SHOW: Another word for PROGRAMME.

SNEAK: To have a piece of music come into the BACKGROUND (*sneak-in*) very slowly, so that the listener is hardly aware it is happening. It also may mean to make the sound softer so gradually (*sneak-out*) that he will not be aware of it (also see FADE).

SOUND EFFECTS (see EFFECTS and Appendix X).

SPOT ANNOUNCEMENTS (or SPOT): A *short talk* or *commercial announcement,* usually about a minute long or less. *Spot announcements* are often put between the RECORDINGS on a music programme. For a more complete explanation (see *D10–12*).

SPLICE: The means of joining two pieces of MAGNETIC RECORDING TAPE together. It is not difficult to do, but it must be done very carefully. There are machines you can use to *splice* TAPES. Before you use a machine, however, you should know how to *splice* without it. In that way you will not only know how to make a better *splice* with the machine, you will also know how to do it when you are in a place where there isn't any machine. Here are the steps:

> Take the two broken pieces of TAPE, one in each hand. Put one end on top of the other so that the two pieces overlap about 2 centimetres (an inch). You will notice that one side of the TAPE is shiny and the other side is not. Be sure your have the shiny sides of both pieces facing up (see Drawing W11).
>
> Hold the two pieces together, so that the edges of one TAPE are even with the edges of the other. With a pair of sharp scissors or a sharp

W11.

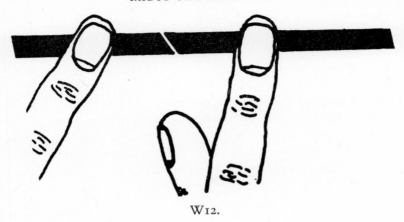

W12.

razor blade, cut across the two ends of the TAPE at an angle (45°). Remove the two little pieces that have been cut off (see Drawing W12).

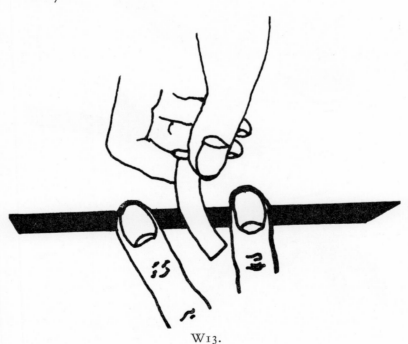

W13.

Hold the two cut ends together so that they are just touching each other (there should be no space in between, and one should not be on top of the other). Put a short piece of *splicing tape* over the place where they come together. The *splicing tape* should always be put on the *shiny* side of the TAPE. Press the *splicing tape* down hard with your your finger (see Drawing W13).

With your scissors or your razor blade, cut off the extra *splicing tape* from the sides. Be sure you remove all the *splicing tape* that can be seen on the sides, even if you have to cut away a little of the MAGNETIC TAPE to do it (see Drawing W14).

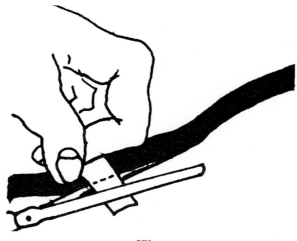

W14.

Always use only *splicing tape* specially made for use on MAGNETIC RECORDING TAPE. Ordinary cellulose tape, or any other kind will cause damage to your TAPE-RECORDER and your TAPE. Ordinary tape will come apart very soon.

STAND-BY PROGRAMME (or EMERGENCY PROGRAMME): An extra programme which is kept at the station in case the one usually prepared is not ready on time.

STATION IDENTIFICATION (or STATION BREAK): The time when a radio station gives its name (or CALL LETTERS), so that the listeners will know what station they are hearing. Most stations do this between every programme, and sometimes in the middle of a programme as well (see INTERVAL SIGNAL, PROGRAMME JUNCTION, and CALL LETTERS).

TAPE (MAGNETIC TAPE): A long thin strip of plastic on which you can put sounds you wish to keep and hear later. One side of the plastic (the dull side, see W15) has a material pasted on to it which RECORDS the sound. There are many kinds of *Magnetic tape*. If you are preparing programmes to be used on the radio, be sure that you have the best kind for your work. The best kind is not always the kind that is the most costly.

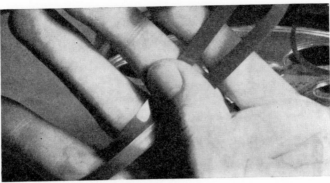

W15.

Magnetic tape (like GRAMOPHONE RECORDS) can be damaged by tropical mould and dust. If possible, keep your *tape* in an air-conditioned room. If you are going to keep a programme on a *tape* for a very long time, put the *tape* on a machine every six months. Run the *tape* quickly through to the end (FAST FORWARD) and back to the beginning (RE-WIND). This will prevent "print-through", which is the sound going from one layer of the *tape* to the next one. The sound RECORDED on a *tape* can be damaged or destroyed by anything *magnetic*, such as an electric motor or heavy electrical wires. Ask your technician to examine the place where you keep your *tapes* to be sure this doesn't happen. When *tapes* get old, they sometimes become brittle and break easily. There is very little you can do to prevent this, except by RE-RECORDING important things on a *tape* that is almost new. Sometimes it is only the beginning of the *tape* that becomes brittle. If this happens, cut off the damaged part and SPLICE on a new piece of the same kind of *tape* (also see RE-WIND, FAST FORWARD and HEAD).

THEME (see SIGNATURE).

TIMING: Making sure that each programme lasts exactly the length of *time* necessary. This is very important, since a programme that is even a few seconds too long or too short can be a major problem to a busy radio station. To *time* a programme, use a *stop-watch* to find out how long each part of your programme is. If necessary, cut out some parts to make it shorter, or add more to make it longer, but be sure your programme is *exactly* the right length.

TRANSITION (see BRIDGE).

TRANSLATION: To take something written or spoken in one language, and put it into another. For a more complete description of *translation* see *Project C.*

VOLUME: The *loudness* of the sound, or LEVEL (see GAIN).

VOLUME CONTROL: A knob to control the loudness of the sound (see GAIN).

V.U. METER (VOLUME UNIT METER) (see PEAK PROGRAMME METER).

APPENDIX X

Sound Effects

Sound-Effects Sources:

Sound effects come from three sources. They are as follows:

gramophone records,
locally made tapes, and
live studio productions.

Recorded sound effects are often more convenient than those produced live. Here are the advantages and disadvantages of each:

Recorded sound effects are very easy to use. Commercial sound-effects libraries, or those put out by the large broadcasting organisations, are usually on high-quality gramophone records. However, these are often expensive and the small studio may not be able to afford very many of them. *Locally made tapes* can be very useful, provided they are recorded carefully. Such sounds on tape are almost as easy to use as those on gramophone records. The main disadvantage is the work of recording, and the problem of finding some of the sounds.

Recorded sound effects whether on tape or gramophone record sometimes do not allow the director as much freedom with mood and timing as he would like.

Live sound effects can offer a high degree of *mood* and *timing*. For instance, a man who is very angry will open and shut a door in a different way than a thief who is trying to enter the building unnoticed. Footsteps can reflect the mood of the character very clearly. They can stop and start, change speed, and even fit in with the breathing of the character. Timing is another very important feature of sound effects. There is always an exact moment when it is "right" to close a door and pour the coffee. The "right" moment can only be determined by the director and the sound-effects man if they listen to the dialogue and try to feel the movement of the play. To be effective, a sound must happen at exactly the right time. Almost the right time is not good enough. This mood and timing is usually easier to get with live effects.

Sound effects produced in the studio are often a great deal of work and bother. Sometimes they are expensive, but they do not usually need to be, if the sound-effects man has a good imagination.

We will not say very much about those sound effects which your studio may have on gramophone records. Even if you have them, there are still sounds you will want to gather in your own community, and there will be some sounds you will want to make in your own studio.

Recording Local Sound Effects:

Every studio will need to collect sounds of its own area. There are many sounds which can be found nowhere else. The only way to get them is to take a tape-recorder and find them. Here are some such sounds:

traffic in your city and in the countryside,
the market-place,
the cries of pedlars or vendors on the streets,
people in your area making things for themselves and for selling,
a restaurant or eating place,
animals and birds, and, of course, many others.

The sounds we mentioned and others like them would form the main part of your sound-effects library. Later, you will probably find the need for other sounds.

Whenever you go out to record sound effects, try to tape different varieties of the same sound. For instance, there are many kinds of traffic in a city:

rush-hour traffic,
busy traffic but not rush-hour,
a time when there is little traffic on the streets,
the traffic on a paved road,
the traffic on a dirt or gravel road,
traffic in the poor part of the city, and
traffic in the wealthy part of the city.

It is wise to get two or three examples of each. Also be sure to get enough of the sound on tape. Traffic sounds should each be recorded for three or four minutes. Other sound effects might not need as much time.

x

There will also be times when you go to a lot of trouble to make a certain sound effect in your studio. When you do this, it is wise to tape it and add it to your library. Next time you need that sound you simply use the tape.

Keep an accurate list of your sound effects, and work out a system that will make them easy to find. Sound effects are usually listed something like this.

```
TRAFFIC:   Down-town Sao Paulo.

Late afternoon rush-hour, recorded

near City Hall.  Many cars and trucks

stopping and starting near traffic-

light.  Occasional cry of street

vendor.

LENGTH:  3'25"
```

Give as many details of each sound effect as possible. This will save a lot of unnecessary searching and listening later on.

Live Sound Effects:

The most valuable thing a sound-effects man can have is imagination. If he has imagination, he can do almost anything. Without imagination, even the most expensive equipment will not really help.

Anyone who begins to take a real interest in sound effects soon collects quite a wide variety of odds and ends, or "junk". A sound-effects man may have bottles and cups, pieces of glass, a chain, a bag of gravel, a broom, and any number of other things.

The second most valuable thing a sound-effects man can have is a willingness to experiment. By trying several dozen different things, a good sound-effects man finally finds the method that gives him the sound he wants.

Remember that the sound must be judged only when heard through a speaker. It can often sound different in the studio than it does over the loud-speaker.

Develop the habit of listening to sounds. For instance, what kind of a sound does the wind really make? Listen to it some night as you lie in your bed. What do the footsteps of an old man sound like? How are they different from a young girl? What is the rhythm of a boat paddling up the river? If you develop the habit of listening, not only will the sound effects in your dramas be very much better, but you will also gain more pleasure from the use of your ears.

Live Effects and How to Make Them:

There are many sound effects that are made just as they are in real life. For instance, to get the sound of coffee being poured into a cup, you simply pour coffee (or water) into a cup. We won't mention this kind of sound effect in the list. We will tell you how to make some sounds that need to be imitated. There is really no limit to the different kinds of effects that are possible, and so this list is intended more to give you some ideas, than to tell you how all sound effects are made.

There are often several ways to make the same sound. The ones listed here seem to be the easiest for most studios.

AEROPLANE MOTOR: Fold a heavy piece of paper, and hold it so that the blades of an electric fan will hit it. Try many different thicknesses of paper until you get the one that seems best. This is not the sound of a jet plane, by the way. If you do not have the sound of a jet on a record, you will need to take a tape machine to an airport and make your own recording.

ARROW GOING THROUGH THE AIR: Use a long thin piece of bamboo, or a stick less than a centimetre (or half an inch) thick and about a metre (3 feet) long. Hold one end and then swish it through the air about 2 metres (6 feet) away from the microphone.

ARROW STRIKING: If the arrow is striking wood, lunge a heavy knife into a large block of soft wood. If the arrow is striking a person or an animal, use the same method as for STABBING.

BELLS: Many kinds of bell sounds can be made with the brake drum from an old automobile. Set the brake drum on a piece of wood, so that the open part is facing up. To get different bell tones, strike the brake drum with various kinds of wood and metal.

BLOWS: For *blows on the head*, strike a large melon, papaya (papaw) or pumpkin with a wooden hammer or a piece of rubber hose; or you can hit a leather mitten or glove with the rubber hose. For *blows on the chin*, put on a thin leather glove and hit your bare hand with your gloved fist. For variety, use slaps of the hands to the chest and thighs. Also look under FIGHTS.

BUSHES: Rattle or twist a dried palm branch, or twist a broom close to the microphone.

CHIMES: Fill several thin glasses with water, and strike them gently with a small wooden hammer. Change the amount of water in the glass to make the note higher or lower.

CLOCKS: If you can find a clock that has a fairly loud sound, just hold it close to the microphone. Otherwise, take a fountain-pen and turn it back and forth over a small metal box so that the clip hits the metal (see photograph below).

Kyung-Do-Kim, HLKY, Korea.

CRASHES: Simply fill a wooden box with pieces of broken glass, small pieces of metal and old tin cans. Nail down the cover of the box. The crash sound is made by simply turning the box over.

Glass crash: Fill a cloth bag with pieces of glass. Be sure the bag is strong enough so it won't be cut by the glass. Drop the bag on the floor and shake it a little to get the right sound.

Wood crash: Very thin light wood, such as a match box, is crushed or broken close to the microphone.

CREAKS: Twist and squeeze a paper cup close to the microphone. Better yet, find a rusty hinge and mount it on two blocks to make the hinges squeak.

DIGGING AND SHOVELLING: Fill a small wooden box with dirt, gravel or sand, depending on the sound you want, and dig in it with a small shovel. The walking flats (WALKING) could be used for this.

DOOR: Most of the sound of opening or closing a door comes from the lock and the door jamb. You can get this sound just as well by building a small door, about half the size of an ordinary door. You would probably need two kinds of doors, at least: the kind found in the traditional buildings of your

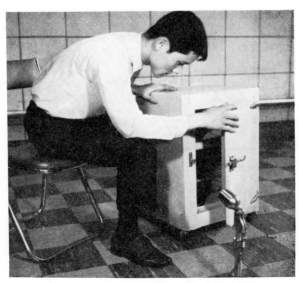

Kyung-Do, Kim, HLKY, Korea.

country, and the Westernised doors found on some buildings. Be sure the doors are on a good solid frame or they will not sound right.

Car door: You need an actual car door mounted in a heavy wood or concrete frame, or you can use a small refrigerator door (see photograph on page 325).

FIGHTS: It takes quite a bit of practice before several actors can produce the sound of a good fight. Often it is best to have the actors who play the fighting characters do the sounds themselves, so that the words and breathing fit in with the hitting and wrestling. Do not make a fight go too fast or it will sound like a scramble. Look under BLOWS to find out how these are done.

FIRE: Gently twist a piece of cellophane close to the microphone. To make a larger fire, add the crackling of pieces of a match box by breaking it with your fingers.

FOOTSTEPS: *Barefoot:* Either remove the shoes or else use rubber-soled shoes that do not squeak.

Soil and gravel: Build some walking flats. These are shallow boxes, about 10 centimetres (4 inches) deep and about a metre (3 feet) long and wide. Fill them with sand, gravel, concrete, or whatever walking surfaces you need. Place a microphone on the floor beside the flat (see photograph below).

Leaves: Rustle some old recording tape in the same rhythm as walking, or stir some cornflakes in a small cardboard box.

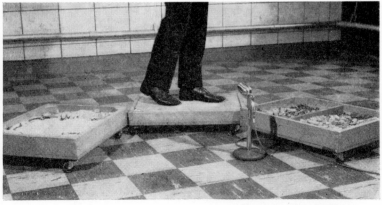

Kyung-Do, Kim, HLKY, Korea.

Mud and slush: Use a wet floor mop to walk on, or a large pan filled with soaking wet newspapers (see photograph below).

Kyung-Do, Kim, HLKY, Korea.

Snow: Squeeze a small bag of cornstarch or very fine rice flour in the same rhythm as walking.

Floors: Build a piece of floor about one or 2 metres (3 to 6 feet) long of the kind you need for your dramas. This should be raised up on pieces of wood so that it is about 5 or 10 centimetres (3 or 4 inches) from the studio floor (see photograph on page 328).

Stairs: Walk using only the ball or the front part of your foot. Do not use your heel. If the stairs are of wood, you should walk on a wood surface, or whatever your drama needs.

GUNSHOTS: Try hitting various surfaces in your studio with a flat stick and listening to the sound through the microphone. A leather cushion often works well. You can also prick a balloon with a pin or, of course, use a blank shot from a pistol.

LIGHT SWITCH: Mount various kinds of switches into blocks of wood. The switch will not make the right sound unless it is set right into the wood (see drawing below).

LIGHTING MATCH: There are two sounds to lighting a match: the scratch, and the flare of the flame. Use large wooden matches, and scratch them on sand-paper or a matchbox about 15 centimetres (6 inches) from the microphone. As soon as the flame comes, quickly move the match as close to the micro-phone as you can.

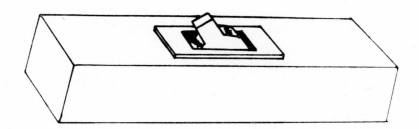

MACHINERY: *Electric motors:* Any small electric motor operated close to the microphone will give you the right sound. For a bigger motor, just turn up the volume.

Small one-cylinder motor (such as are often used on small boats): Pat the opening of a large shell or bottle with the palm of your hand (see photograph below).

Kyung-Do, Kim, HLKY, Korea.

MARCHING: You will need to make a "marching machine". To do this, make a frame of wood, about half a metre (18 inches) square. Make about forty-nine wooden pegs measuring 10 centimetres (4 inches) long and 2 centimetres (three-quarters of an inch) thick. Drill small holes about 2 centimetres (three-quarters of an inch) from the top, one hole going each way. String the little blocks into the frame. To make the marching sound, make the wooden "feet" march in rhythm on whatever surface your drama calls for, by moving the whole frame up and down on to the surface.

POURING A DRINK: Simply pour water into a glass or cup, but always touch the pitcher or the bottle to the glass to get a little "clink" sound. This helps the listener identify the sound.

SPEECH: You can get many different kinds of speech effects by having your actors speak through something or into something. The most useful is a small wooden box with an opening at one end just large enough to fit over the mouth. By speaking into this, the actor will give the impression of being in another room. Try having your actors speak through pipes, into barrels, etc., and find out what results you get.

SQUEAL: Twist the opening of a metal cup on unglazed pottery, such as part of a flower pot. Try twisting and scraping various bits of metal against each other.

STABBING: Plunge a knife into an unripe papaya (papaw), melon, or cabbage.

WATER SOUNDS: Most water sounds must be made by using real water. Many of these sounds can be made in a splash tank. This is a large tub, which should be about a metre (3 feet) across, and 60 centimetres (2 feet) deep. Such a tub must be lined with canvas or some other material to remove the metallic sound or the wooden sound.

Falling into water: Take a small bucket or pot and place it completely under the water before the drama begins. When you want the sound, pull the bucket or pot quickly straight up and out of the water.

Swimming: Use your hands to paddle the water. Practise the sound carefully, and ask someone who can swim to help you if you do not know the sound yourself. Remember that if one of the characters in the drama is swimming, he must breathe and talk as if he is swimming.

Boat: If the boat is moved by paddles, then use a flat piece of wood. Various boats make different sounds. With some, the paddle also scrapes or squeaks on the side of the boat. For a motor boat, in addition to the sound of the motor, there should be a slight ripple of water which you can make by very gently stirring your splash tank.

Surf, or waves on the shore: Use a stiff scrubbing brush and rub it on the face of a drum, or roll some dried peas or rice on a window screen.

Stream or brook: Use a straw or a hollow reed to blow into a small container of water. This could also be *boiling water*.

WEATHER EFFECTS: *Breeze:* Fold two parts of a newspaper in half. Cut these parts
into narrow strips about 2 or three centimetres (about an inch) wide. Sway
these strips gently, close to the microphone.
Hail: Slowly pour rice or dried corn on a piece of board or glass. The board
should be slanted so that the grain does not pile up and deaden the sound.
Rain: Roll several dried peas or some rice around in a flat tin pan, or crackle
some cellophane close to the microphone.

Snow: Falling snow does not make any sound. Walking on snow does have
a sound which you can find under FOOTSTEPS.
Thunder: This can be done with a good drum, by striking one hard blow
followed by several lighter blows, each one softer than the one before. The
best way is with a thunder sheet, which is about the easiest of several kinds
of thunder machines to make. Use a piece of sixteen to twenty-four gauge

sheet iron, at least one metre (3 feet) wide and 2 metres (6 feet) long. At the top and bottom of the sheet, put the metal between two pieces of wood. These must be on very tight, or the sound will not be good. Use bolts to fasten the wood. Put a handle at the bottom. Hang the sheet from the ceiling, and make the sound by shaking the sheet from the bottom. It is best to give the sheet one hard shake, then some smaller ones (see drawing on page 331).

Wind: There are many kinds of wind machines. One of the easiest to make, and perhaps the least expensive, is made from a small electric motor, usually an old fan. Remove the blades from the fan, and put in their place four dowels or thin, round pieces of wood, about half a centimetre (one-quarter inch) thick. Be sure they are firmly in place, and the same distance from each other. Tie a piece of fine copper wire between the four pieces of wood. Be sure everything is exactly balanced, or the machine will fall apart when you turn the motor on. Connect the fan through a rheostat (this allows you to control the amount of electricity going to the motor) so that you can make the fan go faster or slower. This is important, since the wind never stays at the same speed but keeps changing from harder to softer.

WHIP CRACK: Sharply slap two thin pieces of wood together.

APPENDIX Y

Suggestions for Further Reading

A SELECTED BIBLIOGRAPHY

For the Student:

ABBOT and RIDER, *The Fundamentals of Radio and TV*. New York, Toronto and London: McGraw-Hill Book Co., 1957.

ATKINSON, B. H., *Fiction Writing for West Africans*. London: MacMillan and Co. Ltd., New York: St. Martins Press, 1962.

BARNOUW, ERIC, *Mass Communication*. New York: Rinehart and Co., 1957.

CHASE, STUART, *Power of Words*. New York: Harcourt, Brace and World Inc.

NIDA, EUGENE A., *Message and Mission*. New York: Harper and Row, 1960.

NISBETT, ALEC, *The Technique of the Sound Studio*. London and New York: Focal Press, 1962.

PERROW, MAXWELL V., *Effective Christian Communication*. Richmond, Virginia: John Knox Press, 1962.

SCHRAMM, WILBUR, *Mass Media and National Development*. Paris: UNESCO, California: Stanford University Press, 1964.

VAN HORNE, MARION, *Write the Vision, A Manual for Writers*. New York: The Committee of World Literacy and Christian Literature, 475 Riverside Drive, New York 10027.

For the Supervisor:

BERLO, DAVID K., *The Process of Communication*. New York: Hold Rinehart and Winston, Inc., 1960.

DOOB, LEONARD M., *Communication in Africa*. Yale University Press, 1961.

GORHAM, M., *Training for Radio*. UNESCO, 1949.

MAGEE, BRYAN, *The Television Interview*. London: Macdonald and Co. Ltd., Gulf House 2, London W.1, 1966.

MARTY, MARTIN E., *The Improper Opinion*. Philadelphia: The Westminster Press, 1961.

MCWHINNIE, D., *The Art of Radio*. London: Faber & Faber Ltd., 1959.

SCHRAMM, WILBUR, *Mass Media and National Development*. Paris: UNESCO, California: Stanford University Press, 1964.

Recordings:

In addition to various programmes which the student should be asked to listen to and analyse, we recommend the following recording.

A Documentary History of Broadcasting: 1920–1950, Folkways Records, 165 W. 46th St., New York, U.S.A.

Side One: *A Word in your Ear* (Language), recommended for use with *Project C*.

Side Two: *I Know What I Like* (Music), recommended for use with *Project J*.

Caution: English is spoken very rapidly on this record. Some students may be helped by having the script (included with the record) before them as they listen. The material is presented from a distinctly North American viewpoint.

Note: This record also is an excellent example of documentary programming and as such could be used with *Project M*.

Selected Periodicals:

Audio Visual News. The Christian Association for Radio and Audio-Visual Service, 15 New Civil Lines, Jabalpur, M.P., India.

Better Broadcasts Newsletter. American Council for Better Broadcasts, 423 Pinchney, Madison, Wisconsin, U.S.A.

BBC Television Review. British Broadcasting Corporation, London, England.

The Broadcaster's Organ. P.O. Box 1373, Lusaka, Zambia.

CETO News. The Studio, Nuffield Lodge, Regent's Park, London, N.W.1, England.

The Christian Broadcaster. 475 Riverside Drive, New York 10027, N.Y., U.S.A. or:
2 Eaton Gate, London, S.W.1, England.

Journal of Communication. National Society for the Study of Communication, Michigan State College, East Lancing, Michigan, U.S.A.

The Listener. British Broadcasting Corporation, London, W.1, England.

NAEB Journal. National Association of Educational Broadcasters, 119 Gregory Hall, Urbane, Illinois, U.S.A.

UNDA Review. General Secretariat, case postale 211, 1701 Fribourg, Switzerland.

Write! A Magazine for Christian Writers Fellowship of Africa. African Literature Centre, P.O. Box 1319, Kitwe, Republic of Zambia.

A more complete bibliography and periodical list, covering most of the available literature on the subject of the mass media, is available from the World Association for Christian Broadcasting.

APPENDIX Z

Supervisor's Notes

Introduction (S1):

This training manual is designed for use in the developing nations of the world. It is intended for those working in the field of educational broadcasting. These two statements need some explanations.

There is great variety in the situations faced by broadcasters in Asia, Africa, the Middle East, and Latin America. Some nations have highly developed radio systems, while in others broadcasting is still in its infancy. Similarly, there are any number of cultures into which large and small stations and studios are sending their programmes.

Educational programming also takes on a wide variety of forms. The term is used most often to describe programmes made specifically for use in classrooms, even though these would more accurately be called "in-school broadcasts". Educational broadcasting, as the term is used in this manual, means a more general type of programming intended to contribute to the betterment of the listener. This could mean everything from formal instruction for organised listener groups, to general entertainment programmes containing information or ideas.

The basic techniques of programme preparation are somewhat similar in all these circumstances, and it is these which this manual will try to teach. However, because situations vary so greatly, the supervisor who administers this manual will need to be extremely flexible. He will need to adapt portions of almost every project to fit the needs of the studio, the type of broadcasting, and the audience he is aiming for. In this introduction, we will attempt to explain some of the things that are necessary if the best use is to be made of this manual.

The Task of the Supervisor (S2):

When we began our research tour through four continents, most of the people we interviewed agreed that such a manual would be almost completely useless, if it were simply given to a young broadcaster with the words, "Here, go to it."

In the first place, it would be a rare person indeed who would have the will-power to go through all the steps described in this manual, without constant encouragement from a teacher or superior. Secondly, every student can benefit from another's insights and observations.

We were unable to determine exactly what sort of supervision would be available to students using this manual. In some cases, it would be administered by people highly trained in the field of radio. These people would use the manual as a competent teacher uses a textbook, primarily as a supplement.

In other cases, we found that this manual would be supervised by persons who had little or no training in radio. Men and women, extremely competent and well trained in other fields, have of necessity been given positions of responsi-bility in various educational radio studios and stations. They are often keenly aware of their own need for training, and the training needs of those over whom they are given charge. It is this sort of person we had in mind as we wrote these supervisor's notes. These are people with experience in a field other than radio, who are faced with the training of others in the difficult field of broadcasting.

Supervisor's Preparation (S3):

This manual will not be effective if the student is left to do the work on his own. The supervisor must supervise! In order to do this, there is need for some pre-paration.

General study of the manual. The extent of this will depend on the radio experience and training of the supervisor. If he has little training in radio, he should carefully read through the entire manual before beginning to work with the student.

Reading from the bibliography (Appendix X). Once again the extent of this reading will depend on the experience of the supervisor. In any case, every attempt should be made to have as many as possible of the works listed in the bibliography available for use by the student.

Survey of local helps. The supervisor should investigate the resources of the community, to discover the persons and materials available. In many cases, the manual asks the student to locate people with some particular type of training or experience. The supervisor's knowledge of such people will certainly facilitate the training.

Every attempt should be made to gather or locate reference materials related to (*a*) the culture of the audience to which the station or studio is aiming its programmes, (*b*) the music, drama and art of the nation, and (*c*) the particular area of education in which the studio is working.

Programme examples. A great deal can be learned through listening. The supervisor should gather a good assortment of sample programmes, not only of the kinds dealt with in the manual, but others as well. These should be local programmes in so far as they are available, plus other examples from different parts of the word. A check through the various assignments in each project will give an indication of the tapes needed. If they are not available locally, the supervisor may wish to ask one of the agencies listed in *S11* for help.

The students should also have access to a good radio, so that they may locate and listen to programmes originating not only in their own country, but also those coming from abroad.

Final preparation. Before assigning each project to the student, the supervisor should again check through it carefully. This should be done far enough in advance to allow for the preparation and gathering of materials. The supervisor should also study each project to see where it would need to be adapted to fit the local situation, and to discover in what ways local materials or persons might be included to enrich the project. Particular attention should be paid to the assignments, the check-lists, and the supervisor's notes for that project.

Working with the Student (S4):

There are two things which have been emphasised throughout this manual.

The first is the need to adapt, not only the manual and its instructions, but radio programming generally to fit the local listener. It is the opinion of the writer and editors of this manual, that all thoughts and planning in regard to programming must begin with the listener. The listener's needs, his background, tastes, and culture are constantly emphasised. The broadcaster must communicate in relation to these, or he will not be successful.

This requires study and research, something at which broadcasters are often not very good. They are impatient to get on with programming, not recognising that communication will take place only on a "hit or miss" basis unless this is done. More about this is said in the manual itself.

Secondly, we have tried to develop the habit of critical analysis in the student. This is very difficult in many cultures. Often there is a strong tendency to accept uncritically everything that comes from an instructor or from a book. Similarly, programmes produced by more experienced people may be accepted as "perfect".

We have already explained that this manual deals with such a variety of situations, that it would be impossible to say anything that would hold true for all situations. For this reason, both supervisor and student must constantly ask, "Does this apply to us here in our circumstances?" If not, the necessary changes or adaptations must be made.

Even more important is the development of the student's ability to criticise his own work, and to accept good ideas and reject the bad from the work of others. The student should be helped at every point to realise that the successful broadcaster is not one who has learned a great many rules or principles laid down by another. The successful broadcaster is one who can tell the excellent from the mediocre; one who has developed taste, discretion, and responsibility.

Adapting the Manual (S5):

Many of the studios using this manual may have a very small staff. That is why this has been written primarily for use by one student and his supervisor. It has also been assumed that the student is in the employ of the studio, and may be already involved in day-to-day programme preparation.

Where this is the case, it is suggested that the student set aside a definite portion of each day or each week for training. A *minimum* of *two hours a day* is suggested, although it would be possible to work for as little as one hour a day. We have found it impossible to estimate the actual amount of time necessary for the completion of the work outlined, once again because of the variety of circumstances and students.

The day-to-day programme work of the student, and the work in this manual should be co-ordinated as much as possible. Where programmes are fairly flexible, this may be possible to a large degree. For instance, it would be extremely useful for the student to be assigned to the production of a series of short talks during the time when he is working on the opening projects, then moved on to translation work, spot announcements, interviews and so forth. In this way he would be able to apply the instruction of the manual directly to his work.

We frequently suggest that assignments be used on the air. There will be many circumstances where this is impossible, of course, but actual use of the materials prepared will give the student a great deal of extra incentive and practical experience.

In situations where the studio or station already has a staff of more experienced persons, the student could be made an apprentice to the various departments while he is working on a related project. In this case, the student should be under one over-all supervisor, who would re-assign supervision to other staff members as occasion permitted; that is, to the music director while working on the music projects, and to the news director while working on news.

Working with Two or More Students (S6):

In some cases, the manual will be used in workshop situations where a number of students are involved. In these cases, a great many of the assignments can be done by teams of two or three. This is particularly true of those assignments involving the gathering of information. This teaming up may be essential where equipment such as tape-recorders and studios are in short supply. When this is done, however, the students should check their work individually, and each should be responsible for the quality of the work done.

Often the assignments call for reports or written analysis. It is always useful for the student to give a verbal report on his findings, and to answer questions from the group to which he reports. Work is usually of a higher quality if the student knows he must give a "public" account of his findings. Furthermore, those who hear his report will also benefit from his studies. These reports, by the way, could as well be made to fellow staff members as to other workshop students.

There are a variety of listening projects suggested. Where a workshop situation exists, some of these projects should be done by the students individually and in pairs, while others should be the object of the entire group's study.

Whenever possible, the students should be encouraged to make their reports and do all their writing and other work in the language they will use on the air. This will be a further exercise in the development of their language ability. There are, of course, situations such as in the case of international workshops, where this is not possible.

Training Outsiders (S7):

By "outsiders", we mean those people who are not regularly employed by a studio or station, or who are not studying radio on a full-time basis. These may be persons who are in a position to contribute to the work of the studio in one way or another, and who are therefore in a position to receive at least some training.

The manual is designed as a total course. None of the projects is self-contained, in the sense that it covers its subject completely. As we pointed out in our introduction to the student, all the projects are interrelated, and skills learned in relation to one kind of programme can usually be applied to a variety of other programmes as well. Therefore the manual is not completely suitable for such a situation.

However, where a short course of some description is necessary, we would suggest the following:

> *Projects A* and *B* are essential. The manual should not be used in situations where these could not be completed as a minimum. This would require three or four full days.
> *Projects C, I* and *H* would be next, in that order of importance. An extra three days should be added for each project.
> Where training in specific areas is required, the projects related to those particular areas should be added to the above. In addition, the supervisor should check the table of contents for other paragraphs or portions of the manual which deal with the subject at hand. These should be given as reading assignments to the students.
> In situations where the students come for instruction occasionally and return to their regular employment in between workshop sessions, it is suggested that extensive listening assignments be made. For instance, if the students come in for instruction each week-end, the supervisor should give them "homework" assignments. They should be given certain programmes to search out and listen to, along with some written suggestions as to what they should look for in each case. When possible, this should be a specific programme known to be heard in the area, or at least a specific *kind* of programme. The results of their listening could provide the basis of a fruitful discussion among the students.
> Workshops designed specifically to train writers should not ignore production. Although actual voicing and production of programmes need not be

emphasised, knowledge of the problems and techniques involved will certainly be beneficial to the writers. It will also give them an appreciation of the differences between the written and the spoken style of language, something which writers have a tendency to overlook.

Encouraging the Student (S8):

It will be the task of every supervisor to do all he can to encourage the student in his work. Every student is different, of course, and it is assumed that every supervisor will take the time to get to know and understand his students. He can then provide intelligent guidance and encouragement. Most supervisors find that generous praise of real progress, tempered by well thought-out and sincere criticism, is the most helpful formula.

Although due praise should be given when a student makes progress, both he and the supervisor should always keep in mind that this manual provides only a beginning in the art of radio.

A broadcaster should never stop learning, of course. The student must realise that this manual may provide a foundation, but that a polished technique can only be developed through further study and practice.

None of the projects give more than an introduction to the kind of programme they deal with. The student may develop a false confidence if he is not made very much aware of this.

The Glossary Assignments (S9):

In most of the projects, one of the assignments calls for the translation of certain terms from the glossary. In many countries radio terms have been adopted from European languages. Frequently there is no equivalent in the local language for the term given. The purpose of these assignments is simply to help the student understand the process or the technique which the term describes, and to do this he should be able to describe it in his own language. The object then is not necessarily to find an equivalent *word* in the local language, although that would be helpful. The object is to have the student describe the meaning of the term in his own language.

The Glossary Assignments, if they are all completed by the student, may have an additional benefit. In some cases, they may be useful for the instruction of other staff or for the outsiders providing programme material for the studio.

Research and Idea Files (S10):

Frequent reference is made to the research and idea files. It is hoped that the supervisor will encourage each student to develop these files. He should not only add those items suggested in the manual, but should also constantly be on the look-out for other materials which might be useful in his work after he completes these studies.

The purpose of these files is two-fold:

to help the student realise the importance of building informational resources in an organised manner, and

to start the student in the use of such materials in his programming, a use which should continue following the completion of the manual.

Where to Go for More Help (S11):

There are often many agencies and organisations which can give help of one kind or another to a radio studio. These are other radio stations, government agencies, church organisations, schools and universities, etc.

We include here a list of some international organisations which are prepared to give information and some forms of assistance to educational broadcasters. A letter to one or more of these may bring information about resources available to the broadcaster.

The United Nations Educational, Scientific, and Cultural Organisation now has offices in many nations. Contact the office in your country, or write to the headquarters at:

UNESCO, Place de Fontenoy, Paris 7ᵉ, France.

World Association for Christian Broadcasting, 2 Eaton Gate, London S.W.1, England.

UNDA, General Secretariat, case postale 211, Fribourg, Switzerland.

Radio, Visual Education and Mass Communication Committee, 475 Riverside Drive, New York, N.Y., 10027, U.S.A.

National Association of Educational Broadcasters, 119 Gregory Hall, Urbane, Illinois, U.S.A.

Most of the world's larger nations have overseas services, as well as facilities for assisting broadcasters in other countries. Many are very co-operative in the matter of providing information and assistance.

Translation of the Manual (S12):

Ideally, this manual should be adapted into the language and the situation faced by each studio. This is not possible, of course, although it is hoped that some translation may take place. In fact, studios using this manual are encouraged to undertake the translation and adaptation of all or part of it. Where such translations are to be printed or mimeographed, permission must be obtained from The World Association for Christian Broadcasting. The address is given above. This Association will do everything possible to co-operate with such a project, and may even be able to provide some assistance.

Future Revisions (S13):

It is hoped that this manual will be revised within a few years. This will be necessary to bring it up to date with new developments, and to correct problems brought to light by the use of this present edition. For that reason, the author and the Association urgently request all those who use this manual to write, telling of the uses to which the manual is put, and the problems which have arisen with its use. Suggestions for improvement would also be most useful. All such comments will be greatly appreciated, even if they take the form of harsh criticisms. They will be very seriously considered when a revision of this manual is undertaken.

PROJECT A

(A6–8)

The importance of research cannot be over-emphasised. Communication most frequently fails, because we don't know who we are talking to. For example, one country beamed radio programmes at the "poor, illiterate, rural people". This went on for some time, until it was discovered this class of people had no radios and no access to radios.

Therefore, the supervisor should insist that the student do his research thoroughly. This research may also be of general use to the studio in providing information relevant to programming decisions.

This research takes two forms:

study of existing materials, such as those which may be found in government offices, university libraries, etc., and

a field trip.

(A9)

In this case, we have asked the student to study and write for that group in his country having the *most radio sets*. The student should look in the libraries first to find out which group this is. He should also observe various segments of the population and consult with people who might be able to throw some light on the matter. Having learned this, he should make every attempt to interview this specific group of people in their homes (probably five or six interviews will be sufficient for this project) to find out more about them. He should write up his research report in a systematic manner.

When the student presents his research to the supervisor, there are a few things to watch for:

attempts to fit the picture of his audience into his own preconceived idea of what he believes it should be like,

tendencies to overlook major problems of society in favour of his own personal criticisms,

failure to explore available resources for information, and

tendencies to draw firm conclusions from this research. The student must understand that these are only "clues". Even the most systematic sociologists hesitate before drawing definite conclusions.

If the student has not grasped some of the problems of communicating with his listeners, it would be advisable to undertake additional work in this area. The following are some suggestions:

interviews with sociologists or anthropologists (or people who have a deep interest in this subject),

readings related to the nature of their culture, and

further interviews among the group of listeners mentioned earlier.

(A10–14)

The student should bring to his supervisor the edited version of his first writing draft, along with his outline and his research. It should show evidence that he has really wrestled with the problem of "how to say it", and "what to say".

The most common problems likely to be encountered will be:

> a tendency to "preach" or "lecture", with large words and complicated phrases,
>
> a failure to grasp the "one-idea-per-talk" concept, and
>
> a tendency to use illustrations and idioms not meaningful to the listener.

It would be well for the supervisor to review with the student the sample script shown under *A13*. Questions one to ten of the Evaluation at the end of the project might be applied to this sample script. Going over the sample with the student may help him to understand his own work better. The student should not imitate this script and every attempt should be made to encourage originality.

If the student has not grasped the ideas presented in the second portion of the project, it would be wise for him to begin again with his outline. Perhaps the use of another subject for his talk might be helpful.

(A15–19)

If the student has at any point voluntarily decided to abandon a script outline or to completely rewrite a script because of dissatisfaction with it, he should be praised. To recognise the inadequacy of one's work is a mark of maturity, provided it is not carried to extremes.

We are trying to emphasise the fact that it is highly unlikely that any work will be satisfactory on the first or even the second writing. "Good scripts are not written; they are rewritten," should be emphasised throughout this course.

We say very little in this project about radio speaking, although we hope to eliminate some of the more obvious problems related to microphone technique, such as shouting, tenseness, and too much stumbling. It would probably be wise to assign additional "out loud" readings on tape.

It is most essential that the student learn the extreme importance of evaluation. He should be led through a review of the various steps and suggestions in the introduction, as he listens as often as necessary to his tape-recording. If the project assignment has not been completed satisfactorily, it would be well to assign another two or three similar talks which the student should write and record. In fact, the assignment of at least one additional talk is recommended if the time-table permits. It is suggested that these talks and other assignments be used on the air whenever possible.

The Glossary Assignment is explained under *S9* and in the instruction to the student (*A2* and *A18*).

PROJECT B

(B1 and 2)

Read over and become familiar with the lesson before it is given to the student.

The lesson is divided into *four* parts. The student should report to the supervisor after each part. Do not allow the student to proceed until he has reported.

Success in learning the lessons of Part One will depend largely on the encouragement given to the student. It will also depend on whether the supervisor is able to sustain the student's interest in developing the "notebook habit" long enough for it to become a firm habit.

(B3 and 4)

It would probably be wise to buy a small booklet to give to the student as he begins this project. It would also be best for the supervisor to spend some time talking to the student about the community in which he lives.

In some cases, it might even be possible to give the student a camera and a roll or two of film along with instructions to bring back a series of photographs about the various aspects of life in his community.

Perhaps it might be possible for the supervisor, or some other perceptive individual, to walk a short distance with the student pointing out the evidences of conflict, love, hope, sorrow, and the entire gamut of human emotions evident everywhere.

(B5)

Success in developing the reading habit also depends to some extent on the encouragement given to the student by his supervisor. It follows that reading materials must be made available, even though this may lead to problems in their use and handling.

The underlying factor behind Part One is the fact that no staff, no matter how brilliant it may be, can sustain an intelligent programme series entirely on its own resources. Unless staff members are constantly stimulated with new ideas and new insights, they will certainly become mentally sluggish, a symptom soon reflected in the programming.

(B6)

Studio resources, in addition to the periodicals suggested in Part One of this project, should also include a basic reference library. There should be several dictionaries, at least one good encyclopaedia, a thesaurus, if possible, as well as a good collection of the standard works related to the area of programming in which your student specialises.

There should also be available, if possible, some of the better works dealing with your nation's geography, history, politics, art, religions, culture, and economics.

These are basic tools in any studio which aspire to produce intelligent and effective programmes. A certain amount of every budget should be set aside for the purchase of newspapers, magazines and books so that the studio library may be kept up to date at all times.

Students should be encouraged to search out the several viewpoints that may exist on any given subject. They should look to persons of varying opinions and viewpoints, and should consider these divergent ideas with an open mind.

(B7)

The "idea file" has proved useful in any number of radio studios and publication offices. Much of its success depends upon organisation and persistence.

Organisation will depend largely on specific needs. It is important that items can be filed and found easily and quickly. Many studios find that the idea file works best when one staff member is assigned specifically to its development. This also ensures to some extent that the file will be given consistent attention. Other staff members should, of course, be constantly encouraged to go to the idea file for information and ideas and to contribute items to it.

(B8)

After the student has completed Part One of *Project B*, the supervisor should try to determine if he has really learned the value of his notebook, his reading, and the idea file. Questions such as the following might be asked. They are intended mainly to help the student think clearly about these issues. The actual answers are not as important as the thinking they exhibit.

About the notebook: *(B3 and 4)*

Where did you go in your walk?
How many people do you suppose you saw altogether?
What do you think was the saddest thing you saw?
What was the happiest thing you saw?
Did you see anything that made you angry?
If you were a tourist from another country, what do you think you would see first?
Do tourists from other countries fail to see things in our country as they really are? In what way?
What did you see that you think should be changed?

About his reading: *(B5)*

What is the most exciting book you have ever read?
Why was it exciting?
What kinds of books should we have here in our studio? Why?
What kind of magazines should we have here? Why?
In what way do you think you could make use of these books and magazines in your programming?
What part of your day can you set aside to reading good books and magazines?

About the idea file: *(B7)*

Do you think the idea file is useful in our studio?
Is it worth the work that is needed for it?
How do you think we can be sure that people contribute things to it and continue to use it?
Have you any suggestions for ways in which we might improve the file?

If possible, the student should visit a newspaper or magazine office, to discover the way in which it gathers and files material. He might be asked to give a report to the rest of the staff on the way in which this newspaper or magazine keeps up the supply of interesting materials and ideas, giving both the good and bad points of the operation he studies.

(B9 and 10)

In this section, we hope to help the student understand some problems of communication as well as some of the techniques he may use to solve those problems.

It is important that the student understand very clearly that radio is a means of communication with its own unique capabilities and limitations. Although there are areas in common, he must learn not to confuse the techniques of radio communication with those used on a public speakers' platform, a classroom, or a place of worship.

(B11 and 12)

Another important idea the student must grasp is that of focusing his programme on *one particular listener*. The reasons for this are simple. If he does this, his programmes will take on a personal character both in writing and production. At the same time, he will tend to keep the content and presentation within a given framework, avoiding the hazard of working under different assumptions about the audience at various points in the programme.

Therefore, as an exercise, be sure he creates in his mind an image of one particular listener, and that he writes his script in relation to this one imaginary person.

It is a difficult concept to grasp, but one vitally necessary to successful programming. Too often, in an attempt to gain a wide audience, broadcasters think of their listeners as a mass audience. Although the audience for a radio programme may indeed be "the mass audience", experience has shown that these listeners are usually gained by selecting one *typical* representative individual and then designing the entire programme to meet the needs of this person.

> Radio is at its best when it gives the impression of one person reaching out to one person.

Another tendency among broadcasters, particularly those who are doing educational broadcasting, is to be much too academic. Frequently their programmes have excellent content, are well researched and would be of great value to the listener. However, such programmes reach only those listeners already interested in the subject.

If this is the kind of person you wish to reach, then by all means be academic in your approach. However, if you wish to capture the interest of those who may have only a slight interest or may even be antagonistic to your message, then you must of necessity use the more simple and "human" approach.

By this we mean relating your subject to the human events which the listener knows and understands, and more important, to the kind of people he knows and understands. "People are interested in people", is a maxim worth remembering.

This does not imply that programme material should not be accurate and factual. It does mean that it must be presented in terms which the normally disinterested listener will find interesting.

(B16 and 17)

Another problem the supervisor may find in this project is related to the techniques described under "the first draft". It will be the task of the supervisor to help the student relate these techniques to the particular language and culture in which he is working. Some may need modification. There may well be others not indicated which may have particular relevance to your situation.

We recommend that the supervisor spend some time discussing with the student, the particular problems of communication dealt with in this project. A close check on the edited first draft of the script may reveal some of the problems that need investigation.

If the conversation and the check on the script seem to indicate that the student has failed to grasp the ideas put forth, a point-by-point discussion may be in order. This should be followed by a rewriting of the first draft.

(B19)

Part Three should not be too difficult for the student. The student should have grasped the idea of "cutting" and "padding" his script while actually recording. He should have made sufficient provision in his script so that he may remove or add a few sentences near the end, to make his talk last exactly five minutes.

We have been emphasising *timing* during programme preparation. At first sight it may seem to be over-emphasised, but in view of the friction which so often develops between producers and those responsible for the total programming of the station, it was felt wise to emphasise this aspect at the outset. Hopefully, the student will develop the habit of accurate timing, to the point where it may cease to be a problem for him and will automatically be taken into consideration.

(B21–22)

We have asked the student to practise his script seven times before actually going to the microphone to record. In *A15* we listed the things to look for during each of these seven readings.

If it seems the student is having difficulty in doing an effective reading of his script, it would be wise to have him record all seven rehearsals on tape. Then the supervisor should listen to a portion of each rehearsal with him. In this way, it may be possible for the supervisor to point out some of the problems and help overcome them.

Discourage any inclination to do less than the rehearsal suggested, unless the student already has considerable on-the-air experience. The success of his script is determined finally by the type of reading it gets. Good announcing or reading takes a great deal of practice.

Real progress of this area would be hastened by additional assignments of out-loud reading as suggested in *Project A*. Even if the student in question does not intend to make a career as an on-the-air performer, his understanding of the technique and the problems will help him considerably as a radio-script writer. We will be dealing with voicing techniques again in *Project D*.

In the meantime, it may be helpful for the student to listen to some of his nation's best radio speakers. He should listen as analytically as possible, making notes on the ways in which the speaker handles his voice. He should then give a written report to his supervisor. However, when he does this, he should be warned not to imitate or mimic the style of others. The student may gain new ideas from other speakers, but should concentrate on developing his own personal style. Anything else will be false and artificial.

(B23)

The check-list is intended to help the student become as analytical about his own work as possible. This is why he is requested to spend considerable time with the check-list before coming to his supervisor. When the supervisor goes over the list with him, he should be encouraged to use his own evaluation, the supervisor pointing out only those elements which he may have overlooked.

Once again we would wish to mention the great psychological value of using the student's programmes on the air whenever possible. This will provide a good deal of added incentive, and help him to sense the importance of his work.

PROJECT C

Read over and become familiar with the lesson before it is given to the student.

The lesson is divided into two parts. After each one, the student should bring his completed assignments to the supervisor.

(C1)

The object of Part One is to help the student to an appreciation of his language and a critical attitude towards it.

By appreciation, we mean a love and respect that will make him want to know his language, to work with it, and to develop its possibilities. There are sad instances where young people, having been given a "Western" education, begin to think the language or dialect of their homeland is of low value.

(C2)

Linguistic science has shown that there is no such thing as an "inferior" language. Some languages have developed a larger vocabulary than others, but this does not make them better. It means the language has more words. Even a dialect from a small remote village has a richness and colour that can be used artistically by the writer.

It is also true that if real communication is to take place, the best tool is the *first* language of those with whom you are communicating. Even though the listener may have some knowledge of another tongue, you will communicate better if you use the language he uses with his wife and children.

When speaking of a critical attitude to language, we are using the word in its good sense. Perhaps a better term would be "analytical". In other words, we hope the student will try to dig beneath the surface of the language to discover some of its characteristics and traits.

(C3–8)

There is a danger the student may feel that since he already speaks the language very well, he knows all there is to know. His ability to use the language is, of

course, very important. He will use it even better, though, if he would understand some of its inner workings.

It is for this reason that a talk with a linguist would be most useful. It may be
that the supervisor would wish to invite such a linguist to talk to the studio staff,
with the questions in *Project C* as the basis of his talk.

If there is no linguist in your area, a competent sociologist or anthropologist
may be able to help you. Persons teaching language subjects in a school may be
helpful or perhaps an author, an actor, or a well-known speaker.

It is the task of the supervisor to see that the student does everything possible
to come to a better understanding of his own tongue.

(C9)

The second assignment of Part One, has to do with the discovery of language as
an art. It is very difficult for us to lead a student into this study, not knowing the
language in question. It will, therefore, be necessary for the supervisor to guide
the student, and change the lesson where necessary to fit the local situation.

(C10 and 11)

The third assignment is of lesser importance, and not much time should be spent
on it. However, it can show rather well the problems in communication. In fact,
such an exercise could be carried out at a staff meeting, and might provide both
amusement and instruction.

All three assignments should be checked carefully, to be sure that the student
has come to understand the basic ways in which his language works. It might be
wise to ask him to make a report on the matter to the staff of your studio or
station.

(C12 and 13)

There is a common idea that translation is simply taking words from one language, and changing them into the words of another language. This is far from
the truth. In fact, many will claim that translation is more difficult than an
original work.

Poor translation is easy. Good translation is difficult. Good translation of a
book, for instance, can take years.

(C14–16)

The main reason for the fourth assignment (the adaptation) is to help the student see the different structural forms in his language. The differences between his language and English may be hard to see and it is hoped the supervisor may be able to guide the student in his understanding of these differences.

Also of great importance is the knowledge that an idiom cannot be translated. An equivalent idiom may be found perhaps, but the idiom itself (except in a few cases) is not translatable.

(C17–19)

In the fifth assignment, we hope the student will begin to find the mood and the basic idea behind the English news item when he translates it into his own language. Once again, it will probably be necessary for the supervisor to guide the student in his understanding of the article.

It may not always be possible for the student to talk about his understanding of his own translation, or to explain its structure. Although he should be encouraged to do so (since the art of expression is the art of the writer), it may well be impossible for him. The test, then, is to have him read the translated item to another person to see if some of the meaning is communicated.

The supervisor should spend quite a bit of time discussing both the adaptation and the translation with the student, particularly using the check-lists supplied.

In some cases, it may be possible to find articles, poems and stories that have been translated. In this case, the student should be asked to go over the original and the translated versions, to compare the differences and to make critical comments. Where this is possible, several assignments might be worked out to be done before the student undertakes Assignment Four. The check-list for Assignment Four may be used in relation to this.

It may be that the student has trouble with translation. In this case, the supervisor should assign two or three adaptations and translations from a foreign language into the student's own. They should be chosen from a variety of sources, such as perhaps a poem, a very short story, and a newspaper article. If these additional translations can be used in your programming, so much the better.

In this project, as in all others, the supervisor should encourage the student to judge himself as much as possible. The supervisor should guide the evaluation rather than do it himself. The ability of the student to judge his own work will, in the long run, be the most important thing he can learn through this course of studies.

PROJECT D

(D1–3)

The most difficult part of *Projects A* to *D* may be the research. There may be a temptation to leave this part and concentrate on the development of the programmes.

We strongly advise against this. A full and clear understanding of the audience is essential to successful programming. Some of the most skilled writers and producers have failed, because they did not take their audience sufficiently into account.

Audience research is not necessary for every programme one produces, of course, but the student must build an appreciation of its value and maintain a constant interest in the subject. Hopefully, as he begins to write programmes regularly, he will develop the habit of a continuing study of his audience.

(D4 and 5)

The student may need some guidance in locating the best books and people during Part One of *Project D*. Some preparation of usable materials by the supervisor, and some thought towards the selection of suitable resource people may speed up the research considerably.

(D6 and 7)

If you can find professionally-done questionnaires designed for use among people in the area concerned, they might serve as a guide for the student in the preparation of his own questionnaire.

A possible difficulty that often occurs is that surveyors assume the answer to a question is always correct.

Not long ago in an Asian nation, a commercial firm tried to find out if people liked their kind of tooth-paste. They asked many people, saying, "I am working for the makers of Brand 'X' tooth-paste. Can you tell me what you think of it?" All the people claimed they liked Brand "X" very much. Later another group of surveyors asked the same people another question. "I am working for the makers of Brand 'Y' tooth-paste. Can you tell me what you think of it?" These same people, it turned out, claimed to like Brand "Y" just as well as Brand "X". It seems the people were more interested in pleasing the workers who questioned them, rather than saying how they really felt.

(D8)

If at all possible, have the student prepare a complete report on his work to present to a gathering of staff members or a similar group. Encourage the group to ask questions of the student, so that he will be forced to think carefully about his conclusions. Similarly the supervisor should carefully question the student, to be sure he has not reached conclusions on the basis of little evidence. It would be best if the student recognised that he cannot really arrive at more than an intelligent guess. However, the more research done, the more intelligent the guess will be.

We would suggest that the supervisor ask the student to apply the results of his research in Part One of this project, directly to his writing of the spot announcements in Part Two. This is to impress upon him the fact that research must be taken into consideration when doing even the smallest segment of radio programming.

(D9–15)

The circumstances under which a studio may use spot announcements will vary considerably from place to place. It is suggested that the supervisor take these into consideration, and if necessary change the instructions to the student accordingly.

Some studios may not use spot announcements at all, but the discipline and exercise of preparing them will be useful nevertheless.

The subject matter should be related closely to the type of programmes and material the student will eventually be preparing, and if possible, should be designed for actual use on the air.

(D16–20)

The supervisor should check and discuss with the student his outlines, the notes made while listening to spot announcements on the radio, as well as the first and second drafts of the scripts. He should also find out how much the student has taken his research into consideration while planning and writing. The announcements should be written a third or fourth time if necessary, if the second draft is not satisfactory.

If the supervisor has access to recordings or scripts of other types and styles of spot announcements, it would be well to have the student listen to them. Although he should not be encouraged to attempt other styles at this point, he should know that the assignment he has just completed represents a basic style, and that infinite possibilities for variations exist.

(D21–24)

The instructions concerning the speech variables, such as mood, texture, intonation, etc., will also need to be adapted to fit the language being used.

Similar changes may be needed in the method of marking the script. If there is a marking method already in use at the studio, the student should be encouraged to use this. If there are devices in the language for marking stress, tone, accent, etc., these may be adapted for use in marking scripts.

Basic to this section is the concept that language is a *spoken* medium. The writing is simply a system of symbols representing the spoken tongue.

There are, in most languages, differences between the written style and the spoken style. In radio broadcasting, we can use only the spoken style of language, even though the words may be put into a written script before the language is spoken.

(D25)

The supervisor should go over the check-lists carefully with the student as he listens to the recording. If it appears the student has not grasped the ideas presented, the supervisor should assign additional reading and script-marking exercises of varying length and subject matter. Announcements or programmes written by others may be useful for this.

(D26–29)

We have also included some suggestions for ways in which problems of speech may be corrected. These exercises may help in overcoming some of the more common problems, but they are, after all, simplifications of a highly-developed science of speech therapy. Do not expect too much from these simple suggestions.

Most students can benefit from their use, although the results will vary. The supervisor should encourage each student to do each set of exercises daily for several months or longer. Even a good speaker will improve to some extent, and a poor speaker may be helped greatly. Nevertheless, it must be said there is no substitute for long hours of practice in reading scripts, poems, newspapers, books, anything!

PROJECT E

(E1–5)

The first part of *Project E* is designed to sharpen the student's powers of observation, and to increase his ability to transfer these observations into words.

The exercises seem rather simple at first sight, but could easily prove very difficult for the student. Extemporaneous description is more difficult, and it is not expected that the student will reach a high degree of proficiency at this point. If he can produce a reasonably smooth description without too much repetition, without undue pauses, and without much searching for words, this will suffice.

If several repetitions of the exercises mentioned do not produce results, and it would seem that further exercises are needed, it should not be difficult to think of an infinite variety of situations, scenes, incidents, etc., that could be described. It is suggested that these exercises should not be carried on beyond the point where the student begins to lose interest.

(E6–17)

The purpose of Part Two is to help the student develop self-confidence in interviewing people, by asking him to begin with people he knows, who will be more sympathetic and helpful. In fact, where there are several students working on this manual together, it would be well for them to begin by doing a series of interviews with each other. In the process, the student should also learn some of the basic skills and techniques necessary in interviewing, as he prepares to move into *Project F* where interviewing will be discussed in more detail.

It is suggested that the student be given extra interviews to accomplish, if it seems that his own anxiety causes him the most difficulty. Until he has overcome this anxiety, he will find it difficult to progress to higher levels of technique.

Watch for unconscious interjections by the student as he listens to the replies of the guest. In many English speaking countries this runs along the lines of a repeated "Ah ha", or "ummm" or "yes". It will vary according to the language and cultural situation in which you are working. Unless such interjections are essential to good manners, they should be strongly discouraged.

The supervisor is also asked to ensure that the student refrain from remarks that simply delay the programme, remarks such as, "Oh yes, well, thank you for that information. And now I'd like to ask you, what the situation is in the other parts of our country." Rather he should simply ask, "What is the situation, etc."

In other words, encourage the student to keep his interviews lively and fast-moving. One of the secrets of this is a thorough research into the individual concerned. The interviewer should know enough about his guest that he can select from the most interesting possibilities.

It should be pointed out that only the "personality interview" is dealt with in this project. This is because personality is the ingredient that makes interviews more interesting and lively than many other kinds of programmes. Interviews in which other aspects are emphasised will be dealt with in the next project. Personality, however, is a vital ingredient in all programmes.

PROJECT F

(F1–9)

It is important for the supervisor to study the instructions to the student, since he may find it necessary to discuss these at a number of points. The student should report to his supervisor twice during *Project F*.

The supervisor should encourage the student to consider the instructions in the light of his own cultural situation. The style of conversation, the method of questioning, the relationship of the broadcaster to his guest, will vary from one area to another. None of the instructions in this manual are intended as the final word. They are guide-lines, which we hope will help the student see the methods most useful in his own particular situation.

If your studio has a policy with regard to interviews, or to matters that might be discussed in an interview, the student should be made familiar with it before he begins Assignments Three and Four.

(F10)

Assignment One is designed to sharpen the critical powers of the student in relation to interview programmes. It is important that he have a variety of interviews (in his own language if at all possible) which he can study and analyse. Every effort should be made to locate such samples, either from radio programmes heard in the area, or by obtaining tapes from elsewhere. Some possible sources are indicated at the beginning of the Supervisor's Notes (S11).

Encourage the student to be sharply critical. It may be that the student will hesitate to criticise, especially if the interviewer on the programme is a prominent person or someone in his acquaintance. For this reason the interviews selected should, if possible, be by persons whom the student does not know. Failing that, it may be necessary to assure the student that his criticisms will be held in confidence by the supervisor. In any case, the student should be made to understand the reasons for the exercise, and that its usefulness depends on his willingness to be harsh in his judgement. Of course, the supervisor should be familiar with the interviews being discussed.

(F24 and 25)

Assignment Two is intended to familiarise the student with the process of splicing and editing. If possible, he should receive personalised instructions from someone in your studio who is familiar with the technique. It is important that he learn to splice initially without the use of a splicing machine, even though machines usually do a better job. Machines are not always available, and a knowledge of the technique gained through doing it by hand will help him use the machine more effectively.

Every student should know how to splice a tape, even if this is normally done in the studio by a technician. He will invariably run into a situation (perhaps outside of the studio) where there is no technician to do it for him. Anyone with normal use of his hands can, with a little practice, learn to splice a tape.

(F26)

If possible, the person whom the student will interview should be someone the supervisor knows to have a friendly nature, and who would be sympathetic to the insecurity of the student. The student will be much more encouraged by this experience, than if he is exposed this first time to someone less sympathetic.

The supervisor should impress upon the student the importance of doing a complete research and preparation before beginning the interview.

(F27)

Once again, it would be best to choose a gathering or an organisation that would be sympathetic to the aims of the studio and the insecurity of the student. We do not, of course, mean to imply that studios should restrict their interviewing to sympathetic persons and organisations. Our interest at this point is only the morale of the student.

The supervisor should decide if it is possible to use the interviews done in Assignments Four and Five on the air. If this can be done, it would provide additional incentive for the student.

If it appears that the student needs additional practice in interviewing, and this will most likely be the case with most students, the supervisor should reassign numbers four and five, using different persons and groups in each case.

The instructions given in *Projects E* and *F* are simply an introduction to interviewing. They provide a few basic rules, all of which must be proved or disproved by local use. The student should not expect to become really competent until he has had a great deal more experience.

PROJECT G

(G1–4)

The most serious problem most people face in doing both interviews and panel discussions, is the tendency to make them without proper preparation. So often broadcasters will simply find one or several people and begin to talk to them.

A broadcaster with a quick tongue may be able to do a programme in which there are no pauses. Occasionally he may even be able to do an outstanding interview or panel discussion, but this is usually because the person being interviewed or the panel members were particularly interesting.

(G5–10)

The only way to have consistently high-quality programmes is to do the necessary research and preparation. Only then will the broadcaster know that he has not just filled up some time on the air, but he has been able to draw out the *best* ideas, the most *important* information, the most *interesting* personality, from the people he uses on the programmes.

Therefore, the supervisor must ensure that the student becomes aware of the importance of the preparation, and uses these techniques in this assignment and all future broadcasts.

As with the other projects in this manual, *Project G* will probably need to be adapted to the local situation. The traditional or accepted manner of carrying on a conversation may influence the style of a panel discussion. Also, the radio stations in your area may already have established a style or a convention for this type of broadcast. The supervisor should spend some time investigating these matters before assigning this project to the student.

As always, we emphasise that this manual is a guide. It is not a book of rules. Intelligent consideration should be given to all the ideas, and those which are not useful should be changed or discarded.

(G11)

If the supervisor has at his disposal some good tape-recorded panel discussions, it will save the student considerable time during Assignment One. In some cases, a taped panel discussion may be the only one available to the student. However, if there is a well-known panel discussion programme being heard in the area, it should be included in Assignment One. If at all possible, these programmes should represent several different formats. If it seems the student has not really thought through his criticisms, or has not understood the instructions in the project, the supervisor should assign additional panel discussion programmes for his analysis.

(G17)

It would be well for the supervisor to give some prior thought to Assignment Two. If other panel discussion programmes are being done by the station or studio, it would be helpful for the student to observe the moderator of that programme throughout his planning, preparation and recording.

In choosing panel members, the supervisor should help the student select people who would be sympathetic to the training needs of the student. In some cases, it may be almost impossible to find suitable panel members. In such a case, the supervisor and one or two other staff members might serve on a panel discussing the work of the studio.

Additional assignments of a similar nature may be given if the student appears to need them. Whenever possible, the completed panel discussion should be used on the air.

PROJECT H

(H1 and 2)

Project H is difficult in that it deals with something much less concrete than other projects. It may, however, be one of the most important projects, and therefore the supervisor should do everything possible to impress upon the student the importance and urgency of the work.

This is underlined by the fact that the manual can only be partly useful in any one situation. In fact, we encountered great difficulty in the writing of this project, because editors from each area were concerned with their specific problems. To include all these considerations would have been impossible. For that reason, the supervisor will need to do a great deal more "teaching" and guiding during this project than in many others.

(H3 and 4)

If some of the information relating to your area could be obtained ahead of time, it may be very useful to the student. The supervisor should also assist the student. The supervisor should also assist the student in every way possible to locate the necessary information in this project. This is important not only from the point of view of the student, but also it is information every studio should have readily available.

Information may also be available from many groups or agencies. A list of some of these agencies is provided near the beginning of the Supervisor's Notes at *S11*. There may also be other radio stations or studios, government departments, church groups, community development organisations, etc., that have relevant information. All of these should be explored.

(H5–13)

We have encouraged the student to begin work on a notebook or a file. If this has not already been done by the student, this notebook could provide a useful source of information to all studio staff, provided it is constantly revised in the light of new information. Such a study becomes out-dated very quickly, and for that reason the loose-leaf form may be advisable.

It is suggested that the supervisor ask the student to make a spoken report to the rest of the studio staff or some other group about his findings. This will not only be an added incentive to the student, but also may stimulate some creative thinking among others.

(H14–17)

Assignments One and Two are designed to help the student come to grips with his own society, and in particular the type of cultures into which he is broadcasting. He should understand that there are many groups (sub-cultures) within any society, a concept which the supervisor should help him understand.

The student should also be helped to understand that even though he may have lived within that culture all his life, there are many things he will learn if he "stands back and takes a look". It is most difficult to analyse something we are intimately involved with, and thus the student may need considerable guidance in developing an analytical attitude towards his nation's cultures and sub-cultures.

(H18)

The following listing is adapted from a book called *Sociology in the Philippine Setting*. We include it here for use by the supervisor, in order that he may see the types of differences we are hoping the student will discover in Assignment Two. If this listing is shown to the student, the supervisor should be careful to warn him that these descriptions are much too short and too general to be of practical use. The student's study should be much more complete.

*PRIMITIVE OR FOLK	CHRISTIAN FILIPINO	WESTERN
(A few minorities in Luzon)	(The majority of Filipinos)	(North American)

Parents:

(1) The father (or sometimes the mother) decides things for everyone.	The father always decides, although in a few things the mother can speak.	Mother and father decide equally.

Family:

(2) The family is important because it owns property together and works together.	The family is important because it owns property. They may work in different places.	Family does not usually own property together and seldom works in the same place.

Family Group:

(3) Large family group includes many relatives. Older children sometimes live in separate buildings. Many children are born but many die when very young.	Large family group includes three generations and many relatives in the same house. Many children born, but not as many die as in the primitive culture.	Small family group includes only two generations and no relatives. Not as many children born and not as many die.

Value of the Family:

(4) Family is the way to get some wealth and to be honoured by others in the village.	A closely related and a wealthy family is wanted by all members.	Happy family is important, but this is mainly because it helps make each member happy.

* Adapted from: Hunt, Coller, Espiritu, de Young, *Corpus Sociology in the Philippine Setting* (Phoenix Publishing House, 1963), pages 67–69.

PRIMITIVE OR FOLK	CHRISTIAN FILIPINO	WESTERN

Children:

(5) Children are not usually punished for mistakes. The strong values of the village make the child act like the others.	Children are sometimes strongly punished, and sometimes allowed to do whatever they want.	Children and parents tend to consider each other equal.

Marriage:

(6) Marriage arranged by families. Very little romance.	Romantic love is very important, but the parents must always agree.	Romantic love most important. Agreement of parents is not usually necessary.

Courtship:

(7) Rather free relations between boy and girl before marriage.	Always a third person around when girl and boy meet.	Seldom a third person when boy and girl meet, but there are rules about things that must not be done.

Sex:

(8) Fairly wide range of sex relationships before and after marriage. Very little prostitution.	Fairly free for men, but very strict for women. Men sometimes have a mistress, or visit a prostitute.	Fewer rules, but the same for men and women. Fewer prostitutes or mistresses.

Divorce:

(9) Divorce is easy to have for many reasons. Does not cause money problems for man or woman.	No divorce. Man and woman can be separated but cannot remarry.	Divorce easy for many reasons, but there are many laws and many money problems.

(H20–23)

One of the great pitfalls of the beginning broadcaster lies in the comments of kind friends and relatives. His first programme may be hailed as a masterpiece by his friends, and future programmes may also be greeted with compliments. Being "on-the-air" may make him feel a celebrity. All of these things in themselves are not necessarily bad. The initial "celebrity glow" may be very useful, and often spurs the student to greater efforts in self-improvement.

There must be a time, however, when every broadcaster begins to understand the comments of friends for what they are, and to judge their value in terms of programming on an objective basis. This is much easier said than done. More than one experienced broadcaster has kept a poor programme on the air because: "Everyone I know likes it."

On the other hand, some broadcasters have become so cynical of personal comments that they have almost gone to the other extreme of taking the programme off the moment a friend issued a compliment. Our aim is to help the student reach a more logical position somewhere between these two extremes.

(H24–27)

Letters present somewhat the same problems as personal comments, although generally speaking they have greater value in judging programmes. The main pitfall lies in judging letters *individually*. As a rule, the only way letters can say anything useful is when viewed together systematically over a period of time. Even then, they are frequently overrated as a means of judging the type and size of the audience.

(H28 and 29)

A major study of audience with scientific sampling methods and detailed cross-tabulation of results probably could not be undertaken by your student. Indeed it should only be undertaken by people trained in this area. If, however, your organisation does have a scientific method of gathering information, the student should be thoroughly introduced to both the method of gathering the information, and the results obtained.

It might also be added, that failure to gather audience information scientifically is often the greatest failing of non-profit radio stations and studios. Experience all over the world has shown that such reliable information is essential to the successful work of any such educational studio.

(H30)

If at all possible, the supervisor should gather fifty letters, all addressed to one programme. The student should be able to analyse these in a relatively short time, although he should understand that results would be more accurate if he used a larger number of letters. If no letters are available right at the studio, it may be possible to borrow some appropriate letters from another station or studio for this exercise.

PROJECT I

(I1–11)

We have tried to avoid "theories" in the writing of this manual in order to be as practical as possible. It seemed necessary, however, to spend some time explaining the process of communication as a theory, not only to give the student a grasp of what happens, but also to give him a grounding for further study in this field. We have used some technical terms in our discussion of communication, because it will make it easier for the student to move on to other readings where he will encounter these words.

(I12–28)

We would strongly recommend that the supervisor obtain and read the book *Mass Media and National Development* by Dr. Wilbur Schramm. For the student, we would suggest the abridged version of this book, which is called "The Role of Information in National Development", also available in French and English from UNESCO. If the student has had difficulty with this project, the reading of this pamphlet should be assigned at the end of the manual. If the supervisor feels the student can handle it at this point, it could be assigned before he goes on to the next project.

If the student has any problems in his understanding of English (or French), the supervisor may need to offer considerable help in his understanding of the Schramm study.

As in other projects, it will be necessary for the supervisor to read the entire project in advance, and make necessary adaptations to fit the local situation.

(I29)

Assignment Five is designed to help the student focus on basic purposes and motivation. A thorough study of this kind is essential to the successful operation of any studio. If the studio already has well-developed objectives, this assignment could be used as a helpful re-examination. The student should be encouraged to be critical of the existing objectives. If the objectives are sound, they will easily withstand the student's criticisms. If they are unsound, they will benefit from a re-examination.

If the studio does not have a statement of objectives, the student's work may possibly form the basis for such a necessary development.

In either case, the supervisor should arrange a discussion among studio staff or other interested persons (perhaps the committee or board that sets the studio's policy), based on the report and the findings of the student. This will not only offer additional incentive for the student, but also may bring out some creative thinking among those taking part.

The supervisor should be particularly watchful to be sure the student avoids the use of worn-out phrases that do not mean very much, large impressive words he does not fully understand, flowery but relatively meaningless phrases, and ideas borrowed from other sources which do not have a real application to the situation at hand.

(I30)

The supervisor should, if possible, choose three widely different kinds of pro-grammes for the student to analyse during Assignment Six. This might include one programme which is of very poor quality. The student would be asked to suggest ways in which it could be redirected along a better course. It may be necessary for the supervisor to assign additional programmes for the student to analyse, if it seems that his work on these first three does not show a grasp of the problems discussed in this project. If the student is working in a situation where there are other staff members, a group analysis of one of the programmes, led by the student, would be of value to all those participating.

PROJECT J

(J1)

Because of the great variety of musical traditions found in the world, it is difficult to be specific in our instructions to the student in this project. Nevertheless, the material presented can serve as a guide-line for student and supervisor towards better music programming.

The supervisor's most important task in relation to *Project J* is to find and use the music resources of the community to assist the student. Everything possible should be done to acquaint the student with the various types of music used in his area, as well as any foreign music that might be used in the programming. Because music is used to such a large extent in radio, it would be difficult to offer the student *too much* instruction. In any case, a broad general understanding of music (not necessarily a technical understanding) is essential if the student is to do intelligent work.

(J2–11)

This instruction should, if possible, include ways of evaluating music in terms of its quality. Unless the broadcaster has some means of judging between good and bad, he will certainly not be discriminating in his choices. This can only result in inferior programming.

Such instruction unfortunately cannot be given on the printed page, especially for such a variety of musical situations. It must therefore be the responsibility of the supervisor to arrange for such instruction. The guide-lines in this manual should give some direction, however, in the preparation of programming.

(J12)

In matters such as *cues* and *fades*, the student may find some difficulty in understanding what is meant by the instructions. He may not be able to *hear* the differences between the good and the bad. It would be useful if the supervisor, or a more experienced staff member, could listen to various programmes to point out the pacing of the cues, and could listen to a number of possible signature tunes to find the best places for fades.

If the student is reasonably familiar with Western music, he might find it easier to hear the phrases in Western popular songs, folk-songs, and hymns. Of course, if musical phrases are easily found in the music of his own country, then this is the music he should work with first.

Most important is that the student be made very conscious of these technical points of programming. Such consciousness in a sincere student, will certainly result in a gradually improved technique.

Throughout this project, the student should do as much listening to music and music programmes as possible.

(J13)

This study of music in this assignment should be as extensive as possible within the resources of the community. The student should be encouraged to interview all kinds of musicians: those highly trained, and those without formal training who simply play for their own pleasure. If possible, the student should be asked to make a verbal report to his fellow staff members or to some other group in addition to his written report to the supervisor. He should be ready to answer questions and to lead a discussion following the report.

(J14)

This assignment may also be the subject of a discussion or a report to an interested group. The supervisor may decide to choose one of the programmes the student has analysed, have the group listen to it, then have the student give his analysis followed by a group discussion.

In selecting the three programmes for the student to analyse, it would be best to choose three widely different kinds. If the student has difficulty with his analysis, he should be asked to review the information provided in the project, and then to analyse other programmes assigned by the supervisor.

(J21)

This assignment is self-explanatory, although it should be suggested that additional music programmes be assigned if the supervisor feels the student has the time to do them. If the programmes can be designed for use on the air, this will give added incentive to the student.

PROJECT K

(K1)

There will certainly be a wide variety of ways in which this project will be approached by the supervisors. This will depend very much on the circumstances of the studio in which the work is taking place. It should be emphasised, however, that even if the studio is not now involved in the kind of work described, the student should study the material thoroughly in order to broaden his horizons beyond that of the studio in which he is working. Furthermore, skills developed here can be put to good use in other programme areas.

(K2–7)

This project opens with a look at the ways in which non-staff talent is used. Obviously there will be studios that rarely use such talent, but the matter should be considered in any case.

Although there is no assignment in connection with this portion of *Project K*, here are two possible assignments the supervisor may wish to give to the student:

> If the studio has on its staff (or if there is someone in the area) a person involved in the use of volunteer talent, the student should talk to him in order to find out about the problems and advantages of the system used. He should then prepare a written report on the matter for the supervisor, or should give a verbal report to an interested group.
> If the studio does not presently use volunteer talent, the student should be asked to make written suggestions for the ways in which talent could be found, trained, and used in programming. If possible, he should discuss the matter with others who might understand some of the problems involved.

(K8–14)

The second portion of Part One deals with techniques of microphone use and recording. This is done in the full realisation that in many studios regulations do not allow the programme person to handle technical equipment. Nevertheless, it is the feeling of the writer, that a working knowledge of the subject will give the student a much more intelligent approach to his work, and will enable him to work more meaningfully with the technical staff.

If the programme person serves as his own technician, which is the situation in many cases, then a knowledge of these technical matters will be even more necessary.

Wherever possible, a person with technical training should help the student with this project. It might be arranged that the student watch a technician in the course of his work for a period of time, if it is felt that the technician could explain things meaningfully to the student.

If this is not possible, the supervisor should do everything possible to become familiar with the techniques and problems involved, in order that he may assist the student in his learning. It is doubtful if the average student would master this section without such assistance.

(K15 and 16)

The main purpose of this portion, and of Assignments One and Two is to help the student develop a more sensitive ear. If he can develop the habit of listening critically to the acoustic quality of all the broadcasts he hears, it is probable that he will learn many of the skills necessary to bring about a high standard.

(K19–28)

The main aspect of Part Two of *Project K* is to help the student realise that he must maintain control of all programmes, even under pressure from listeners. All too often, such programmes become rather bad, because the person responsible feels he must use everything the listeners send to him, or must meet every request for music or information.

(K30)

It may not be possible for each studio to provide letters for Assignment Four. It may be that the supervisor should ask another studio for some examples. In an extreme case, the supervisor should write some letters himself. It is best if the student can be given long letters that demand cutting, or more letters than he can use, so that he is forced to edit his materials.

PROJECT L

(L1 and 2)

The purpose of this project is to introduce the student to radio news. We begin by trying to help him to face up to his responsibilities as a news reporter, and to do everything possible to bring factual information to the people he serves. Even in countries where complete freedom of information has not yet been reached, the broadcaster can do a great deal. He can act as a responsible and honest reporter within whatever regulations he must follow, and at the same time he can keep alive in himself and others the ideal of complete freedom of information.

(L3–5)

In order to do this, he must know the differences between opinion, news, and propaganda. As we use the terms in this manual, *opinion* means a responsible presentation of a well-studied viewpoint and is presented *as* opinion, not as fact. *News* is the presentation of facts which are accurate and impartial as far as this is possible for any human being. *Propaganda* is the conscious slanting or twisting of news in order to form a certain viewpoint in the listener.

(L6 and 7)

Unfortunately, news-men sometimes unconsciously slant stories to fit their own viewpoints. In fact, there is almost always an element of unconscious slanting since we must select certain items for broadcast and leave others out. An honest news-man will use legitimate news even when he knows it will reinforce a viewpoint with which he disagrees.

(L8–17)

Some of the basic methods of writing, editing and compiling are introduced in this portion. The supervisor might well decide to add further assignments or to find more instruction and reading for the student.

The instructions in this entire project, as in the rest of the manual, will need to be adapted to fit the local situation. The student should be encouraged to disagree with any statements in the manual that he feels do not meet the needs of his people. News broadcasting techniques and styles will differ from place to place, and these differences should be pointed out by the supervisor.

In the use of this project, the supervisor may find it useful to enlist the help of a local news-man if this is possible. A person from the studio with news experience, someone from another station, or a newspaperman could help the student see the local application of this manual more clearly. In fact, it might be made an assignment for the student, that he tape an interview with such a person on the matter of news gathering. It would not only be a useful exercise but might also make a good programme.

(L18 and 19)

Assignments One and Two are intended to help the student listen critically to news broadcasts. It would be wise for the supervisor to listen to the news broadcasts in question, in order that he might discuss them with the student and make observations which the student may have missed. One question not included in the check-list, but which would lead to a useful discussion with the student, is this: "What are the differences between the newscasts coming from outside the country, and those which were made here in our own nation?" The student and supervisor should look for differences of content, style, approach, and accuracy. Other staff members might be invited to share in these discussions.

(L28)

In order for the supervisor to evaluate Assignment Three, he must be quite clear in his own mind about the differences between radio and newspaper styles. A careful examination of the two will usually reveal the differences. Additional newspaper items should be assigned to the student for rewriting if necessary.

(L29)

Assignment Four can easily be adapted to fit a local situation. The names might be changed, although this is not necessary for the exercise. The supervisor may also wish to make additional assignments of this nature. It is quite easy to make a list of the facts from a news item the student has probably not seen, and then ask him to write this into a news story. Also the supervisor might find a well-written radio news item, make a list of the facts and give them to the student. Later he might ask the student to compare his own writing of the story with the original. Be sure, however, that the student understands there may be several good ways to approach the same news item. The fact that his item is different from the original does not make it wrong.

(L30)

The supervisor should be prepared with several suggestions in relation to Assignment Five. If the student has a choice, or can even suggest his own news assignment, his interest is likely to be higher. Whenever circumstances permit, the student should be asked to cover something which might be usable on the air. He should rewrite as often as necessary to bring his items up to station standards.

If circumstances permit, the supervisor is encouraged to ask the student to prepare first a 5-minute, then a 10-minute news broadcast from news items available in the studio. If possible, the student should also accompany an experienced reporter when he is on a news-gathering assignment. In fact, the more general news experience the student can obtain in the course of this project, the more he will be able to benefit from *Project M*.

PROJECT M

(M1)

This project is a continuation of *Project L*, and develops more sophisticated forms of news and information broadcasting. In some studios and stations, the student may not be involved in these kinds of programmes at the present time. His study will be useful, however, since many of the ideas suggested here can be applied to other programme forms. The student will also gain more from his radio listening, which in turn will assist his development in other areas of programming.

There are several references in this project to previous work covered by the student. The supervisor should encourage the student to review this work at the points suggested.

If possible, the student should begin this project by listening to examples of the types of programmes covered, and he might well listen to further examples following his completion of each part.

(M8)

There may be instances where the supervisor would choose to have the student do both portions "A" and "B" of Assignment One. In this case, "B" should be done first. The purpose of the assignment is to give the student the experience of on-the-spot coverage, and to integrate various kinds of materials. It is important that he gather more material than can be used in the news story, in order that he may further develop the art of editing.

(M10–23)

The magazine programme, in one form or another, is usually within the possibilities of most studios. This portion should therefore be given some emphasis. Documentary programmes on the other hand, are much more difficult and should not be undertaken by the newcomer to radio. Nevertheless, the student should try at this stage to understand documentary forms and to prepare himself for the time when he could undertake such a programme.

(M24)

The purpose of Assignment Two is to help the student learn to look below the surface of printed publications, and to see what use they might have in radio. It is also intended to help him see the differences in both style and structure between materials intended for print, and those developed for radio.

(M25)

The supervisor should be prepared to assist the student in locating suitable materials for Assignment Three. The length of the broadcast could be altered, if the supervisor felt the programme might be used on the air. The student should not present simply "a magazine programme" but one that is in line with the purposes of the studio or the station.

PROJECT N

(N1)

The two projects on drama are perhaps among the most important in the manual. If a student can really learn the art of radio drama, he will also have learned many of the skills necessary for the making of other kinds of programmes. These two projects, therefore, are longer and more difficult than most of the others. The supervisor should be prepared to give more time and attention to them.

It would be most useful for the student to spend considerable time listening to radio dramas, both before he begins the project and after. In each case, the student should write a one- or two-page summary of the drama, and should criticise these productions in the light of his own audience, using the lists at *N18* and *N34*.

If there are books or articles written about the performing arts (drama, dance, music, etc.) in your country, the student should be encouraged to read them. If there is someone in your area who has a good knowledge about drama, such as a literature teacher in a school, it would be useful to have him speak to your student. Perhaps the student might be asked to prepare a series of radio interviews about drama with such people, or he might be asked to make a report on drama to the rest of the studio staff.

(N2)

Whenever possible, local forms of drama should be emphasised. If your nation has its own indigenous drama- or story-telling tradition, the student should investigate this as much as possible. At the same time, he should also study other forms of drama.

The suggestions in these projects are for the beginner. As with any art form, he will, as he progresses, no doubt find many exceptions to the rules laid down here. Nevertheless, he must become familiar with the rules, and should break them only after he has enough experience to do so intelligently.

(N4 15)

This section deals very quickly with the short-story form. It is unfortunate that space does not allow us to deal more fully with this subject, since the short story can be a most effective radio form.

The supervisor may well choose to have the student go into the subject more deeply. This can be done through listening to short-story programmes on the radio, with the student summarising and analysing each story. Where these are not available, short stories in printed form can be used as exercises. The student should analyse each story first, then rewrite it in his own language for radio.

Where there are persons in the community who can speak with knowledge on the short story, their help may be sought and used in much the same way as suggested for the dramas.

In some cases, the supervisor might ask the student to prepare a series of short-story programmes following his study of Part One, as a preparation for his study of drama. Some stations have been most successful in their use of short stories, and in many cases have adapted them into a semi-dramatic form. This was done by having one or two of the main characters performed by actors, while all the other characters and the narrative are handled by the story-teller. Sometimes a few sound effects and music are added.

As always, we suggest that students' projects be used on the air whenever possible.

(N16)

The supervisor may choose to have the student adapt this story (N5) into his own language and cultural setting before completing the analysis as suggested in Assignment One.

(N17)

Whenever possible, the student should be encouraged to write in the style and form of his own tradition, rather than to copy a foreign style. The supervisor should encourage the student to write and rewrite the story in Assignment Two as often as necessary, to be sure that it is not only a good story, but that it is also useful to the listener. Additional story assignments could be made to good advantage.

(N19–29)

The difficulty of a manual such as this is that a subject as complex as drama can only be touched on. Radio drama deserves a separate volume for itself. However, these suggestions will help the student get started. May we emphasise again, however, the importance of developing in the student the habit of critical listening.

We would like to include a suggestion for a very valuable exercise which the supervisor may give to the student. Unfortunately, it might not be possible in many circumstances, and so it is not included among the other assignments. Where it could be done it would be excellent preparation for Part Two of this project.

Ask the student to prepare a report for his fellow staff members or a talk for any interested group of people called, "The Ways My People Speak". In this report he should discuss the different style of speaking (not regional dialects) used by various economic and social groups in his society, and as much as possible, should illustrate his talk with taped examples. The student should be asked to spend considerable time searching the community and taping the different styles of speech. In doing so, the student will listen carefully to styles of speaking he may never have noticed before. Then later, when he prepares his report, he will need actually to describe the differences between the styles. If he can do this, he is a long way towards the writing of realistic dialogue.

(N30–31)

There is a tendency among students to regard anything printed in a book as being beyond criticism. The student should be helped to realise that in the field of art (the radio programming is an art, not a science) there is no ultimate standard by which things can be judged. The student's evaluation may have as much value as yours or mine, and he must be trained to have respect for his own judgement. This is the main object of Assignments Three and Four. If the student shows that he sincerely tried to find the good and bad points of the dramas he analysed, then the purpose of these assignments is fulfilled.

(N33)

Assignment Five may take considerable work, and certainly a great deal of writing and rewriting. The supervisor should emphasise to the student what was said earlier in the manual. Good scripts are never just written. They are *rewritten*.

The script he develops in this assignment, plus "The Contrary Wife" should be saved for production in the next project. For this reason, the supervisor should ensure that sound effects, music, and other technical matters are within the capacity of the studio to produce.

Where time allows, several extra drama-writing assignments may be given to good advantage.

PROJECT O

(O1)

This project attempts to give the student some further insight into the art of radio drama. Although it deals largely with the production of drama, the information contained here is also needed by those who write dramas.

(O2-26)

It is even more urgent at this time to have the student again spend a good deal of time listening to dramas, both before and after he works through the project. To be useful, the listening must be extremely analytical. Extensive note-taking is always an aid to such analysis, as is a report on each listening project, which should be given to the supervisor and discussed with him. If several students are working on this portion at the same time, they could be put into teams of two or three to analyse the drama, and prepare a joint report.

Unfortunately, space does not allow for a complete coverage of drama production. For that reason it should be impressed upon the student that this manual is but an introduction. Much hard work and practice will be necessary following the completion of this manual, before the student can consider himself competent in this field.

(O32-45)

The suggestions in Part Two would really be more appropriate after the student had considerable experience as an actor and writer. If possible, the supervisor might arrange for the student to leave this portion for the time being, and concentrate on writing, acting, and possibly some production (if he can work under a more experienced person). Then, when it seems he is ready to launch out as a director of dramas, Part Two will be much more meaningful and useful to him.

(O46)

The student should show real evidence of having thoroughly studied the dramas mentioned in Assignment Five. It may well be he will need to discuss Part Two of this project point by point with the supervisor, and then repeat Assignment Five. If at all possible, at least one indigenous drama should be included among those he analyses.

(O47 and 48)

Assignments Six and Seven may prove somewhat difficult. If a more experienced staff member is available, it would be better for the student to work under his close supervision. If there are several students in a workshop situation, it would be best to use them as actors, sound effects people, etc., rather than using talent from outside the studio. The supervisor may also find it necessary to simplify the dramas concerned, in order to make them possible within the limitation of the studio and the capabilities of the student-director. In any case, the supervisor should discuss both dramas thoroughly with the student, to be sure he understands the problems involved in the production.

In Conclusion (O52):

We must state again that radio broadcasting cannot be taught from a book. A manual such as this can offer some guide-lines and suggestions, but in the final sense, the student must learn for himself.

For this reason, we suggest that for a considerable period, perhaps a year, the student should use a check-list for the programmes he is doing. This check-list could be based on a combination of several check-lists included at various points in the manual. He should then use this to review his work constantly. At the same time, the supervisor or an experienced staff member should review at least one of his programmes each week. This person may wish to use the check-list also, and certainly should go over the programme point by point with the student.

The emphasis, however, should not be on keeping the student within a rigid set of rules. Rather the student should be encouraged to think of his own work, to study it critically, and to look for new and more imaginative methods of communication. The object is to stretch, not to restrict.

Included in this manual is a short bibliography (Appendix Y). These books have been carefully chosen, and are recommended for study by the student and the supervisor.

There are available a number of magazines and journals related to the area of broadcasting. The supervisor should make himself familiar with these, then subscribe to several that seem to deal with his general field of broadcasting. Some of these are also listed in Appendix Y.

A magazine has little value, however, unless it is read. There should be one or several people in each studio or station, who as part of their assigned task, review the articles in the magazines and pass on to the staff those that are of particular value.

All of this is intended to keep the broadcaster growing. There is a very great danger of becoming so engrossed in the production of programmes, that new developments are neglected, and new techniques left unlearned.

The human mind must be constantly stretched. If it isn't, it soon hardens and loses touch with real life.